Great Eagle Rising

True Confessions of a Missionary

Millie Camille Eehn-Toms

iUniverse, Inc.
Bloomington

Great Eagle Rising—2nd Edition
True Confessions of a Missionary—*"Noquivi for the Soul"*

Copyright © 2011 by Millie Camille Eehn-Toms.

Revised March 19, 2013

All rights reserved. No part of this book may be used or reproduced by any means, graphic, electronic, or mechanical, including photocopying, recording, taping or by any information storage retrieval system without the permission of the publisher except in the case of brief quotations embodied in critical articles and reviews.

All scriptures taken from the New King James Version Bible. Copyright © 1979, 1980, 1982 by Thomas Nelson, Inc. All rights reserved.

Only scriptures on page 21 of Isaiah 52:14 & 53: 4,5 & 8 taken from the Holy Bible New International Version Bible®. Copyright © 1973, 1978, 1984 by International Bible Society. All rights reserved.

Cover design and graphics, and the photographs featured on the cover of this book were taken by the Author's husband Will Toms. We are grateful for permission from Megan Jenkins (the Hopi maiden in the cornfield with her headdress) whose photo is on the front cover of this book. She is a friend of the Toms family.

All profits derived from the sale of this book will go to the work and ministry of YWAM Tribalwinds among Native Americans.

ISBN: 978-1-4620-4927-1 (sc)
ISBN: 978-1-4620-4928-8 (ebk)

Biography/ Autobiography/ Memoir/ Native American Missions/ Hopi/ Christian spirituality/ Native American spirituality

First Printing 2011

For information contact:
YWAM Tribalwinds
P.O. Box 30776
Flagstaff, Arizona, 86003
www.tribalwinds.org
928-527-0104

For the glory of our beautiful Creator!

This book is dedicated to my husband
Will Toms
You have brought love and joy to my life and you have certainly made my life interesting. And I still like holding your hands.
Thank you Clover Esther & Tim David Jacobs
Naphtali Toms &
Johnny & Kayti Grace Toms for walking with our awesome Father above!
Dr. John H. & Margaret H. Eehn
Daniel & Kathryn, Westin & Bethany Eehn
David Oliver Eehn
And to Ranen Kai and all my future grandchildren

And to all those who supported this ministry of YWAM Tribal Winds! We are truly grateful!
Your name should be on this page.

And to all past & present Sea & Summit Expeditions & Winter House staff & students & participants
& YWAM Tribalwinds staff
And okay, to all my friends who don't fit into any of the categories above but still call me a "friend"

And of course, to all my beautiful Native American & indigenous and island friends around the world!

Thank you Deborah Schaulis, Lynda Mitchell, Jan Gowey
for getting together with me almost weekly
to read and edit this book.
Your dedication so touched my heart!

True Confessions of a Missionary

Reviews on Amazon & Etc.

By <u>Jen Anderson</u> - **Touched me in amazing and unexpected ways!**

Your book touched me in amazing and unexpected ways. I don't know that my words will do it justice. There are so many "inspirational" Christian books but this one truly brought me closer in my relationship to God. I read it while I was going through a difficult decision-making time in my life. Each chapter felt like I was sharing a delightful cup of tea with a wise woman of God who was willing to share her deepest struggles and triumphs in her relationship with God, and with the sometimes-narrow path He had her on. I could apply the wisdom she shared to my own situation and I found the path that God was providing for me.

Her honesty and humility with the Lord are rare commodities and even remind me of the writings of Corrie Ten Boom. I would even encourage the author to consider writing another book as a daily devotional for missionaries. I finished this book, hungering for more, hungering to know this honest, humble, wise woman who was willing to lay her heart bare for the possibility that the reader might be encouraged. It is certainly a book that would be of great value for anyone in ministry--any ministry--because the lessons Millie speaks of are universal. I am not a missionary, but I would imagine that this book would be of great encouragement to anyone on the mission field!

By <u>Virginia Setters</u> (Santa Fe, New Mexico) 91 years old

I could hardly put your book down to eat or sleep. You take your reader through the personal thoughts and struggles that are a part of every missionary's life. This is vital information that others need to know, to bring understanding to an entirely different level. You are an excellent communicator. This is where the "rubber meets the road".

By <u>Korina Dove Schneider</u> (Oklahoma) **Eye-opening and awesome!**

This review is from: Great Eagle Rising: (Kindle Edition)

I laughed. I cried. I could not put this book down! I not only have a new understanding for missions workers but a new love for the Hopis as well. A must read for anyone wanting a glimpse into Native America. The author is humorous, loving, and honest to the core.

By <u>Sarah Hine</u> (England, UK) **You've inspired this white British woman!**

A friend bought me this book in France while she was on a holiday as it w as a gift to inspire me as I have wanted to work with Native Americans since I was 13 years old. And this is exactly what it did - it inspired me. It also made me laugh and cry in equal measure as Millie so eloquently shares her experiences as a missionary in Arizona.

The honest and real way that Millie writes engages the reader to participate in the joys and frustrations in being a missionary. I love the way she does not shy away from the realities of her calling, and also how she brings a beautiful insight into the Native American culture and

its people. What I loved most about this book was reading about someone who lives several thousand miles away from me, yet still holds the same visions/values and outworks her faith in a relevant and practical way. Thank you Millie for writing this book - you've inspired this white British woman to keep focused on her long-term dream.

Great Eagle Rising

By **Ashley Porter** ((Part Hopi, Apache)– **Brutal honesty, Refreshing, contagious, an eye opener, moved and challenged**

Her brutal honesty in this book is refreshing. I think most "religious" people would say "shame on you", gasp, and snub up their noses. But I love it because she has the courage to be transparent. This is what I long to be. Her words are contagious; they make me want to act and not to stay stagnate in my walk with the Lord.

While reading this book you need a tissue for the moments when you are so consumed by the trials she faced but then the next chapter you are laughing hysterically at her humor and honesty. I definitely think God gave her laughter to cover all the tears she has had over the years. I was moved and personally challenged. This book really helped me take a deeper look into my walk with God. It is a book for those who want an eye opener into the Hopi people's lives as well as those who just want honesty for once to fully fall in love with Him.

By **Jeff Harkins**– **Unique, beautiful, unpolished style but clear as a bell**

Millie Camille Eehn-Toms' honesty in "Great Eagle Rising" comes through in a life-transforming, attitude-changing way, clear as a bell, not only because she is speaking the truth in love but also because of the unique and beautiful, unpolished style in which she expresses herself. You will get what she is saying. You will have a far better understanding of the challenges which the Body of Christ faces (and sometimes avoids) in cross-cultural evangelism and ministry. And you will absolutely fall in love with our Native Americans. I hope this book ultimately gets circulated far and wide in the Body of Christ so that it can help shape the attitudes and destinies of mission-minded believers everywhere.

Jeff Harkins is the Author of Grace Plus Nothing

By **Gordon Dalbey** - **Pioneering journey, rare balance of both truth and grace**

This book pioneers a fresh journey of faith in an often forgotten frontier. Too often, churches either withdraw passively from Native American ministry out of politically correct tolerance or preach aggressively out of religiously correct judgment. Here's a rare balance of both grace and truth, a credible story of ministry from the heart, struggling against traditional stereotypes and prejudices to rely on Jesus alone for vision and power. Yes, indeed: how can the Church use incense in the mass and judge it as "false" among Native Americans who embrace Jesus?

Gordon Dalbey is the author of Books: Healing the Masculine Soul, Fight like a Man, Broken by Religion, Sons of the Father, No small Snakes etc. "A real man is a man who's real"-www.abbafather.com

By **mountaingirl** - **Rare look into the life of North American missions**

This review is from: Great Eagle Rising: True Confessions of a Missionary (Kindle Edition) It's written from a very genuine heart, that has experienced and is sharing what many Americans have no grid for but for which they hold much responsibility, the plight of Native America. The author shares the trials, joys, breakthroughs and cultural differences, as they move in with a people group known for having the most well-preserved Native religion/culture in North America. I found myself laughing hard out loud more frequently than most books I've picked up, surprised by her honesty, and engaged by her knowledge, experience and love for an intriguing, fun-loving Native tribe. I loved reading it the second time too. A fascinating book!

By **Aslander**—**True confessions**—**Authentic and Real!**

I was touched by Millie's story and her authenticity and indeed her "confessions as a missionary". I found myself absorbed in her book; the dynamics of the Native American culture, the struggles to work with the people in it, the difficulty and conflicts in working with other Christians in ministry, and the personal

True Confessions of a Missionary

emotional and spiritual pain one must fight and endure to stay true to God's purpose without succumbing to it in the midst of constant spiritual battles. Of great importance for each Christian seeking to bring the Gospel to the lost is reaching them where they are. The author is authentic, real, humorous, and engaging. I think you, too, will be inspired by sharing in her story.

By **Sarah MacLeod** (Indiana) –**There is so much to be learned from First Nations.**

The book's format was a little difficult for me to get through, simply because of my analytical mind wanting more information. But once I grasped the idea that it was written in a conversational, storytelling way, I started to get into it more. I found it delightful that to show respect and deference to the elders, the "gatekeepers", is still appreciated. The whole tradition facilitates a communal society that values mutual understanding.

Throughout the book were hidden little nuggets of the Hopi culture. Often throughout the book moments of the church's narrow-mindedness and unintentional oppression were pointed out. To be honest, this surprised me. Yes, my heart is moved. Now, my spirit rises up when I think about the American Church that is still oppressing her Native brothers and sisters. It is obvious that the church has not realized that there is so much to be learned from First Nations. It is obvious that the church has forgotten that the Native People are also made in God's image. So I pray for the eyes of the American church to be opened; for Godly sorrow to break our hearts to move to action where we were previously apathetic, and extend a hand of respect and friendship. 'Our Native friends tell us, "You deal with your sin-stained culture and we will deal with ours." (Pg. 124)

By **Ruci Rogoyawa** (Fijian)- **It doesn't sugar coat missionary life**

I'm a proud Fijian woman and I will fight for my home if I see others coming and not respecting our culture. It's heartbreaking to hear about cultures that have been forgotten or overrun. It's happening now. Until I read this book I haven't questioned how indigenous people all over the world have felt. I would definitely recommend this book to anyone going into or considering missionary work with Native Americans and those going into missions. It doesn't sugar coat missionary life, but at the same time it shows the faithfulness of our God who calls us into it. I was very encouraged to read about Nita's story. The Hopis are amazing people. Nita's story challenged me as a Fijian.

By **Priscilla Mueller** (Cree, Canada) – **A Great read if you want to know more about Native American Missions or Missions in general.**

Reading this book I have learned not everyone's Walk with God is the same, God loves every culture, and it is not wrong to worship God in our own culture. One thing I am having a real hard time with is letting go of my assumptions of everything I have been taught up until now. It is okay for me/us to worship God in our different cultural songs, dances and prayers.

I am a Cree native from British Columbia. I do know that native people are a very hard people group to reach because of the past years of being forced by outsiders to leave their families and learn English and forget about their culture. They were told that it is wrong to be a native person and practice their culture. This is the reason that I don't know much about my culture; it was lost over all these years. I grew up in an area where there were only white people. It has been a never ending battle inside of me to figure out my true identity. Eventually I just went along with what everyone said I should be and how I should act. I am just discovering my true identity. I only want God to show me who I should be.

By **Chelsea Cullen** (New York) – **Sprinkled with stories, splashed with analogies**

The book "Great Eagle Rising," was a book that carried a lot of thoughts that is nice to hear being said for once. There are so many facts, sprinkled with stories, splashed with analogies but all coming from pure honesty. This book shatters the glass cased image we have of the term missionaries. The author is a missionary that breaks the mold! *This book sparked up a lot of thoughts in me*

Great Eagle Rising

I digress. From reading this book, there were a lot of things I have come to understand in my own life that had finally been written on paper. She had the nerve to say things most people are too afraid to say or cannot find the words to express.

By **Mary Harris** (born & raised in Japan) - **Inspired me to pray for freedom for the native people to rise up and cultivate their own, unique relationships with the Creator.**

Many missionaries in the past required Native Christians to give up their indigenous identity and conform to western culture as they were told that their dances and instruments were evil. Today, missionaries and Native Christians alike find themselves caught in the middle of this question, with pain and hurt on both sides many times. She shares how it broke her heart when Native forms of worship were blindly rejected because they did not fit the 'western mold of Christianity. In her book, Millie highlights the importance of honoring the native culture and customs.

The idea that stuck out the most to me in this book was that of letting the Native peoples decide for themselves what is right or wrong in their cultures. This seemed very radical to me. I realized, however, that not letting Natives make this decision for themselves can spiritually stunt them, as they cannot learn to ask God directly and may become reliant on the missionaries to know God.

This book is very inspiring, for both the aspiring missionary and the intercessor. God has placed so much potential in the native peoples. This book inspired me to pray for freedom and for the native people to rise up and cultivate their own, unique relationships with God; or, the Creator.

By **Tina Lovaason** (Hopi) - **Forgive me for not pursuing who I really am**

There are emotions that are very hard for me to deal with like a woman in labor, who is trying her hardest to push out that which is inside of her. I feel like a lot of what I am feeling is guilt because here are people who are not even Natives who have such a burden for the Hopis. Something is going on inside so deep, I prayed and I ask God to reveal to me what these labor pains are all about. All I can say is Father forgive me for not pursuing who I really am. I can see now that in my flesh I would have walked away from my inheritance in a heartbeat. I have always just walked away. And it was not necessarily because I was afraid but it was because I just did not know how. So as I am confronted by situations that I must face and am doing my best to learn that I must face them.

By **Inawantji Scales** (Aboriginal, Australia) – **Not white man's way but Jesus way!**

This is about Millie's life, straight forward nothing hidden every bit of her life shines out. Oh she is so brave to do this, to write this book. I don't think I could do it, open my heart and life to others to read it. I would feel shamed and think people will judged me. And what about Will this is about him too- wonder what he felt, but it's not really about our feeling it's all about Creator and what He wants us to do.

She didn't want to move from Santa Barbara to the remote desert to northern Arizona. Will was the one Creator touched and changed in the high mountains of the Sierras. Creator showed Will about the Native people of America and was calling him to them with songs, dance, and others things, after more dreams and visions and especially confirmation to Millie. Two years later they packed up and moved to Hopiland. They made friends and love the people and showed Gods love through friendship and to worship the Creator the way he made them to be not to turn into white man's way but Jesus way.

Millie and Will support, encourage their Indigenous brothers and sisters to worship and be Hopi, Paiute, Chumash or Anangu Pitjantjatjara (mine). But of course, not all culture is good. Every culture there is bad and good, like what Jesus did- He challenged his Jewish tribe to change and get their hearts straight and turn them back to the Father. We, the Indigenous people need to take what's good in our culture and redeem our songs and dance and worship and praise our loving father creator and be followers of Jesus.

The Great Eagle Rising

Table of Contents

Reviews on Amazon & Etc. -- v

From the Author-- 1

Chapter 1 - Not a "Missionary" type ----------------------------------- 4

Chapter 2 - Kill the Indian and save the man ------------------------- 13

Chapter 3 - It is not up to us to redeem the Culture ----------------- 18

Chapter 4 - Daring to challenge the darkness ------------------------- 25

Chapter 5 - My Heart Aches!--- 34

Chapter 6 - Joyous events in Hopi------------------------------------- 45

Chapter 7 - A Garden in Hopi --- 54

Chapter 8 - Our God Is Concerned For the Nations---------------------- 65

Chapter 9 - Centipedes & the Sting of Death -------------------------- 83

Chapter 10 - Hardly a Dull moment------------------------------------- 91

Chapter 11 - Forgiveness -- 102

Chapter 12 - Repent for our arrogant ways and
               Take a position of Humility------------------------- 113

Table of Contents - Continued

Chapter 13 - Dragonflies and Roses --- 129

Chapter 14 - Clash of Two Cultures --- 134

Chapter 15 - The Koreans are crazy in good and bad ways! --- 148

Chapter 16 - A Garden Near the Mountain --- 160

Chapter 17 - Our Lives on this Earth, Such a Mystery to Me --- 174

Chapter 18 - Rising Up! --- 189

Chapter 19 - Polished Arrow --- 196

Chapter 20 - "Is It You, Jesus?" --- 199

Chapter 21 - Life's Lessons --- 212

Chapter 22 - Dream Keeper --- 220

Chapter 23 - Blessed is the One who is Full of Quiver --- 229

Chapter 24 - Can we ask the Wildest Questions? --- 241

Chapter 25 - "Every Bush Is a Flame with the Fire of God" --- 254

About the author --- 266

From the Author

I purchased some delicious strawberries to give out to some people, but, I kept them too long and they went moldy. Stories can be like gifts of fruit which need to be given away when you sense it is the right time, or they may go sour or have no effect to do anyone any good. I thought this is the time for this story as I did not want to keep it too long and have it go moldy. I want to tell it while it is still fresh.

According to some, I am considered a bad missionary because I don't fit into their paradigm of how to minister among the Native Americans. I cannot help that. I need to walk this life on earth the best I can. I cannot dictate to the original people of North America the same old European ways of doing church. The church has been there and done that for five hundred years. It has proven only to be a dismal failure as there are still only 2-5% believers among all the native tribes.

There was an awful thing called "apartheid" in Africa. But this still goes on in the U.S. The natives of North America who are also called the "Red Indians" have nothing except casinos these days. They have lost their land, culture, language and dignity through boarding schools and many abuses. And the church is often still saying the same thing to this present day. We want them to cut their hair, sing white hymns, not do their cultural dances (good or bad) in order to be called "a Christian."

I believe we cannot fully see the beauty of God in the Native American world, if we try to make them white European. This would be to ask God to turn all the multi-faceted colors of the dragonflies into just one gray color.

This is just my own story which no one can argue or take away. It is simply my own journey of living among the Hopi Indians in Arizona and learning who I am as a child of God.

This book is a continuation of The Great Eagle Calling. I am not about to pretend that we have had some great revival out in Hopiland. In fact, I sometimes think that the Native American expressions of church may never happen at the rate we are seeing.

Culture is not in existence just for a people group or tribe, but to bring honor to the Creator. What are all the dances and ceremonies about, if they don't bring awareness of the Creator's heart in those things? No culture is positive or negative in itself, for every culture has uniqueness which honors our Heavenly Father and things which break His heart. I simply shared what we experienced in Hopiland, neither glorifying the culture, nor putting it down.

Even within our own mission, YWAM(Youth With A Mission), most people know nothing about Native Americans. They pray for every other country but forget the tribes within this nation. This is a conscience-raising book to say that our God has created more than 500 beautiful Native American tribes, which need to be respected and allowed to choose how they can worship the Lord as Natives and not look White any longer in order to follow Jesus.

I believe that God hears the prayer of the saints. We are His children, set apart for God, and when we pray He will honor our prayers! The prayers of the saints brought deliverance to many of the nations, because someone brought those nations to the attention of those who pray. I want to bring attention to North America and cry out to God to bring deliverance to the Hopi and other Native tribes, who suffer with depression, hopelessness, alcoholism, drugs, suicide, etc.

The name missionary simply means a messenger and we should all be that—God's messenger to this world.

I am in fear and trembling about publishing this book as I am brutally honest of confession of many things. It is easier to disappear into anonymity, where no one can see or hear you and you won't be criticized.

But I am going to stand before the throne of God someday, just as you are, and I am going to live my life to the best of my ability to bring Him honor. I desire to do all that I feel He is requiring of me, and this book is one of them.

The beginning of birth pangs, travailing to bring in something new, always has a heavy price. Matthew 24:9 says at that time, people will be handing men over into pressure of tribulation and affliction and treated repeatedly with ill will and constantly hated by all the ethnic nations because of the name of Jesus. I do believe that something is about to burst among the Native American nations and that we are at the beginning stage of a birth of something great!

"Noquivi for the Soul" was suggested as a sub-title by a Hopi sister, Lorna Joseph. Noquivi (a traditional mutton and hominy stew) is much more than what is a bowl of chicken soup for the white men. It is a traditional Hopi stew which is presented at all the special ceremonies and dances and all the other social gatherings. I am grateful for her suggestion that this book can be food for the soul. I felt so honored that she would even suggest this that I just had to somehow fit it into the book cover.

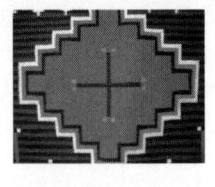

Chapter 1

Not a "Missionary" type

The word *missionary* comes with much baggage. It intimidates many people. It puts the missionaries on a spiritual echelon above normal people. I don't appreciate being a missionary sometimes.

Remember how God made Balaam's donkey talk? God cannot make people become missionaries because free will is involved. I believe most of those who became missionaries became that because God is irresistible and not because they think they are so holy. I probably have more than a couple of hundred confessions in this book without saying "I confess". I just want you to know that we are only human.

It seems to me that a missionary should have certain qualities like some quiet Amish people or a Franciscan monk. Well, neither Will nor I am like that at all. One should know that if God chose imperfect people like Will and me to be missionaries that He can choose anyone.

When my Christian girlfriend in college found out that I actually liked Scarlett O'Hara in "Gone with the Wind", she almost had a cow. My friend's mouth was opened from the shock so long that a fly could have gone in and out of her mouth about five times. She acted like there was absolutely nothing good in that character. I like Scarlett O'Hara because she is a fighter and not a quitter. She lived tenaciously and did not give up. She is not a wimp at anything and met all the challenges of life with both sleeves rolled up. Of course, I don't like everything about Scarlett O'Hara—her terrible and bratty ways. She really should have gotten a good spanking.

Everyone has something good and something evil in their hearts somewhere, like every culture. There is no one or no culture that is perfect. My friend acted as though I liked only the deceitful side of Scarlett. It is amazing how some people could leap to a conclusion like that. She kept saying that she just could not believe that I liked Scarlet O'Hara, like I had killed somebody. She was terribly disappointed in me. Before that, she really liked me and had me on such a pedestal, like I was really something.

I think I disappoint a lot of people because I cannot seem to fit into their perfect image of how a "Christian" should be, no matter how hard I try. I have mostly stopped trying to please men, but only my heavenly Father.

I am always asking the Lord to help me not be like Scarlett, as much as I want to be sometimes in order to get my way. I don't want to meet the Lord face to face someday and have Him ask me why I was up to no good. But it is much more that I want to please Him because I love Him.

If I were a true missionary, I should not like Scarlett at all, not one bit, only sweet Melanie. Scarlett seems a lot more interesting to me and real with all of her human tendencies and follies. I've thrown a thing or two against a wall. I just know that I have felt nearly as desperate as Scarlett during the Civil War. I have felt famine and defeat. Melanie seems too sweet to be true. If someone came after my husband the way Scarlett did with Ashley, I would want to scratch her eyes out. Scarlett really needed to get a life concerning her infatuation with Ashley. She really irritated me with her conceited face, her selfish behaviors and with her pathetic longing of Ashley. I just wanted to shake her silly. She could have made up her mind to call Ashley a "varmint" just as she called Rhett Butler, if she really wanted to. After all, love and hate is also a choice.

I am terrified that any of us could have any resemblance to Scarlett. I know we can all be just as selfish, conniving and evil as Scarlett and even worse. It is not like we are so high and holy on our own. I just know that we have a choice. It scares me sometimes that we have a choice. I also know that there is death and darkness somewhere deep inside of me without God. I am no better than Scarlett—the only difference is that I have found life and light in the Son of God.

Now, about Will—He had a rough childhood. His father died when he was only five years old. His parents had taken him, his younger sister Bonnie, and his baby brother John to a Christian camp. Both of his parents contracted Polio, and his father died within a few days. Will's dad was studying to be an engineer and was a very loving husband and father. One can imagine the shock and sorrow of Will's mother, now being a widow with three children, all five and under.

When the newspaper carried the story and the photo of Will's mother, regarding this first incident where one spouse had survived but not the other, she received hundreds of letters from suitors wanting to marry her. God made men to be the protectors and fighters. I suppose most men have these tendencies inside of them. Perhaps these men thought they were going to save Will's mom, who was a beautiful poor maiden who was in trouble. They all wanted to be a knight in shining armor on a white horse.

I wish she had kept those letters, so I could have read the soggy and good intentions of those men. But, of course, only an egotistical woman would do such a thing and lug them around from one place to another. Besides, no one would keep such things after almost fifty years, unless they were a packrat.

Five years later, Audrey did marry someone who ended up being very abusive. Will's mom recalls how one time, his step-father had him on the ground with his knee on the small of his back and was beating him. When she tried to stop the beating, she ended up getting a black eye and had to run over to the neighbor's house to get help. Will had somehow blanked out this memory, although he recalls other incidents. He felt totally powerless at times.

A person's past is like a shadow that is always sewn to you, it is not like Peter Pan's shadow which has to be sewn on. It is amazing how our past history can creep up on us so suddenly. It is like a shadow hiding somewhere deep inside of you. Angry and weird emotions suddenly appear, when something reminds you of an awful event that may have happened to you long ago. I admire people who don't have a temper. They seem so noble and don't appear to need any self control, while I have to work so hard at it. It would be nice to have a perfect husband, and if I were perfect myself. But what is the use of talking about that?

It is not easy being in a full time ministry together as missionaries as a couple. Two people could have a thousand different opinions on a thousand different matters. A marriage is a clash of two cultures. It is like being in a promised land, and still being a pilgrim in a strange land. One minute one feels that he or she is so blessed that one pities all those poor singles who are not yet married. The next minute, one counts them to be the most blessed.

It is like coffee and milk coming together. Some say you should drink coffee for its taste only, but I think it is nasty. Without milk or crème, it tastes like a bad cigar (not that I know what that would be like). Who needs that? Most men desperately need a woman like thick black coffee needs milk.

Many of us could never be good enough for our earthly fathers. This resulted in such a deep longing for me to be loved and accepted that it felt like a black hole in the galaxy. Not even a loving spouse or a friend could possibly fill this vast hole in a person; only the Great Spirit of God. With Him, there is great redemption! He will make ALL things beautiful in the end!

As someone once said, "It is better to light a candle than curse the darkness." I don't want to complain about not having an earthly father. That would be like cursing the darkness. I want to light a candle and say that I have an awesome Heavenly Father.

Once in college, I had to have a meeting with my Campus Crusade ministry leader, Betty Hartley, who told me that I should not wear this one long shirt dress on the college campus because it showed my figure too much. She said that men think things and that their brains were wired differently. This was a very long time ago, but I remember this slinky dress since I had been confronted by Betty. It was just a simple, comfortable cotton dress which went down to my feet. I told Betty that if one of my roommates wore the same dress that she would not be having a meeting with them, and she said that was true. She should have just told me that the same dress cannot be worn by a flamingo and by a hippo and that I should just be quiet and that I was being rebellious when she was only trying to help me be godly. I am not saying that I was some gorgeous flamingo and that my roommates, Kim and Marianne were some fat hippos, because they were not even fat at all, but the point I am trying to make is that I was not a good candidate for a missionary. I confess I liked that dress. And now, looking back, I see that Betty was right.

I really got it once I married. The Lord has made physical and sexual intimacy for a reason. It was the Lord's way to make men to be aroused. If He didn't make it that way, the men would be oblivious to what the women need. The men would go out and work and forget all about that they have a bride. But, he must try to please his wife because if she is mad at him, he can't touch her.

In my mind, it is a miracle that we have as many honorable men on this earth as we do. I am talking about those men who try to have pure hearts and have self control to keep their minds and hands to themselves.

I think it is very important for the female race to dress modestly so that the men would not want to grab what the Lord has made only for the bride groom to grab. I don't think it is right for women to be all covered up in black or in a Mumu dress either.

There is bound to be some rebellion when there is such a lack of self expression. I believe if men are going to think impure thoughts, they are going to think it even if a girl wears a Mumu dress which shows no figure at all. How we dress is very important. In certain inner cities, the way you dress could get you killed.

I often feel like Scarlett and Melanie are fighting inside of me. It may appear all too schizophrenic with these warring thoughts in my mind. Maybe you are too, except you did not write a book which reveals your inner wrestling.

For instance, I have an elder Christian brother who pets me and kisses me on top of my head when he comes over to our place. I am going to tell him to knock it off the next time he pets me like a dog. Missionaries shouldn't think such thoughts. After all, he is only trying to show his affection and love. But, missionaries are just human beings. They can be just as selfish, ambitious and think bad thoughts as anyone else. They have to repent as any child of God if they are to continue in missionary work.

One minute, I wish I could be sweet and delicate and kind and the next minute, I want to be like Peter who literally cut off one of the ears of one of the men who came to arrest Jesus. It is a good thing that Jesus picked up the ear and put it back on the man. I wish all my mistakes were that easily taken care of on this earth. One minute, I want to look like a "typical" missionary and then the next minute, I don't want to look like a "missionary" at all, whatever that means. I want to dress like some hip young lady or a stylish and classy woman like I came out of some Beverly Hills shop, not that I have been to any. I really don't care.

I told Betty once that I was thinking of going into a nunnery. I was attracted to the idea of being able to serve the Lord with all my life. Betty told me that there were other ways of loving God fully in the communities through my life, with all my heart. She didn't say it, but I think she was thinking that I would not enjoy being a nun. Besides, I like having kids and having a house and decorating and having people over and all that stuff about married life. And, if I had not married Will, I never would have experienced all the beautiful people we got to meet in this ministry, on this planet earth.

And, that is another thing. I love having all kinds of special memorabilia and artsy things around our home. I was an Art major and I think God made me this way. I am fascinated by colors and shapes and all the beauty of how things are made. In other words, I am a bit of a packrat. I don't know whether a missionary should be someone who has too many things, because that would be materialistic. A missionary who is a packrat should not enter the kingdom of God, doesn't the Word of God say that somewhere?

Truly, I do have too many things, but much of my things bring me memories of where we have been and the love of those who gave to us. I do know that I need to curb my appetite concerning the things of this world, even though they may be on great sales and may represent art and God's creativity through human beings to me. What is a decent missionary? Someone who has bare walls? I think some people don't care about art or interior decorating, and that is fine, but don't ask me to be the same in order to be a decent missionary.

I am not pleased to be a missionary sometimes. They are always being watched. If one is a lawyer or a company executive or a model, they don't have to give an account to anyone, and they probably make a whole lot more money than missionaries. They don't have to give an account as to how they are spending their money. I used to run into some of our financial supporters at the grocery stores back in California. I worried about what I had in my shopping cart. Perhaps, I had purchased some expensive-looking meat or ice cream.

And how did I look that day? Perhaps, I had on a designer dress, and I feel I have to explain to them that it was a miracle of a find at a second-hand store. I sometimes felt like I was a fake, because I had purchased these nice designer jeans and dresses from the thrift stores and wore them. But, who is a fake anyway? What makes a person a fake? Just because someone spent a lot of money on a dress and the other only a few dollars, does the amount spent on this earth make one genuine and the other a fake? Well, in that case, I may just choose to be a fake.

Some people tell you that you should not be going to thrift shops. "You are a child of God," they say, and you should not have to bow low to second-hand items. You are doomed either way, no matter what you do. The fact is, I like antiques and thrift shops because they are interesting. I can't stand the malls. Everything looks the same.

There are people who may look expensive, but never buy anything. Yep, they are the missionaries who are counting every dollar in their minds, while they pick up everything in the store thinking that they need to use their money for something else. But there is something good about having these warm bodies in the stores browsing around, because no one likes to go into an empty store. These missionaries are good as decoys to bring other customers into the store as one warm body attracts the others to come in.

By the way, this word, "missionary" is not very well-received at all among the Native Americans, as it had often brought much pain of bringing the "white man's religion" to them. No matter, God did call Will and me and our three children far away from all that we had known in California. It doesn't matter if anyone else thinks we are fit to be missionaries or not, because it was not our idea to be called. If anyone does not like it that we have been chosen to be missionaries, they are simply going to have to talk to the Lord about it. Arizona was the last place we wanted to come to at that time. I say "at that time," because now I think it is one of the most beautiful places in the world. If it was up to us, we would have said, "No thank you, God! We would rather stay where it is warmer in winter and more near to the ocean and where I can grow roses."

What is frustrating is that everyone thinks that a "missionary" is someone who goes to some places like Africa or India or China or somewhere overseas, but not here right inside of America. It stinks (pardon my expression as this pun is intended), sometimes to be a missionary among the Native Americans, because it already has such a stench of bad history.

It is like going into a marriage to a person who had been previously in an abusive relationship where she had been robbed of all her true identity and personality through physical, mental and sexual violence. No matter how much you try to love that person, she will always be suspicious of you. It takes such a long time to build trust, and such a short time to tear it down with one misunderstanding or one wrong action.

For the past hundreds of years, the missionaries wanted the Native Americans to all look like them. It was just like the religious leaders who wanted Jesus to act and look just like them. They got so angry when he refused, that they finally hung him on the cross. It really is still like that and it really would be a lot easier to start from scratch somewhere else.

Not a "Missionary" type
Will & Millie, 1980

Chapter 2

Kill the Indian and save the man

It has been said in the past, "The only good Indian is a dead Indian!" or "Kill the Indian, save the man." I know that you might be gasping right now as you just read that. Our friend Ida Walking Bear was sent to a boarding school when she was very little. She did not come home back to the Hopi reservation until she had graduated from high school. She lost all her language and culture for she was not allowed to speak her language in school. In fact, the kids were punished if they were found speaking in their native language to one another. All boys' long hair was cut and their native garments were replaced with military style uniforms. The church was often working alongside our US government in conducting these schools.

Sadly enough, nothing has really changed much. The government run boarding schools are much more respectful of native culture these days. However, the Church at large is still telling our Native American brothers and sisters that the only good "Christians" are those who are "dead Indians." They only approve those who will shun and die to their culture and not play their drum songs, nor go to any of their ceremonies.

Yet the Church may know nothing about what these songs or ceremonies are about, and they reject them, simply because they look or sound so different. If it doesn't feel good and seems foreign, it must be evil, right? We have traveled to many other places in the world, and I get sick thinking what we as "Christians" have done to these nations. We still see pastors, even near the equator, wearing a suit and a tie to preach their sermons on Sunday morning services in almost hundred degree Fahrenheit weather with over ninety percent humidity, because this is what is expected of a man of God. I wonder what was wrong with their own cultural garb.

For over a century, the Hopi Christians were told that they could not be involved in any of their Hopi ways, and therefore they could not really witness to even their own loved ones. I believe this was a reciprocal reaction. When the Hopi believers were prevented by the church from attending traditional dances and ceremonies, they were no longer the salt and light within their community—not because they were living unrighteously but because they were no longer involved in most of the community's doings. It is our prayer that the Hopis would dance for the Lord beyond what they've done in the ages past.

If one has found a tree with the most sweet and delicious fruits, it would be such a shame not to be able to tell your loved ones about it. But this is how it was and still is that as Hopis, they are told that they must not attend any of the tribal ceremonies or dances, as they are all evil. How is a missionary to know and say that everything about someone else's culture is evil? To a degree I understand this, as we were running a discipleship house when we were first married. We ended up having to ban all other types of music except Christian or classical. This was not because we thought all country or jazz songs were evil, but because we simply could not go through every single person's cassette tapes and listen to every song to determine what was godly and what was not. We simply asked that they hold off for the short time being while they were with us. Our goal was to see them follow the Holy Spirit, leading them into godly decisions regarding the culture that they were immersed in.

Was this the reason why the Natives were told by the missionaries not to go to any of the ceremonies or the dances? However, it was not just for a short time of refraining, but permanently, so they could not be who they are. In order to be a Christian, they had to look European because that was holy. Only a cult would want everyone to conform and look exactly like the leader's description of what is holy. Everyone starts looking and talking just like the cult leader.

I find that most Native people are a very polite kind of people. If someone of the rank of a "pastor" or a "missionary" tells them that they must not do this thing, they would not disobey or question this order. And what is worse is that, if the parents and the grandparents have been under this kind of a regimen, they would not betray their elders or ancestors because it would be saying their parents were wrong, and that would not be respectful. One may argue that the missionaries and the pastors were not saying that these Hopis not go to their relatives, but only to the ceremonies and dances. But, it does not work that way in Native American world. When you don't go to their ceremonies and dances, they don't want you hanging around them, either, because they think you are not one of them. I am not saying that one has to attend the ceremonies and the dances either, but only that we as outsiders cannot determine that for them.

Nita once struggled with this question as to whether she could enter back into her kiva to pray among her own people. It is not because she felt a lack in any way as a follower of Jesus, but simply that she felt that there were good things of her culture which were worth keeping for the glory of our Lord's name. She was given a picture of a shopping mall, as she inquired of the Creator in her prayer. One can walk down the mall, but that does not mean that one believes in the products being sold at every single store at that mall. And yet, one can choose to go into some of those stores to purchase an item or to buy gifts for the loved ones. No one would think that one is in sin because there might be one store which sells provocative night gowns or that there might be a store that sells adult movies at the mall.

Although there are disagreements among the Hopi Christians as to what they can and cannot do in their culture, we're very much amazed to see how some of them are being moved in their hearts to still go to their dances, ceremonies, and into the kivas (traditional ceremonial chambers) to pray for their people. We are genuinely seeing their hearts for their people, and they are praying in the name of Jesus and to no other.

> Who has ascended into heaven, or descended?
> Who has gathered the wind in his fists?
> Who has established all the ends of the earth?
> What is His name and what is His Son's name? If you know!
> (Proverbs 30:4)

The Hopis have an old testament with good laws but not the fulfillment of God's Son. It is amazing to me that just as the Hopis have their ancient prophesies, God gave a hint of His own Son in the book of Proverbs a thousand years before Jesus ever came to this earth.

It seems that there had been many full churches in the mid twentieth century, but there were hardly any believers when we arrived in 1996. Perhaps the older ones did not care to share their faith with the younger generations, as a Calvinistic teaching seems to have been prevalent with some. One old Hopi saint would not join us for jail ministry, because he said that if they were of the elect they would be saved and nothing could change that.

In talking to people it seems that the churches emptied out in the 1960's and 70's around the time when the American Indian Movement and others were saying that Natives needed to reclaim the fullness of their identity, which had been stolen through the abuses of the past couple centuries. This may have been more attractive to that next generation of Hopi young people, as well. After all, to be a Christian in both the US and Canada meant one could not be a Native American, but must actually be more "white" than Native. We believe this is a lesson that must be learned for the Native church of today.

The Native American believers must take up their godly stand to live righteously and in the fear of God. And as for the rest of us, name changing from Indians to Native Americans is not enough. Yes, we did commit genocide in this nation. By the early twentieth century, we had reduced them to a quarter of a million from what used to be millions. We must live our apologies much more in action than just in words.

We are so in awe of some of these ladies who are taking authority to do exploits in Jesus' name and that they have the great courage to believe that they can take back what Satan has stolen, by going right into their ancient places of worship, and being truly the "People of Peace." It is like taking back all the art and music which the enemy had stolen from Christians through fundamentalism in the past century.

Chapter 3

It is not up to us to redeem the Culture

When your reading glasses get too foggy from the steam of a hot bath water, it is best to immerse the lenses into the steaming hot water. This will take care of the problem as now the lenses will be almost the same hot temperature as the bath water and you would be able to see. Likewise, one needs to immerse oneself with the people of the land if one desires to see more clearly rather than judging with their own foggy lenses through their own world view.

Someone asked me, "What is redeeming the culture?" I answered, "It is not up to us as cultural outsiders to determine what is redeemable and what is not, but that it is up to every Hopi and the other Native American believers. They need to hear God and determine for themselves what, within their culture, is honoring to Him and what needs to be discarded." We, at Tribal Winds, have come under criticism, because we do not tell the people to stop going to the Dances or Ceremonies, cut their hair, sing their songs, etc.

We recognize that we are not the Holy Spirit, to tell the Hopi believers what to do and what not to do, but that they have the freedom and responsibility in Christ to obey the Lord and to honor Him, with the Word of God as their guide. It would make our lives a lot easier to act like we know it all and tell them to do as the traditional Church had been teaching for the past 120 years. That approach only produced Native American believers who talk, sing and act like the white people. If they went out to the rest of the world, no one would see the beauty of their cultural heritage glorifying the

Creator and His Son. Who wants to see a bunch of Native Americans with suits and ties, who dance and sing like the Europeans? Why is it okay to hear the Africans sing and dance in an African style, but not the Native Americans? It is no wonder that the enemy seems to be threatened to cause such an upheaval and commotions about this, as well as so much fear. If this is not something which is an affront to the kingdom of darkness, we would not be running into so much opposition.

Anytime I have found so much resistance, I found it worth fighting for, as it most likely is the cause which will bring advancement to the Glory of our Father.

So, we have some who believe that they need to enter into the kivas, because they believe Jesus would have gone down there to pray for the people right where they are and to pray for the eyes of their people to be opened. Some of the new believers think they ought to attend and even let their children dance at the social dances so that they can be connected to their own people. In the past, European missionaries told them that all of Hopi ways are not to be mixed into this Westernized Christian faith. Thereby they almost completely severed any relationships with their own people and have made it difficult to witness at all.

We also have those we have worked with, who feel that they, as believers in Christ, need little of Hopi ways. They are very happy to sing Western European hymns and not attend any ceremonies out here, and yet they bless others who feel differently because they know each one will stand before the throne of God some day and be accountable for only their own actions.

We have another, who is a "holy water carrier" in a very traditional village. She feels she ought to continue this job to bring the water to her people for the dances and ceremonies, because she believes this is where she can pray for her own people to come to know the Lord as she did. We must encourage and pray for these, our sisters and brothers in Christ. They are trying their best to follow and obey Jesus, but are coming under persecution by the church, which seems to believe anything that resembles Hopi is evil.

In redeeming the culture, we have been asked at times about stumbling our "weaker" brothers. In Hopiland, it is hard to know who exactly the weak ones in Christ are. Some people seem to have an agenda of weakness, meaning they are always worried that somebody else may be too weak to handle our freedom in Christ. Perhaps instead, we and they need to educate and disciple people into the fullness of what Christ offers us. In this case that Hopis can be Hopi and follow Jesus. Hopi after all means, "People of Peace." Let us not throw out the baby with the bathwater.

As the Hopi are turning to Christ, we are now faced with certain matters to a much greater degree. One is the issue of their "Massau," the god of the underworld and death in Hopiland, as defined in the Hopi dictionary. Some say that he is the Great Spirit. Some others say that he is Jesus or Messiah. Massau, who first met the people when a remnant long ago emerged from the judgment of the Third World into this the Fourth World, has been depicted as wearing a scary, bloody mask. Many of the children and even some adults are scared to death of him. Some old Christians will say that he is really Satan.

To make things even more confusing (or more interesting), it is told and also written in books that there are two Massaus—one who is poor and humble and good, the other who is greedy and evil. One friend believes that Massau, usually depicted with a bloody face, is the same as Jesus, the Suffering Servant. She challenges us to think of Him in the *Passion of the Christ* film. He was bloody and bruised, with thorns on his head and not recognizable.

Isaiah 52:14(NIV) says, "Just as there were many who were appalled at Him; His appearance was marred more than any man." In Isaiah 53:4-5 and 8 we read:

> Surely our grief He Himself bore, and our sorrows
> He carried; yet we ourselves esteemed Him stricken,

smitten of God, and afflicted. He was pierced through for our transgressions, He was crushed for our iniquities . . . He was cut off out of the land of the living, for the transgression of my people to whom the stroke was due.

This is a matter that needs much prayer, as the name of God is very important for any people group.

Let me give you an example from my own nation. When missionaries came into Korea (there was no such thing as South or North Korea as it was all one nation then), my people had their own name for God. The name was and is "Ha-na-nim". When we count, we say, "One, two, and three . . ." in English. In Korea, we say, "Ha-nah, dul, seht . . ." So the name for God in Korean literally means, "One Sir" or "One God."

Initially the missionaries wanted to use the name for God in Chinese for the Koreans, perhaps because they thought we were all alike. The Koreans and the Japanese are as different in their language and culture as the French are from the Finnish. The Koreans were very resistant to the Gospel and there was not a spiritual breakthrough to be seen. In fact, history has it that the Koreans were so resistant to the Gospel that they even killed some missionaries. Then some wise missionaries allowed the Koreans to use "Ha-nah-nim" in our Bibles and in our prayers. After that, revivals broke out which no one could stop. Only a century later, they became the Asian nation with the most Christians and the biggest missionary sending country besides the USA.

So, for the Koreans, redeeming their name for God in our language was of supreme importance to their acceptance of that name. Now, is it possible for the Hopis to redeem one of their names for God? This is only up to the Hopi Christians themselves.

Encouraging these Native believers to hold onto those aspects of their cultures that the Holy Spirit shows them to be of Him is a challenging process. Some believe it is impossible and wrong; others of us find it uncomfortable but absolutely necessary. We all must learn to find our own personal faith walk in Jesus without clinging excessively to our spiritual parents. The eagle must force its young to find their own wings of flight.

One of the ladies from a very traditional village decided to go into the kiva for all-night ceremonial dances and songs. Only at certain times are the ladies able to use the kivas for their ceremonies. She said that, after a number of hours, she came out with her daughter and went home to sleep because the Lord told her, "You don't have to be down here all night. You can go home and rest, because I paid the price." She went home and slept and rested, and later went back down back into the kiva.

When the ladies were dancing and singing to make fun of the men who are lazy, who are not going out to the fields to plant, the Lord spoke to her again, that He is not pleased with that song. So she said to her daughter, "The Lord is not pleased. We need to sit down." So, they did not dance with the rest of the ladies in the kiva, but sat and repented, instead, for making fun of the men. When all the ladies were climbing up the ladder from the kiva to go to the shrine before the sunrise, she and her daughter came home, because the Lord spoke in her heart that He did not want her going to the shrine.

This sister in Christ obeyed every whisper of our Lord and obeyed, while still being with her people. We are told that she and some others are taking Bibles into the kivas, because they say that the Book is good for their people. One may say that this action may be "syncretism," which combines the Hopi religion and Christianity. However, if they are reading the Word of God in the kivas to some people who will never—and I mean never—enter the church buildings, the promise of God is that this Word which has gone forth, will not come back void.

Three of the Hopi ladies in yet another village felt that they are still to go down to the kiva, to pray for their people. Four ladies in that village are picked every year to come out from the kiva and run in the Four Directions and pray. Surprisingly, three of the women who follow Jesus were picked this time. They were all given this honored role, and each was given an eagle feather to carry the prayers of their people to their assigned directions—north, south, east and west. Only one out of four ladies picked was not a follower of Christ. What an amazing time we live in! Our friend said that she knew the feather did not have any power in itself, as only Jesus can answer prayers. We think that perhaps using a feather, corn pollen and cedar smoke may be valid symbols and actions of prayer for these people—just as kneeling and clasping hands may be acts that are conducive to prayer for many Protestants, rosary beads for Catholics and incense for Episcopalians.

It is still such a puzzle to me why it is holy for the Russian Orthodox to use their smoke as an incense to God, but when the Native Americans do it, it is evil. For me to quietly not say anything concerning this matter would be to sit and quietly allow the Jews to be persecuted, while they are being sent to concentration camps. Or it would be to quietly turn our heads and pretend we don't see anything while an Afro-American is being chained down in a dungeon. It would be turning our heads, when someone is being robbed at gunpoint or when someone is being mistreated with a radical hate crime. Someone has to say something to stop these hate crimes, which calls the European Christianity holy, but still label the Native American Christianity savage.

Once, guitars were considered instruments of the Devil. Are you kidding? One would hardly ever see an electric guitar or a percussion drum set in the sixties in any of the churches. But opinions changed, because the opinions were not necessarily of God, but they are just opinions. If this was God, the Word of God says that He is the same yesterday, today and tomorrow, and would be the same no matter what era. But it did change and now almost all the churches have these instruments. As someone once said, "Everyone can have an opinion, but not everyone can have the truth."

There is a new movement of the Lord coming among the Native Americans and the First Nations people all around the globe.

It is happening sovereignly by the move of God's own hand. Our brothers and sisters in Hopi and all over the world seem to have a desire to be able to sing and dance for the Creator with their own expressions. They are refusing to act "white" at this time, in their desire to honor Christ. These new believers do not want to have their mouths cleaned with soap for speaking in their own native tongues, nor do they want to have their own children taken away to the boarding schools to be educated to be "white"—which was done here for about a hundred years since the late 1800's.

This movement of the Lord includes "contextualization," which simply means following Christ within the context of one's culture and redeeming parts of their culture. This will continue, whether any of us feel comfortable or not because God is jealous for His "First Nations" people groups to come to know Him. We also ought to be jealous for that! We have been accused of stumbling our weaker brothers, who may be tempted to be drawn back to the traditional religion. On the contrary, it is my desire not to "stumble" our weaker brothers or sisters who have just come to know Christ by demanding, once again, that they have to act and dance and speak and sing like the European Christians.

The Lord said that the Good Shepherd left the ninety-nine to find one sheep that was lost. We believe that it is time now to leave the one sheep to find the ninety-nine.

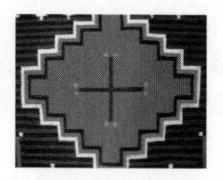

Chapter 4

Daring to challenge the darkness

This is a strange land I have come to on this Hopi Indian reservation. At least, strange to what I was used to anyways. It is a different sort of a place which you don't expect to find in the United States.

Do you see any place where you can see the young virgin maidens dancing in the snow? Yes, the young maidens were dancing barefoot in the snow! They were rhythmically waving their cedar sprigs to the drum beat; it was indeed a magical site to behold. The Hopi dancers wave their cedar sprigs to the drum beat in some of their dances. We are told that the evergreen leaves represent everlasting life.

As we watched a Buffalo Dance today at the village of Mishongovi, large snowflakes were descending beautifully upon the dancers. I realized again the hope I have of seeing that dance someday being danced for our Lord. It was a beautiful dance and I was moved to tears. One could live in Arizona all one's life and not realize that there was such a world with a strong and unique culture right inside our own nation in North America.

Lightning hit the home of one of our Christian sisters in a traditional mesa village. The children were playing outside and saw the lightning hit her house. They say that they thought the lightning had gone back and forth between this house and the house of her sister (another believer), and that it was strong enough that they felt the shock. This is such a bad omen in Hopiland that no one dares to stay and live at the house where the lightning has hit. They believe that it is a curse. Or at least, they move out for awhile, even when it hits something near their home.

We were told that the son-in-law of one of the sisters blamed the ladies for turning to Jesus. What was never even dared to be challenged is now being challenged! He was told by these Hopi sisters that in another culture the lightning means "cleansing" and that Hopi culture may not be correct. Furthermore, they believe this lightning signifies that the Lord was cleansing them. This is a monumental thing which God is doing.

We are very much aware of the fact that we are AT WAR in Hopiland. Let me give you some examples of the warfare and the victories which the Hopi Christians are experiencing.

One of the ladies who has been coming to the Puhuqatsi group, or New Life group, had a fearful experience. Her dog turned vicious one night and went into the sheep pen and mauled the sheep so badly that five were killed and two more had to be put down the next day.

She sensed such power of darkness that she tried to call us at home to come and pray for her and her family and her house and property. Since we were not home, she called a friend who also was a follower of Jesus. They decided to pray and take communion together over where this incident happened with the killing of the sheep. They wanted to let the enemy know that they believed Jesus died on the cross and was broken for them and that HE was more powerful than the one that was in this world. After they took communion and prayed with authority over the spirits, they knew that they had won, for a great peace came over both of them. How exciting when they are taking back this land for themselves by the blood of Jesus!

One lady from our New Life group had a dilemma, because she could not decide what she ought to do in one particular situation.

She called another lady in the group and they met together for lunch at the Cultural Center restaurant. When they saw yet another woman from our group, they called her over and held hands and prayed together for guidance. These are all professional ladies within the Hopi Tribe, yet they were not ashamed to be seen in public and praying together in the name of JESUS.

Yet another kachina mask has come off during the dance this month—this being the fourth! Apparently, a kachina on his way into the plaza, lost his balance and stumbled and the mask fell off. The Hopi people must wonder, for their prophecy is told that when a mask comes off that their religion will die and that they will then go into the church. And as we tell the people the Church is not a building.

There were five different night kachina dances this past weekend. Contrary to what may seem as though the culture is getting stronger, this is showing that the Hopi ways are deteriorating. In the old days, there were fewer dances which were done in an orderly and humble manner. Our Hopi sister says that the time is coming when she knows that she will no longer be going down into the kiva, for the Lord has revealed to her things about her own culture which are no longer as beautiful as they used to be long ago.

We are finding that the Lord is raising up mighty warriors who would not be intimidated easily. One Hopi sister said that the kiva was full when she tried to go down during a Night Dance in her village this past weekend. No one was willing to make room for her, even when she politely asked, because now she is attending church. One of her sisters who was already in the kiva, signaled with her hand, for her to go up to the top of the roof and come down the ladder. This would bring her down to the middle of the kiva.

So instead of letting the others intimidate and shun her, she went up to the roof and went down the ladder. When no one wanted to move their stretched legs to let her pass to find a seat, she sat on a crate, which was right in the middle of the kiva. When she saw that yet another of her sisters was at the door way and could not get in, she, too, signaled for her to go up to the roof and come down the ladder. They both sat and prayed that evening for their people.

How wonderful it is when we have Jacob's ladder, to climb to the throne room of our Heavenly Father! It says in Genesis 28:12, "Behold, a ladder was set on the earth with its top reaching to heaven; and the angels of God were ascending and descending on it." Jesus is our Ladder.

The other day I found myself in a fetal position, feeling so hopeless. I later found myself burrowing my head into Will's chest and sobbing, after feeling so hurt and misunderstood. But I sensed that the Lord was saying that I may be tasting only a portion of what price our Hopi brothers and sisters are paying in this land. They feel so misunderstood and accused, and rejected by not just their own traditional people, who don't want them to follow Christ, but also by some Christians who believe that they must act like the Europeans in order to be a "real" Christian. One Christian young man said, "We're not accepted in the kivas and now we're not accepted in the churches."

There have been kachina dances every week in different villages. Last week, the dance was held in our village of Kykotsmovi, the week before that, in Shongopavi, and this week it is up at Bacavi village. In these villages, the girls have all gone inside to grind corn for days, as part of their passage into their womanhood.

Sheila, Danielle and I went and sat on the roof of a house looking down into the plaza, where all the men were dancing with their masks. All their steps are perfectly matched. The sound of the rattles and songs, chanted in deep tones, echoed quietly over the mesas. Would there be a time when masks can somehow be used to illustrate the Lord's redemptive works?

We are ignorant of many things and it will be up to the Hopi Christians to know and choose. We know for certain that some of the non-religious social dances will be presented before the nations in honor of Jesus. We were invited to so many friends' homes to feast, that by the time we finished eating Noquivi (hominy and mutton stew), roasted green chilies, home-baked soda bread, cakes, pies, etc, we could not possibly eat at the fourth house. When we were coming out of the fourth house, someone else asked us to come and eat. Sheila panicked and almost screamed saying, "Oh, I can't eat anymore."

The Hopi people are beginning to go to look for eaglets to be raised on top of their roofs. The birds will be sacrificed after the summer. The *pahos* (the down feathers from their chests) will be used to adorn Hopi prayer sticks, which are placed on different shrines on top of the mesas in Hopiland. These are believed to carry their prayers to the Creator. Eventually, it is our prayer that these noble birds will be spared, as the Hopis come to know that the ultimate sacrifice has been paid by our Lord Jesus Christ on the cross.

I asked once how the Hopis are able to find the eaglets. Our Hopi friend said that the eagles must not be so smart, because year after year, they go back to the same spot to nest—even when their little ones get stolen. However, they never take all the eaglets out of one nest, but leave at least one.

I would choose to be a hummingbird, rather than an eagle in Hopiland. This is because these eagles, which are now tethered up on top of the roofs of the Hopi homes, will never get to fly! I would choose to be a small and insignificant hummingbird, buzzing all around my garden with its iridescent wings rather than to be chained up and then be sacrificed. But this is what our Jesus did for the human race—submitted Himself to sacrifice.

Four of our sisters who come to our gatherings have not been given eagle feathers as a blessing from the kachinas. These are presented to all the households in the village. They were told by their elder brother that they were kahopi, no longer Hopi, because they have turned to Jesus, the wrong path. Instead of being dismayed and rejected, they stood firm together. They told their brother that they are indeed Hopi, or "People of Peace," even BETTER Hopis, because they are now cleansed to pray to the Creator and the Son.

They told the brother that they have seen answers to their prayers for their families, for their village and Hopiland more than ever before.

One of the sisters smiled and told me, "Besides, we saved a bird!" (meaning an eagle) The Hopi Tribe is the only Indian nation in the U.S. which has permission to take eaglets out of the nests, for our government recognizes this as an ancient religious practice. They name them like children, and raise them on the rooftops of their homes. We heard that the neighboring Navajo nation once also asked whether they can sacrifice eagles, but were refused, being told that this was not a part of their original ceremonies.

We went to see one of the dances on top of the mesas overlooking the vast desert land below. We stood on the roof of someone's house and watched five eagles being fed by some young men, little more than an arm's length away from us. Painted toy gifts were hung before each eagle. One can almost feel the wind, with the flapping of their wings.

We find that we have an Old Testament religion here in Hopiland. It has much has to do with following the Law. The Hopi are the ancient people, who had not been moved to this area by the U.S. government. They do not have a "Trail of Tears" from being relocated, as some of the other tribes. How did they survive in the desert for over a thousand years? They have springs on top of every mesa, where clear water flows out from rock crevices, like when Moses hit the rock.

There have been many good intentions historically by the "white" church, but there have sometimes been bad results. When these ancient people enter into the New Covenant with Jesus and are told, once again, to throw away all that is beautiful along with some things which do need to be discarded, we fear that some new believers will fall away due to hurt and confusion.

A Hopi lady recently had a bad car accident. When she was taken to a well-known Hopi medicine man, he told her that this accident was meant to be a whole lot worse by those who wanted to harm her. However, she had a strong Presence who had protected her. She knew this was the Lord, for her injuries were minor. She went down into the kiva for a women's society meeting and shared what had happened. She told them that they also need this new path. She said that Hopi women are different than other Native American tribes, for they can shoot arrows and be warriors. This is why the first ladies who come out of the kiva from this meeting come out shooting arrows. We pray that these ladies will become mighty warriors for the Lord, to bring dignity and honor to a place where there were only ashes and sorrow.

The Hopi men and women are increasingly singing Native style songs in their own language. One song says, "We, the Hopi men, praise You, because we are happy that we have found this new life." Another song is in English, but undoubtedly a Native American melody, which says, "This little light of mine, I'm going to let it shine." Then the song goes into a beautiful chant of "Hayah," which I believe can be a praise and exaltation of Him, similar to "Hallelujah." Every person who has heard these songs which the Hopi believers have composed themselves, seem to well up with tears, or simply break out and cry. Sometimes, we just all sit stunned with such deep emotions that all we can do is quietly gasp, like an audience at the conclusion of a great and fantastic symphony. We believe that these songs are the songs which our Lord has longed to hear for a long time.

I remember when the Lord met Will back in 1994 in the Sierra Nevada Mountains. Will was chanting, "Hayah, Hayah . . ." in the Spirit. In Exodus, when Moses encountered the burning bush, he asked God what name he should give to the people when they asked who had sent him. God said, "Yahweh," which we now know literally means in Hebrew, "to be" or "I am." According to *Strong's Concordance*, the root for this word, "Yaweh" is "Hayah."

We see that native peoples across this continent chant variations on Hayah. Could it be that Yahweh, in some ancient time, gave the peoples an affirmation of their life and lives founded in

Him, as they chant, "Hayah, Hayah, Hayah . . .", perhaps meaning "I am, I am, because You Are!"

Our one Hopi Christian brother did not go down into the kiva this year for the Bean Dance. When his sister asked why he did not go down to the kiva, he told her that he does not need to go down to plant bean sprouts for the kachinas to pass out to people, for it is God who helps him. He was very surprised, when he saw this older sister, his "mother," at church singing and clapping to songs. Yes, one by one, they are coming into church.

How wonderful it is to finally see some of the Hopi ladies calling forth the "Prayer and Fasting" time for God to heal their land! They have already done this. They will go and bring the spring water from all the villages, in order to pray and fast and take communion over their land, and ask God to break the strongholds of the enemy in the heavenlies. They are doing this and weeping together, as we have been praying for all these years. They are calling for an all-night prayer meeting, as well as coming on Thursday evenings and again on Sunday afternoons to worship, pray and fast. They are tired of the many deaths and tragedies in Hopiland. They know that the Lord Himself can bring victory to them.

Worship songs are important in Hopiland. An experiment was once done with various types of music being played for some plants. The plants which had music which sang about beautiful things and good words of life thrived. The plants with music which sang of death and murder and other bad things, shriveled and died. I believe music matters. Some say we just need to be silent and still. Well, guess what? I believe it is both. We need both.

We are hearing many more stories of God's wonder. A brand new roof of a house in one village was blown off during a fierce storm in Hopiland. Yet many old roofs of the believers were left standing nearby. A Hopi Christian lady did not go to the night dances, for she felt God had told her not to go. This is something new, as it would be the norm simply to go to every event. Her brother, a very traditional Hopi, started singing about the blood of the Lamb and other hymns all through the house. Many Hopis are still deciding to follow Christ—even when there are many persecutions, because they are not participating or helping with certain Ceremonies.

We definitely see variation in how the Holy Spirit leads people, which seems to depend on the person and their circumstances. Another Hopi sister told us that she still goes into the kivas to pray when there are ceremonies. One kachina asked her why she was there, if she is supposed to be a Christian. So she asked him, in all the years while he had worn the mask and prayed, whether he ever felt joy in his heart or had an answered prayer. He said, "No." She then told him that she was there, because she knows who her Savior is and that Jesus has given her joy in her heart. She was there to pray for her people, because Jesus does answers her prayers.

A young lady came into the Hopi YWAM building the other day crying. She was hit in her stomach so hard that she was trying to throw up. She was pregnant. It was a perfect picture of Satan wanting to abort the baby which is to be born in Hopiland. Too many young people are dying and too many tragedies are all around Hopi nation. We really need much bigger break throughs. With Christ, this is possible!

Regarding the Hopi church, we must seek the Lord, our ultimate Expert, as to what His church (not ours) should look like. We felt that He had asked us to imagine with Him what the Hopi church should look like. Therefore, we found ourselves early on, regularly coming to Him in creative partnership, to see His indigenous church raised up. Does it look like the church we have always known? No. We believe that it is His Native born church, which will ultimately flourish in Hopi soil.

Chapter 5

My Heart Aches!

We have new problems among the believers. Sexual immorality, gossip, slanders and infighting is in all the churches. It seems to be a part of Satan's tactic, now, to destroy the Church with these bad and ugly things, since he could not keep them from walking the Jesus Path.

In addition, there are Christian men who were looked up to by others, when they overcame alcohol and other drug addictions. Women were especially attracted to these men, like bees to honey, for these guys were suddenly so different. They no longer beat on their girlfriends and were kind to others. All this attention from the other villagers made them puffed up, and they fell back into sin. Two of the Hopi men are back in jail.

This was also the case with the women, whose beauty was enhanced by the presence of the Lord. They now showed his strength and dignity. We found that their old boyfriends were coming back to claim them. Because some of these were the fathers of their children, the women would take them back and be abused once again.

Being in a ministry is okay, as long as there are no human beings. I wished at times to go and be a hermit somewhere. The disagreements among the believers as to whether they can still be Hopi and be able to participate in any of the Hopi traditional events have caused such sharp divisions and confrontations that it has brought many tears to us. We have been accused so badly at times, that I had asked the Lord to be released from the ministry. I believe that the enemy is scared, as we're beginning to see a small, real movement of the Lord. The enemy would love to kill, steal and destroy the work that God is doing. However, we're very much encouraged, as we're seeing God bringing back and redeeming those who had rebelled against Him.

We have a new minister who has come and acts like he has done all the work and boasts, Sunday after Sunday, of how all the Hopis are coming into the Church because of him. Does he not fear God? Does he not know that there have been many missionaries and the Hopi believers, who paid such a high price for over one hundred years in Hopiland? Sometimes, I just want to kick him in his shin. So now we have "the good, the bad and the ugly."

So much time is wasted explaining and arguing over such unimportant things! I am sure that some people think that these are very important matters which will make certain people go to hell. Will said that if we were not so sure of our clear calling here that we would have quit. I almost flew off the handle when I heard that one of our teachers for our DTS (Discipleship Training School) may speak on "smudging," another controversial topic. That would mean using the smoke from the burning of the Cedar or native Sage to demonstrate one of the Native American ways of praying. I could only take so much rejection. I do not mind being liked once in awhile, you know.

I feel a bit like a woman in her last stages of labor pain—screaming, crying, and pleading, not knowing whether she could possibly live to see the baby born. Some have already fallen back to old ways of sin; they are sick of being attacked by the Hopi traditionals and also by the Christians. Only a few of the Hopis came to YWAM, while we were gone on our Sabbatical. We had left the New Life women and men to their own, rather than to our staff, but it seems that they did not trust in their own ability to lead. We still have a long way to go.

We know, nonetheless, that the baby is coming! We are certain that there will be a strong Hopi church, which will be mighty in the Lord someday. They will go to the ends of the earth to preach the Good News to the nations.

We have seen outsiders get kicked out of this reservation. There is a quiet, but firm pressure by the Hopi people, and then the outsiders are told by the Hopi house owner that one of the relatives wants to rent the house. Afterwards, no one else will rent to them, so they must move out of this land. We have also seen the Hopi tribe putting out a message to their people not to have anything to do with certain outsiders whom they deem undesirable to this nation.

I believe the enemy made such an attempt to kick us out, because he did not want us on the reservation. Our landladies received phone calls from a few Hopis, saying we shouldn't be here. However, these attempts were not successful. Many Hopi people have come to be our friends and became believers of our Lord Jesus. We have purposely gone slowly and relationally. We still choose not to post a YWAM sign out in front of our facility. We are not program driven. We do not want to glorify YWAM. We desire to see Jesus glorified with a truly indigenous church—a gathering of the Hopi following Jesus as a people group.

Have you ever felt totally inadequate for what God is calling you to do in your life? I have! I believe I try my utmost to give all my burdens to God, but try as I may, my body does not seem to believe me. I cannot fool my body.

Shingles is a virus that attacks the nervous system, when one's body is worn out or stressed. Most people get shingles on their abdomen or legs. However, God allowed me to get shingles right on the front of my face. I cannot hide anything. I was sick in bed for many days. After seeing a second doctor, I finally began to feel like a human being; however, I still have some scars above my right eye; people probably think it is a pock mark. I know that the Lord is my strength and my shield; my heart trusts in Him and I am helped.

The cares of this world are pressing in from every side. Our intercessor and a very good friend in Arizona has been found with ovarian cancer and is going through chemotherapy. During a very bad thunderstorm a couple of nights ago, we lost several of our electrical appliances to a severe power surge. And yet, I sense that the Lord is challenging me to truly press into Him, to know the true gladness and joy which the world cannot offer. Yes, He is my gladness and joy!

Lightning struck the house of one of our little Sunday school girls. There was much panic once again, as our staff tried going to that house to pick up the little girl for church. All the children in the van, and even the older ladies, were screaming and getting mad, saying that they should not go there and that we are not being respectful to listen to their advice. Our staff, Tamara Leatherby and Charity Theissen did not pick up the girl, but the little girl walked to church on her own with a friend.

Something has lifted and hope has come. We can see clearly that the harvest is plentiful, but "the workers are few."

Sometimes we feel that we have been given more than we can handle, and the spirits of this land—hopelessness and depression—hover over us like a thick fog. Recently, even with many good things happening, I went into a time of prayer and travail asking, "Has God abandoned us? Are we supposed to really be leaders? Have we really heard from the Lord to start an even bigger operating and training base in Flagstaff? Are we crazy?"

I heard the Lord speak in my heart, "Will you trust me? Will you let Me unfold things the way I desire in My perfect timing? I do have a wonderful plan!"

Yes, He will get the job done with or without us, and He does have a wonderful plan! We do not want to miss out. We want to be a part of this move of God among the First Nations people.

One Hopi man came to our house and said to me, "Now that you've been here eight years, and you're still alive and Will and your children are also alive and your marriage is still together and things are going well, it tells me that your God is stronger than my god." I wondered later what this meant. Were we supposed to have been killed or something

After five months and three different satellite technicians, one from Phoenix (500 miles round trip) coming out to our place in Kykotsmovi, we finally got our computer back on line—hallelujah! One of the technicians had seen similar problems on the Navajo reservation, where the client finally had to get a medicine man to pray over the air—following which the problem was solved. I told him that we had a mighty God, who is more powerful than any medicine men around here. As it turns out, it was a small mal-functioning wire connecter, which the previous two technicians neglected to see—hence taking these three technicians almost 1000 miles round trip all together to figure this out. There is a certain disadvantage to living in the middle of the desert, once in awhile.

We must be like Boramir, in "Lord of the Rings", who fought valiantly, despite all his human weaknesses. After receiving a barrage of arrows from the enemy, he fell on his knees to the ground, looking like a big porcupine with all the arrows in his chest. But his eyes never left his enemies. He got back on his feet ever so slowly and then fought once again, valiantly, until his death. As I watched that scene, I realized that one single tear had fallen from my eye. It actually comforted me. I realized that we had been wounded also, and I saw that it was okay to hurt, as we do sometimes when there is such a fierce battle going on all around us. In the end Aragorn, a type of Christ, comforted Boramir for finishing bravely, in spite of his previous failures.

My best friend, Ida Walking Bear, who is 90 years old, has been put into a Nursing home in New Mexico on another reservation near a Casino. She had refused the offer to live with her relatives and it was dangerous for her to be alone in her home in Kykotsmovi.

More than once, she forgot and left a kettle on top of her stove and the house could have started on fire.

We went and visited her five hours away. Ida played the piano and we sang many songs. I was so afraid that she might get frantic as we were leaving, for she kept saying that she would like to come back home with us to Hopiland. But, the brave soul that she is simply said her good-byes to us and walked briskly off to a hallway leading to her room. I wondered whether she went and cried as she was being left behind almost 300 miles away from home

When we all stopped in at a gas station and Taco Bell down the road, Ruby said to me, "Millie, go ahead and cry it all out." And then, all the tears I was trying to hold back came out. Was this the ending for this retired school teacher who has given so much to others? How do I know whether God would not let this happen to me someday? It is hard to have joy in this.

I have found that I am almost depressed on Sunday mornings. For almost nine years, it was such a part of my identity to go up to Hotevilla Gospel Church. I feel lost now that we are no longer attending there. We believe now that we are supposed to get together in home church style with those who still will not enter the church buildings for one reason or another.

Yet another rock was thrown through one window at the church in Hotevilla after all the glass was put back. Another window got a couple of BB gun holes, but nothing more since then. At a community meeting at the church, eight ladies showed up and had some good advice. They wanted to have a sale to raise funds for the church to replace the windows.

A letter of apology was also asked to be written from the boys who confessed to stealing over two hundred dollars from a summer team who has come for years to help the church. When I tried to follow through with this discipline, I was badly criticized by those who believed that the boys saying "sorry" is enough, and that they should not have to write a letter of apology. Sometimes these attacks come at such a consistent rate, when it is clearly the Lord's standards.

It is good for a child to learn early on to make restitution, not because it is an eye for an eye and a tooth for a tooth, but because the Lord has put His spirit of Justice in all of us. It is good for our soul to simply make restitution when it is at all possible. It is necessary and good for our souls to make things right as much as possible. When I was around thirteen years old, growing up in Los Angeles in the early seventies, I stole a pair of red socks from Sears. I thought I was going to have a heart attack, because I was so nervous. Forty years later, I still remember it. I am not saying that because I feel that I am such a goody two-shoes, but because it just bothered my conscience badly somehow.

The word of God teaches us that if we're faithful in small things, that He will give us bigger things. It is so good for the children, while they are still small, to take back even a small candy cane to the store which they may have stolen. It is all about loving our God and loving our neighbors. If the children know that it is not okay to steal even a candy cane, they may surely know that it is not okay to steal someone else's wife or husband someday when they grow up.

My heart aches that so many people are bound up in what they think is love, which only brings death, when they consistently choose to overlook the need their children have for discipline, done in love. It is said in the Bible that the Lord disciplines those whom He loves. The problems start with ignoring the disciplining of small matters. Things tend to snowball, to where they are indulging in drugs and alcohol when they get older. We have seen so many people in jail who did not learn self discipline at home, so now the state has to discipline them. I understand that discipline alone is not the answer, but it is such a glaring need here.

Two more professional ladies came to Puhu Qatsi (New Life)—an artist who has her own studio and a store, and another Hopi tribal worker. It was precious to see the other Hopi ladies encourage them for coming and tell them that they were brave. Everyone knows the disapproval they would receive from their relatives and friends for coming to YWAM. I was seeing things happening right before my eyes which I had only dreamed of and yet I had a nagging feeling that this is not permanent and that most will fall away. Many come for their own needs and, if their needs are not satisfied very soon, they quickly get discouraged and don't show up anymore. I wish that God would give me a "happy pill" which would make me feel instantly happy and not want more.

One precious Hopi sister, Nita, has been telling us that we need to start having a church that is held outside. She suggested our back garden by the fire pit area. She said more Hopis would come rather, than walking into a Church building. You see, I was thinking big numbers in the future, five years down the line. She was content only to think of the present, whereas I was already unhappy thinking of the future. As a "visionary" person, all I could see was that there was not enough room in my garden.

The Hopi people are supposed to be the "People of Peace," which is what their name means. Likewise, Los Angeles, the "city of Angels," (or "Messengers") was supposed to carry the messages of God, via Hollywood, to nations around the world. Instead, Satan usurped this power and took his own message of corruption, rather than good. Fortunately, God's people are taking back some ground in the movie industry.

According to our Hopi friend, there is so much division and turmoil in the tribal government, which is affecting almost all the families with anger against someone. The Hopi Tribal President/Chairman's power has been usurped by the Tribal council. Now the B.I.A (Bureau of Indian Affairs) has stepped in to bring order. Division, confusion, rebellion, and covetousness are some of the predominate spirits between families, clans and villages. Thankfully, there are people whom God has placed to pray as "watchmen" on the walls.

There was such a huge issue of "offense" of the Native Americans against outsiders at so many different levels, that we did not know whether we would ever get it right. I was so fed up one day, that I almost said, "I am sick of these people." I realized that I had taken on the same spirit which I had disdained. The Lord dealt with me quickly and showed me that true love never gives up! Oh, how I need to know His great love and sacrifice beyond my shallow heart!

I have to tell you a bit about Charity Thiessen. She is from Saskatchewan, Canada. She came to us when she had just turned eighteen. I am so impressed that a girl at seventeen would apply for our Discipleship Training School and then come to live among the Native people for six years afterwards. Most girls her age think only about themselves. Below is a letter from Charity, which she wrote in 2004, at the age of nineteen.

Hi everyone, this is just a little update about some things that are happening. There was a stabbing Monday night at the Hotevilla store. Last we heard the man was still alive, so pray for him that he won't die, and that he would come to know the Lord. Both of the men involved were drunk. Please be praying against alcoholism out here. It is a major part of the battle these people are being faced with. Pray that the people would instead be filled with the Holy Spirit.

Charity McDonald, our staff person, was also in a car accident Sunday night. She was not hurt, and her car has very minimal damage. Pray for the lady and her son in the other car. Their car was totaled but their injuries did not seem to be too serious. Thank the Lord for His protection, and that Charity would not blame herself and be brought down, but that a lot of good would come out of this.

You know about the accident a couple weeks ago. There were also two stabbings that week. One of the men who were killed had come to our jail ministry, and quite possibly had become a Christian. There just seems to be a lot happening right now. The enemy is getting desperate, but he is not winning. One of the men killed was probably a Christian, and this last stabbing did not result in a death. Be praying hard for God's protection of these people, and against the spirit of death. One of our speakers who came out here said he could smell death as soon as he drove onto the reservation. Pray in God's life for these people.

Thank you guys so much for your willingness to pray for Hopi. Each prayer makes a difference in the lives out here.

Another Note from Charity

We have a very important day coming up. We are going to be having 24 straight hours of worship, prayer and fasting for Hopi.

We are tired of the bondages and strongholds that Satan has these people imprisoned with, so we are going to push back his power by just praising our God, and interceding on behalf of the people. Some of the things we are specifically praying against are:

Alcoholism, Drugs (Meth, and marijuana are big ones), and Sexual sin (This is huge and includes every area of sexual sin).

There are so many single mothers, so many kids with kids, so many dads with kids with more than one lady, so many broken relationships and families, so many young girls and guys who are going to be trying to find their identity in sexual relationships. There are sexual transmitted diseases and also things like diabetes, etc. as a result of poor diet and life choices.

Most importantly, pray against a lack of identity. Most of these problems stem from people not knowing who they are, and trying to find something. Pray that the truth of our identity in Christ would be made known, that people would see the truth about themselves and understand that we are made holy in Christ, that we are not worthless, purposeless, hopeless, but that we are a chosen generation. Pray that the Hopi people would find life and find it abundantly, and that life can only be found in Jesus. Pray that people would stop striving, and in turn failing, and that they would give everything to Jesus and let Him be their strength. That they don't have to strive, but that Christ has made them holy. Pray for hope!

Sometimes we only know by faith unseen.

The average life expectancy in the 21st century for Native American men is 48 years. Something is terribly wrong with this picture even though we are supposedly in the land of plenty. I don't know how it could get any worse at times with the killings, kids getting run over with cars and dying, suicides and so many other tragedies.

I feel like the tragedies we have seen and heard in Native American lands have been as heartbreaking as some Shakespeare plays like "Macbeth", "Hamlet" or "King Lear." Once I checked out all the famous operas from the public library and read all the sub-titles of the words being sung, and it was quite depressing. But my melancholy side was quite hooked on these operas. I knew these operas were undoubtedly the epitome of our sin nature. Without the grace and the love of our heavenly Father, we would all be stuck in our own depressing soap operas. Who needs "Madame Butterfly"? It is so pathetic and fatalistic!

There was a flow of Hopi people all last night and one Hopi lady in the morning. This is unbelievable! Oh, praise God! We believe the next time we do this that there will be many more who will come, as something contagious is happening. It is exciting!

I once heard a story of a girl that was lost in a tall wheat field. After many hours and days of attempting to find and save her, finally someone had an idea to gather all the rescuers and friends to link arms in a giant circle and start moving into the center of the field. They found the child, only it was too late, for the little girl had already died.

I want to know why there is such a high percentage of these tragedies among the First Nation's peoples. I want to know how we can circle around these, our host people in North America, to bring them full salvation.

Chapter 6

Joyous events in Hopi

There is an Eagle Dance, as well as another Buffalo Dance in the village of Shongopavi. We were invited to come and eat at three different homes and we were all very full, like a stuffed turkey at an American Thanksgiving meal. We had elk meat, "noquivi" (a traditional mutton and hominy stew), sweet cornmeal pudding, homemade donuts, cupcakes and Hopi bread. The bread is baked cooperatively in an outdoor stone oven by twenty to thirty women. The smell of fresh baked bread is heavenly.

It is not easy for the Hopis to be wedded in a traditional way, as it is very expensive with many duties for everyone in the clan. Many opt to live together during an extended engagement.

For the first time, I was dressed in full Hopi traditional dress by my Hopi sister, Nita, for a wedding in Hotevilla. I was asked by a relative of the bride whether I was a Hopi, for I had Nita's grandmother's moccasins, Ruby's woven cape, the bride's daughter's manta (the Hopi dress) and my green, black and red woven belt. I felt wondrously like the king's daughter, as I walked down the long aisle to the altar with Will, one of the groomsmen.

Will and I had the privilege of being in the wedding party. Will was also the co-officiator of the ceremony with another pastor.

The bride and groom had five beautiful daughters, who had attended Sunday school at Hotevilla Gospel Church for many years.

After the parents began attending our New Life group and Sunday morning services, they wanted to make their relationship right before the Lord.

Many new believers and families helped out financially for this wedding. Many also helped with decorating and cooking the food in order to bring this event together. Tents were put up outside of the church and the wedding was held there, because there was not enough room inside the church. All of the bridesmaids and all the flower girls wore a Navajo or a Hopi dress (the bride is half Navajo).

Yes, the Lord is so great and awesome! This is historical, for this is the first whole family to come to church since we have been here. It is also the first Christian wedding.

The First Hopi Warrior Carving

Hopi Kachina dolls, representing the hundreds of different spirits, or messengers, can be found in museums all around the world. Since ancient times, these dolls have been carved by Hopi men to help their children learn the different names of the Kachina spirits. What used to be very simple carvings are now often very detailed art forms, demanded by art collectors around the world—some costing thousands of dollars for one carved figure. Yet, the market for these Kachina dolls is often very slow, for some of the other tribes who have nothing to do with the Hopi religion are manufacturing them.

We just had a breakthrough! All these years, we could not get any of the Hopi men to carve those things that reflected God's Bible story. Our friend, Skip, finally carved us an Ephesians 6 "Hopi warrior" wearing the armor of God. In front of the helmet, it says, "salvation," however, in the back of helmet, the word was misspelled, "slavation." It is true that when we go backwards that we become slaves to our sins.

Another friend started carving a nativity scene. We asked for Mary to be carved with the traditional Hopi butterfly hair-do, because she was a virgin. Only the young maidens could have this hair-do of "squash blossom" before getting married. I think Princess Leah in the Star Wars Trilogy copied her hair style from the Hopi.

We asked that Joseph be in a Hopi farmer's outfit and the three wise men wearing outfits representing three different tribes (Dine, Apache, Pima, etc.). We believe this is a huge breakthrough. We hope there will be new cottage industries in Hopiland, which will bring honor to the men, who will once again be providers and bread winners for their families.

Increasingly, the Hopi Tribe is including us and asking assistance from YWAM. The Hopi Guidance Center is allowing YWAM meetings to be credited to those who have to attend AA or Anger Management courses. Yesterday, both the Hopi Care Center and Domestic Violence office called to ask for assistance. The Hopi Youth Center also wants our staff to help with their events, and Will has been invited to the Hopi Men's Leadership Summit later this year. We have also worked with Hopi Women's Health. The Tribe did not even charge our staff person anything to have our DTS acceptance letter and visa invitation notarized to send to an applying student from Thailand; whereas, they used to charge us before.

Just last night, the Hopi Police stopped to take our staff gals to a phone. Charity and Danielle had run out of gasoline while doing their daily prayer drive. Some couple heard about it on the police scanner and brought gasoline to them quickly. What beautiful people!

It has become the norm to hear songs about the Lord on the Hopi radio station, KUYI (meaning *water*). Among all their eclectic music, they play, "How Great Thou Art" and other Christian songs, traditional, and contemporary, both Native and non-Native as a part of their regular repertoire.

Also, below is an example of what one may find more often than before in the Hopi "Tutuveni" newspaper. This letter is from a young lady who received the Lord into her heart in jail and who comes out regularly to YWAM.

An apology letter read: *"Ms . . . I would like to apologize to you for the pain, suffering and stress I have caused you because of my unacceptable behavior at your home. I pray you will find forgiveness in your heart for me. May the Lord bless you and your family with His grace. May this prayer give you and your family strength and ease the pain during our time of grief. Our Father in heaven, may your name be honored, may your Kingdom come soon. May your will be done here on earth just as it is in heaven. Give us our food for today, and forgive us our sins just as we have forgiven those who have sinned against us. And don't let us yield to temptation, but deliver us from the evil one."*

Oh, how sweet to hear these Hopi ladies reading out of the Scriptures saying, "Great is the Lord in Zion. He is exalted over all the nations. Let them praise your great and awesome name! He is holy" (Psalms 99:2, 3). Last night, I heard that there were over a dozen ladies at the "Puhu Qatsi" New Life, ladies' group. They are asking each other what the Lord has done and sharing deeply without any outsider's help.

It is a glorious thing now to finally baptize Hopi men. A young man, from the jail work release program, who has been attending our DTS, got baptized. He was immersed in a horse trough under our new arbor, in front of the YWAM building, in sight of the main highway. It was also a glorious thing to hear six native men (students & visitors) sitting and discussing how to glorify God! There were three baptisms at Hotevilla Gospel Church for the first time in over thirty years. One Hopi lady and a Hopi man from two separate villages were baptized. These two people were from such traditional families that this has shocked many people. Uberta's granddaughter also got baptized. And our beloved Hopi sister, Nita, has announced that she is to be baptized on Valentine's Day. Yes, the wave of the Lord is finally hitting in this dry and thirsty land!

There were three more baptisms up at Hotevilla Gospel Church (our recent bride, another lady and a young boy). Next week, our friend, the groom, will be baptized at YWAM, by Will. Satan cannot stop this new move of the Holy Spirit. Yes, the light is penetrating into the darkness little by little!

Many Hopi people are choosing to believe that Jesus is the way to the Creator. We can sense a different atmosphere, even since the beginning of this year. People are praying without any traditional use of the cornmeal and feathers because they now have a personal relationship with the Living God! They now know that they can enter the "Holy of Holies" as royal priests. And yet, I do not want to give the wrong impression that there is not much more to be done. There is still much to be done! We do, however, sense that the dawning of His glory is about to burst like the rising of the sun, which suddenly appears over the horizon in the early morning hours.

There is a two story house built behind our house in Kykotsmovi. Somehow they built the house around a single wide mobile home and the house kept getting bigger. Now, it is called the "Hungry Bear" restaurant. One day, I had a knock on our door in the afternoon and found their young son coming into our house. He asked me to call the police, because he thought someone was prowling around his house when he got off the school bus. It was nice to have their son feel safe enough to come to us. It all went well.

We also have a family of seven staying at the YWAM facility. They have been staying in a tent in the rain, and the children could not get to their first day of school. This couple has five kids ages 5 to 14 years. The father apparently came out of the Jail and told the family that he found a new Path, and that they must now walk this new Way together as a family. They have already been seeking the Lord and wanting to learn more. There was a power encounter with Satan just before the 24-hour prayer time, as Nita and I and a Hopi policeman ended up carrying a young woman out of Nita's house into the police car. It seems she was under the influence of alcohol and methamphetamines.

It is hilarious what can happen with a good intention. For the wedding that was held in our backyard, a Hopi friend came over with the tractor while we were gone. When we came home, we found that he had plowed and made a sand pit about the size of a football field in front of our house. It was the day before the Wedding Ceremony. What was meant to make more parking spaces, instead, turned out be a huge sand trap.

We had to block the front yard with our car so that no one could park there; everyone had to park out on the street. Many cars have been stuck in our yard since then. Many of the plants like the rabbit brush, which the Hopi ladies use for their baskets was pulled out. For all these years, I had tried to save them by weeding around them, and now they were killed. However, we realized how kind it was of our friend to do this for us as it was his desire to bless us.

The Chairman (president) of this Hopi Nation is now a Christian. He is not ashamed to go to church and made the announcement that he is a believer in the "Tutuveni" Hopi newspaper. He began to go to church before he ran for this office. We are amazed that this nation is willing to vote for someone who claims to be a Christian. Also, the newly elected Vice-Chairman is very open to Christ, as he and his wife joined us in the Phoenix area for our last Sunday school outing. Their son, a Hopi Ranger who went to school with our kids, attended YWAM meetings. Their young daughter has attended "Signs and Wonders" camp with our staff gals, Charity and Danielle.

In the very recent past, for one to be voted in politically, one had to have been traditional in Hopi ways and reject Christ. Now we are beginning to see the politics turning. What is sad is that once Hopi people make their declaration as Christians, there seem to be all out attacks of the enemy to bring them down and to bring shame, and not many seem to be able to be able withstand all the trials and temptations. We are so in need of those who will surround these leaders and pray for them that they would not turn away.

It is such an amazing thing to hear our Hopi brother's testimony. He is now a Security guard at one of the most dangerous schools in Arizona. He approached some Apache boys doing drugs and drinking alcohol at the prom. One of the kids socked him from the side, and then several boys jumped in and beat him up. He could have taken on these boys, as not so long ago, several police cars had to be called in when he and his brothers would fight in Hopiland. However, this time, he told us that "to hit one of these boys would be like hitting Jesus." He walked away with a fat lip and a black eye and bruises. Three of the boys came up to him again, one day, and asked for forgiveness. Now one of the boys wants to start a Bible study.

Hopi men played the parts of all three Wise Men, the three shepherds, and Joseph in our Christmas play at Hotevilla Gospel Church this year. The children's pageant was completely taken over by one of the Native believers, and I did not have to do anything. Now, we regularly have 30 to 50 people (this is including the children) coming to church every Sunday. This number may not seem much to outsiders, but it is huge here.

One must recognize that Hotevilla is one of the most traditional villages in North America. When all the other Hopi chiefs and leaders finally gave in to our U.S. government earlier this past century, I have heard that only the elders from the village of Hotevilla remained firm in their refusal to send the children to the Boarding Schools. Unbelievable as this story may sound, a number of men were put into Alcatraz Prison for up to eight years—just for saying they wanted their children to stay home.

Our young adult neighbor across the street now comes faithfully to YWAM and goes up to church with us. The Lord had told us many times to proclaim His love over our neighbors, that they may know Him, and to pray blessings over them. This girl said to us that Hopiland has changed and that, everywhere she goes, she hears others talking about the Lord as well.

We were ministering at the Hopi jail with Hopi, Tewa, Navajo and Apache men. We did a Talking Circle, allowing everyone time to share what was on their hearts. Following that, we all read through Psalm 51, speaking about how God really wants honesty and humility from us, more than any religious practice. They were asked if anyone wanted to enter into a relationship with Jesus—through His one great sacrifice, receiving forgiveness, relationship and eternal life. All the men—almost fifty of them—stood, making much squeaking noises of their chairs.

I don't know sometimes how salvation works. If all of these men were truly sincere and prayed the salvation prayer to receive Christ into their heart, does this one prayer seal the deal for heaven for eternity? What if some of these men go outside into the real world and never acknowledge Christ again, only to die later after having lived an awful life? And what if just one man who had truly encountered the living God that night turns his life around to touch not only his children but grandchildren and many generations to come?

Though we have times like this in the jail, still the discipleship process is normally very slow, with many pitfalls along the way. We have recently learned firsthand more about the reality of the spiritual bondages that have ensnared the majority of the people here. We are praying against the spirits of murder, suicide, manipulation, and false pride.

We now have a young man who had faithfully came to church at Hopi Jail, as he is now out and has been to YWAM for the past few days. He is from another tribe in Montana. He has tattoos all over and one can tell he has already experienced much in life. His heart is soft now and we also need wisdom as he does not seem to want to go back home and cannot find work here on the reservation.

This year, for the second year in a row, a Kachina's mask was blown away by a strong wind during a dance. According to Hopi prophecy, this signifies the end of their religion. The ladies were panicking and tried to put the mask back on the man, as others tried shielding the children from seeing the unmasked kachina.

It is a blast to go to a Hopi Basket Dance. After all the Hopi Maidens and the men are done dancing in their Plaza, hundreds of gifts are thrown out to the public. Some rowdy young men really fight to get the especially good items, and one must be careful not to get hurt in all the commotion. We did very well this year, with many of us from YWAM catching so many gift items in the air. We filled big boxes full of candies, food, toys, plastic ware, fruit, popcorn balls, etc.

An "Indian Day" at Hotevilla/Bacavi school—in Hopiland
It is a joyous thing to go and see the children at their school dance with all the families attending

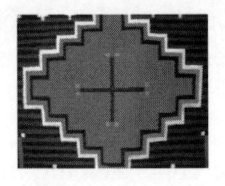

Chapter 7

A Garden in Hopi

It just is not fair. The irises in Hopiland bloom only a couple of weeks out of the year. My garden in Hopiland was all sandy soil and yet when we went back, our mouths all dropped open. The backyard was an amazing array of purple Irises blooming. It was the best bloom in all the years! I had seen these same irises when transplanted to California, where it is sunny all year round, bloom almost continually throughout the whole year in my sister-in-law, Kathryn's garden. But I have other things she does not have, like the beautiful Painted Desert and my Hopi friends. Where we are planted matters a lot!

How sweet it is to see and taste the fruits of our garden! We are harvesting so many delicious cherry tomatoes, yellow squash in plenty, green onions, parsley, basil, mint, and green peppers and rosemary.

There was a wedding in the garden behind our house, officiated by Will. It was a day of miracles! It was about the only calm day without the fierce dust storms. God showed His favor and power to all who came that day.

The bride made her own beautiful white wedding gown, adorned with a traditional Hopi belt. Their five children were in the wedding and wore their Hopi outfits. The groom was from a very traditional village, and his parents were not all together happy that their son had chosen the Jesus Path. However, he had already told them that this is now the only Way for him.

The bride carried a bouquet made of peach colored roses, pink cosmos, lavender snap-dragons, purple butterfly flowers, burgundy petunias, and green apple leaves—all from our garden. The bride walked down the aisle to the Native American flute music of "Amazing Grace."

The groom, the youngest of seven siblings, was warmly surrounded by his family. Will, seeing an opportunity to make a connection with these traditional Hopi, gave a message of the One who came to the people in distant lands, the Polished Arrow hidden in Creator's quiver (Is. 49:1-13), just as it was prophesied long ago by the Hopi elders, that this One was coming.

After the wedding ceremony, the Hopi Youth Cultural Dance team wanted to honor the bride and groom with a dance in our back yard. There were also Hopi singers around a drum. We were very much moved, as we were entering into another phase of freedom in Christ to worship the Lord our God with indigenous dances and songs.

It seems now that there is no stopping this. Oh, we praise God!

The Bride is also getting baptized this coming Sunday. These things are quite a blow to Satan in this land, since he has had the people by their throats for so many years.

The celebration continued with a traditional mud fight afterwards, during the reception, between the aunties and the in-laws. I felt honored to get my face muddied, for now we were part of the family! Somehow Will got away, even though he conducted the wedding.

A sheep had been slaughtered for the wedding and there was so much *nukwivi*, home-made bread and other foods that it took a long time for the ladies to distribute it all to those who came at the end. After the wedding, we vacuumed a bag full of sand from our house—enough to build a small sand castle.

It can get quite crazy with the wind blowing, and sand absolutely everywhere! And yet there is a row of about 75 purple Irises in my garden thriving in this blustery chaos. All things are possible!

Pastor Jack and Jane Lankhorst from Riverside, California, came out with their team of 33 people and threw a big fireworks show and game night at the Hopi Civic Center. Over 3,000 Hopi people showed up, so we threw a garden party for their team. There were over sixty people in my garden out in our backyard. Additionally, the team had a married couple who went up to "Pumpkin Seed" lookout point, right over our village and renewed their Wedding vows. We had a beautiful reception for them, with torch lights, flowers and a wedding cake. The YWAM E.A.R.S. (Environmental and Resource Stewardship) team really helped in setting this up. We had many Hopis come to welcome these teams that evening.

That week they taught the method of using gray water (water that had been used for household purposes) for agriculture and composting, to make the sandy soil more fertile. As much as I liked having this Environmental and Resource group from YWAM, I found out that the Hopis did not put to use anything that had been taught by them.

The methods of using gray water to grow things have benefited many other nations, such as Israel and Africa and other dry places. But the Hopis like doing things their traditional way. They like dry farming, which means they will not irrigate to grow their corn, beans, melons, etc. They have done it this way for many centuries and do their ceremonies and dances to pray in the rain. It is a known fact that some Hopis have starved to death in the winter time in past drought seasons. Even when they can irrigate, the Hopis will not, as this is not their way. Only in the village of Moencopi, where a stream flows year round, do they irrigate.

Uberta had always admired my garden and often commented on how she wished she could have a fence around her home at Hotevilla so that the dogs would not ruin her garden. Dan and Billy, Pastors from California, came out with a small team and the fence was built around her house.

It is not for me to change the things of any culture. I found that when I think I am trying to help the people that I am not helping at all, but rather wasting their time and money.

The Hopis find the journey and the task of going out and watering and being outside to be just as or more important than the "end" in itself. Whereas, I would set up the drip-line system to get the maximum result with little effort, they would rather do this the old fashion way—even at the cost of sometimes having the plants die when they go away for a long period of time. That is just a part of life to them, as death and life go together.

Some Hopis are using tractors these days. A Hopi man said that his grandfather told him that it is better to do things as they have been doing from long ago because when the field is done quickly with all those machines, what are they going to do the rest of the day? The young men will laze around with nothing to do and get in trouble.

Water is very precious to them and they will not waste it. One can actually argue that it may save water by using gray water or putting in a drip line water system. But again, it just is not their way. I once put in a drip line system to water all of the flowers and beans inside of Uberta's fenced-in garden. The black hose looked like a spider web which went in every direction. When I put the timer on, all the little spouts watered every single flower and plant within a matter of minutes every-other-day. They were amazed at first. However, the timer got messed up later somehow. Uberta and her daughter tried to figure it out, but this modern technology became more of a bother than they cared to handle.

Pretty soon, I found the whole set-up discarded in a big pile. They would rather water each flower and vegetable individually. The watering of each plant and praying is more important to them than setting up a system, so that one can skip that step in order to do one more thing at the same time. It does not mean that they don't get disturbed by the lack thereof. I know a few who were pretty upset that their corn and other things did not make it.

The point I am trying to make is that the Hopis don't want to mess with their natural way of farming. On the other hand, I like these drip line hoses. It just takes one or two times of missed watering in this desert place to kill something. Sometimes it takes only one or two times of missed opportunities to minister to someone, which can kill those relationships.

I like vegetables and flowers that live. There are too many unpredictable matters which can come up suddenly in ministry and cause me to miss watering. I don't think it is a sin for me to have a drip-line system in the desert. If it was so, half of the world with irrigation would be in sin. If the Lord shows me otherwise, I will gladly put them away. I am sure that no one else really cares about my drip line in our yard, but it really is so nice to not have to worry about my plants dying when I am gone on outreach. I also like this auto drip line system, because I can get other things done at the same time.

I heard once from a Tibetan monk on the radio, who taught that one should never do more than one thing at a time. Oh, give me a break! I was thinking that this man has never been a mother. If I followed this man's rule, my kids would have all died off during childhood. There are constant interruptions of phone calls, another child needing to go potty, loads of laundry to be done, etc. Some other child may be in danger and you may need to rush over at the same time you are holding a baby in your arms—otherwise, someone's skull or ribs may get broken. And when one is in a ministry on top of that, well . . . I cannot tell you that as good as this theory of never doing more than one thing at a time sounds so excellent, that it is not realistic. I do understand that we need to desire to try to give our undivided attention as much as possible.

I hate wasting time. I like doing two things at the same time. It makes me feel productive. I can't help it. I don't even like to stand and brush my teeth for two minutes without doing something else. My dental hygienist told me that I need to brush for that long. I am not fond of looking at myself in the mirror as I drool my toothpaste all over my chin. So I made up my mind that I am going to use those two minutes praying and thanking the Lord for that day (I don't think God would be offended) or read my Bible. In two minutes, I could read a short chapter in Psalms. Two minutes, twice a day adds to twenty-eight (almost thirty) minutes a week. That is almost two hours a month, twenty-four hours a year. Sometimes I like to space out into far away land with my Lord. That is okay too.

I got bit by a red ant in my garden and I could not believe how nasty that bite was for several days. How is it possible for such a tiny creature to have that much venom? It takes a tremendous amount of self control for me not to scratch my itch. It just drives me crazy. It only makes things worse and makes you itch to scratch even more. Sin is like that. The more you do it, the more you want to do it. You have to slap yourself on the itch and not scratch it. We must slap any temptations of sin in our lives and not do it also.

As far as the ants are concerned, any human being is just the biggest piece of steak for them. I am going to ask God why He made the ants bite human beings. He didn't. I think it has something to do with the fall of men. The red ants love to sting you just before they croak. They are nasty. I had one get in my shoe. I was trying to get it out and it got killed. But, before it got killed, it stung and left a vicious mark on me. I suppose if someone or something that is a thousand times bigger wanted to kill me, I'd let them have what venom I have to let them know I don't appreciate getting killed. Okay, the ants are justified. Cancel that question to God.

Mosquitoes are horrible and even worse because they suck the blood out of human beings literally. Once, my brother Daniel caught one alive and tortured it up in the High Sierra meadows to bring fear to all the other mosquitoes. He was just really being funny. Both he and I are allergic and respond with huge welts to these bites. He took one leg and wing at a time as he threatened loudly to the other mosquitoes that they will be in the same predicament if they come near to him. I wonder whether this is okay with the Native Americans or they would just let the mosquitoes suck the blood out of them. I have seen Hopis slap those buggers dead without any remorse.

Now, I will go back to the dying plants in Hopiland. Dying is just a part of the cycle of life. It is like the animal kingdom, where one gets eaten so that the others can survive. It is a natural cycle of life to eat and to be eaten on this planet earth. Some who are faint-hearted may not like some cute creatures being eaten by some of their predators. But no one tries to go to Africa to stop this natural cycle of life and death by killing off all the lions or other predators which eat their prey.

I can't stand it when I see a cat trying to get a bird. This is natural too, but I chase the cat away. If I see my dog, Zoey, trying to catch a bird, I always go after her to tell her to stop. I love that dog, like I never loved any other pets. She is the only dog I ever have sit on our ottoman, so that she could rest her head on my ankles when I stretch out my legs. She is really something else. Still, I would smack her, if I saw her going after a bird, because it doesn't seems right to sit and watch a dog kill a sweet bird. I think in this case, it is okay to interrupt nature once in awhile. Zoey was not going to starve if she didn't eat that bird. She eats everything else—cottontails and huge Arizona Jack rabbits, lizards, mice and almost anything else that moves.

She had a baby bunny in her mouth the other day. It was rather sad to see it. If that baby cottontail had lived, it would someday be a hundred rabbits which would gobble up everything in my garden very soon, so I don't feel so sad after all.

I do, however, appreciate those in this world who protect endangered species. I think they are way ahead of Christians in being the stewards of the earth whom God wants us to be. It would be sad not to have future generations see Bengal tigers, panda bears or blue whales and many other species in their lifetime. Many of these species would have gone extinct, if it wasn't for the protection of conservation groups. For this I am grateful. I like them, as long as they don't go crazy to the other extreme, where a whole bunch of human beings have to suffer for one owl or some spider species. I don't know what to do about that.

I once saw a documentary of the very last bird of its kind in the Amazon jungle. It had come to the point of extinction for its beautiful plumage. It was the greed of those Amazonian Indians who were willing to hunt these birds down for money. Or perhaps, it was their last effort to survive to feed their families, as their homeland is getting smaller and smaller. It is also the greed of those who want these feathers for their own possession, for beauty on their hats or on their walls like a trophy.

This beautiful bird gave a haunting call over and over again to try to beckon the other bird to come when the recording was played. The bird did not know that the sound it was hearing was just a recording that was done some years ago when there were other birds of its kind. It was one of only a few times I cried watching a documentary about animals or birds. Other times I cried when my breath was taken away by the beauty of all God made. This time I was crying, because I thought this must be how our God feels when a whole tribe goes extinct because of another's greed for power and for their land.

We had a team of young people come and help in my garden with weeding. The hoses were cut in three different places, which made the water shoot up like Yellowstone Geysers. Some of the flowers had been pulled up along with the weeds. Nevertheless, the garden looked beautiful with all the work that had been put in by the students and staff. When many people are working together, mistakes (intentional or unintentional) are almost unavoidable, because some information is neglected or falls through the cracks. In any ministry setting, we ought to remember the times of joy of having worked together and recognize how much good resulted, rather than the few cut lines and flowers.

I felt like a greedy chipmunk which tries to carry too much when I went out with my basket to harvest some cherry tomatoes from our vegetable garden. I had so many that some of the tomatoes kept dropping out of the basket. So, I put some in my shirt, folding it to make a big pocket. And yet, I was losing one, two, three, four cherry tomatoes that kept dropping to the ground from the basket and my shirt. I was so frustrated that I almost said a bad word. A bit of a good harvest should not irritate me so much! If you were here, you would have had a good laugh on my account, because it was like watching a person trying to gather a bunch of scattering cats into a basket, while some are meowing and clawing and jumping out.

Ruby harvested eight truckloads of corn and also truck loads of melons from her field. This was truly a miracle! We had all been waiting for this kind of a harvest all these years in Hopiland. This is the reason the Hopi people danced for rain for centuries. There had been such a drought for over a dozen years that many did not even bother to plant until only the last couple of years. In Hopiland, when a woman has corn, she is considered very rich. Ruby is a follower of Jesus.

Hundreds of my deep purple Irises have bloomed and died while we were all gone for a month on our YWAM Discipleship Training School outreach with our students. All that was left for us to see when we came back were dried up petals on green stems, which I will not see again until next year. I looked forlornly inside our fenced-in front garden and as I walked around the winding path of our garden in the backyard. Why would God have me plant flowers and work so hard, only to have them bloom while we were gone? I heard Him gently say to me, "Millie, but I enjoyed it!" That was good enough for me!

After all, this is not my garden—it is the Lord's. "Awake, O north wind, and come, south wind! Blow on my garden, that its fragrance may spread everywhere. Let my beloved come to his garden, and taste its choice fruits" (Song of Solomon 4:16). He can enjoy my/our Iris flowers all He wants!

My one apple tree does not have fruit, as the winds have blown away all the blossoms. It is a perfect example of the enemy who comes to steal, kill and destroy.

I realized also that I had no right to expect to see the fruit of our labor in Hopiland. We have only to be thankful when we get to see anyone's lives changed. We can till, plant seeds, weed and water, but it is only He who can transform their hearts. The glory belongs to Him!

I don't want to ever have the Cain syndrome. Perhaps it was a generational sin. Adam called his wife, Eve, "Life." He said she was the "Mother of all Living." I don't want to bring an offering that is full of pride. I think pride was involved when Cain brought his fruit as an offering to the Lord while his brother Abel brought a lamb for a burnt offering in the book of Genesis. A gardener could think that it was his or her efforts which brought forth fruits when it was the Lord who created all those species of flowers and trees and the vegetables in the first place. I don't ever want to think that I did it.

It is a beautiful world when I can have the fresh smell of basil, rosemary, mint, sage and lavender in my garden. There is a place for everyone on earth just as there is a purpose and place for every tree and plant and flower. Some flowers grow on the path and no matter how pretty they are I take them out so they don't get stepped on. Sometimes, I transplant them to another location just like God may take us from one position or a place to another where we are more suited for.

Tamarisk and Russian olive trees do not belong on the beaches of the San Juan River. They dominate and take over all the indigenous plants and river banks. What used to be beautiful beaches are taken over by these plants and no one could even camp there anymore. One Tamarisk plant with its feathery pink flowers would be stunning perhaps in a blue ceramic pot somewhere by itself, or growing free in its own indigenous region. "American" popular culture, including the "white" church, is somewhat similar around the world even destroying languages by means of the media outpouring. It may have its proper place in white America but it has come to dominate the Native American churches and cultures elsewhere.

    We thank the Lord for this beautiful day! The snowflakes, like manna, came down once again to Hopiland. However, it was so warm the day before that I was able to weed out in our backyard for a few hours. Oh, how awful those weeds are. They've managed to thrive in this desert land where hardly anything else can survive. In my garden, I have a sign that says, "All my weeds are my flowers." It is really a lie.

    As I sat with my Savior in my garden today, I realized once more how precious our lives, our breath and actions on this planet earth are. It is He who gives us a reason to live, to joy, to be useful. What is simply astounding is that our Maker loves our being even without all our doings. I saw that He was not only watching me but some cloud of witnesses also, with much interest. They were cheering me on with the hopes and dreams which the Father had for me. I realized how pure and good my heavenly Father was once more. Oh, Worship the Lord our God, yes for He is holy, holy, holy!

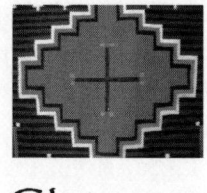

Chapter 8

Our God Is Concerned For the Nations

It was an honor to help out and join into the "Puberty Ceremony" for a young Jicarilla Apache maiden, with our Apache friend, TeAda. For several days we all worked with the members of her extended family, cutting meat and vegetables for stew and frying huge quantities of fry bread for the many guests that arrived each day.

We learned that first day that we were welcome to enter into the ceremony with TeAda's family, the maiden and a young brave. This is not the place to describe all that we experienced. We also learned a very interesting story about the "Wanderer," who visited a hundred some years ago.

Another Apache friend, who is an honorary Chief, told us that his people had this unusual encounter back in the early days of their reservation. They were conducting a ceremony when an outsider showed up, looking a bit bedraggled from traveling by foot. They discussed whether they should kill him, but decided not to as the US government might hold them accountable. After the first day of ceremony our friend's uncles drove down to the lake with this "Wanderer," as he was called. They all washed off and then the two Apaches drove the wagon away together. When they looked back the sun was just shining down onto the lake, when in its bright reflective glare they saw the "Wanderer" step up onto the lake's surface and start walking.

This story picks up again decades later when a missionary was negotiating with members of this same family for an opportunity to build a church on the reservation. The communications had broken down, due to language problems. When the Apaches started to look through the missionary's large Bible, they saw a picture of Jesus walking on the water. They were stunned and excitedly proclaimed that this man in the picture was the "Wanderer" that they had met some years back. The impasse broke, and the missionary was given their blessing to begin his church.

Our friends, Randy and Cheryl Bear Barnetson and their Drum and Dance Team from the First Nations Church are now ministering this month in Russia. They are doing some large evangelism events, as well as Pastors and Leaders Conferences. The Russian leaders want the First Nations leaders from North America to help them "contextualize" the Gospel for the Russian churches.

A Western form of Christianity has taken root in Russia in the last 20 years that does not "look" or "feel" Russian. The Russian church leaders believe that, because the First Nations churches of the USA and Canada have faced the same challenges, we have something to share with them. They want us to help them make the Russian church truly Russian in order to reach Russians, and not just be a caricature of the American-style church.

Principles of contextualization that have been learned by the First Nations believers are a gift to the Body of Christ world-wide. Anita Hensley, our Mohican friend, has been going to Turkey to pray. She is able to drum her songs and speak to the Turks like almost no one else can, because she is a Native American. Anita had an appointment to meet the mayor in the town of Kars on the Armenian border—a courtesy visit. On a prayer journey along the border of Turkey, Iraq, Iran, Armenia and Georgia, Anita and her three companions committed not to talk but to pray. Anita brought a Navajo blanket and told the story of why they had come—to pray to heal his land.

She asked for permission to enter the village of Ani. It was a town of a thousand churches once, but has been deserted since 300 AD. It is on the edge of a field where there are shells of mosques, cathedrals and homes—and not a single soul around. This land had been fought over with much bloodshed.

The mayor grabbed the Native American blanket from Anita and said excitedly that he knew what to do with it. He said he saw many cowboy and Indian movies. He was Kurdish. They believe that they are descended from the Medes, who were among the wise men who came to see baby Jesus. He was able to identify with the Native Americans, because they also lost their land and were persecuted. What was supposed to be a twenty-minute visit turned out to be two hours with coffee and chocolate. They were taken out to eat by his wife. One of the others, a man from a Salish tribe was able to pray a blessing.

As the team quieted themselves to intercede, they could hear the people crying. They had a deep sense of awareness of the devastation of that land. Anita went right over to the Armenian border with her drum and stood. Tears began to come over her. She began to drum and sang a healing song for about an hour.

Then an eagle came right over them and flew back and forth at least ten or twelve times. The eagle soared high above and was joined by two other eagles where they were standing. It was cemented in her at that moment that this was her role to pray as a Native American daughter of God. That was her gifting as an indigenous person to the world.

As she was drumming, she sensed she was not to worry about the opposition which would also come. As she prayed for the awakening to happen, the Lord showed her that negative things will be awakened, as well. Yes, opposition will arise whenever God moves into any city, but we do not need to fear it.

Illegal to Preach the Gospel on the Reservation

One would never guess that anybody could go to jail for doing a Christian activity in the USA. But our friend from one of the other Pueblo Indian reservations in New Mexico was put in jail overnight for having a gathering in the name of Jesus on his property. The next day, when the Tribal Council members had a meeting, they argued among themselves and let him go, telling him not to have another Christian gathering at his property again.

It is illegal to preach the Gospel on his reservation, and one will be kicked out of his own house and property if he does. We were told that some of his people believe in Jesus quietly, as they often have to go to live in the cities to find work and find saving faith there. We need to pray for these 20 Pueblo nations which are most resistant to the Gospel, right inside of our own country. The Hopi Nation is the only one of the 20 Pueblos located in Arizona; the rest are in New Mexico. This friend came and stayed in our home on the Hopi Reservation for a couple of nights. Using a Native hand drum, he sang us some beautiful songs, which he made for the Lord in his language.

Northern Cheyenne, Wounded Knee

During our DTS outreach, we drove to Park City, Utah, to share at Mountain Life Evangelical Free Church and then moved onto Yellowstone National Park. Nita talked to all the strangers, even in the bathrooms. Then we went to YWAM New Waves on the Flathead reservation in Montana. Afterwards, we drove to Lame Deer, Montana, and help set up several teepees and did other preparations for the Lydia Fellowship conference with the Northern Cheyenne people.

I saw a strikingly beautiful Native woman, for whom I felt led to pray the evening that Will and I spoke. Several others eventually joined me to pray with her for deliverance. She told us that all the men in her life had died and that she was called the "Black Widow."

After much prayer, she moved her raven black hair away from her face, and I looked into her beautiful eyes looking up at me. I knew at that moment that she was a child of God and belonged to our Lord. She already knew Jesus, but was being nonetheless tormented by evil spirits. We later met with her family in their home, where we prayed with her mother and learned of the enemy's attacks on the males in her family. Our team prayed all throughout their home, both inside and outside. We learned while there of her relation to "Wooden Leg," who was famous for his account of fighting Custer at the battle of Little Bighorn.

Our team was allowed to enter the Youth Detention Center to share in both the girls' dorm and, later, the boys' dorm in Cheyenne country. These youth asked us to come back the next day, which—according to the guards—had never happened before. So we went in again and shared. We saw again how effective we could be as a team of mixed nationalities: Hopi, Japanese, Korean, Tsalagi (Cherokee), Islander and European.

Some days later, we were also able to stay with native YWAMer, Rod, and his wife, Alexis Wilson, in Spearfish, South Dakota. One day from there we went to see the Crazy Horse monument in the Black Hills, which are sacred to the Lakota Sioux. This region was promised as a sanctuary for the Lakotas, until gold was found and the miners swarmed in to take possession. What an affront it was to the Natives when the government later blasted out the stone images of US presidents at Mt. Rushmore!

Crazy Horse was a revered Chief, known for his selfless dedication and service to his people. The Crazy Horse monument, a work in progress, is the largest mountain carving in the world; when completed it will stand 56 stories high. In 1939, Henry Standing Bear said, "My fellow chiefs and I would like the white man to know that the red man has great heroes, also."

We were blessed to go to Wounded Knee, the location of the last massacre of the Sioux people. Norma Blacksmith, a Lakota elder, told us that much intercession had been done there and that we now needed to worship and praise the Lord on that site. In fact, she said she cannot even recall how many teams she has brought there, as everyone wants to go there. Our team went to help in Whiteclay, Nebraska, which is right next to the Pineridge reservation. This town, just over the reservation border, is notorious for its liquor stores. Because alcohol is illegal on the reservation, they sell unbelievable amounts to the Natives who walk only a few steps to get it. We were able to help out at a ministry site and talked with many struggling alcoholics on the streets. We then drove all day through Nebraska, Wyoming and Colorado to the Jicarilla Apache, in New Mexico.

The Lord is bringing the nations to us. We have already had students from Sweden, Switzerland and France. We have had applicants from Thailand, Nepal, India, Africa and Uzbekistan, but they could not get their visas. We are trusting that the Lord will increasingly bring workers from around the world to reach the Native Americans. We believe that our Native American Christian brothers and sisters will also be built up and go to the ends of the earth with the Good News of our Lord Jesus Christ.

It is a great privilege to be able to send out our DTS team to three different islands in the Philippines. We are also looking toward the Amazon jungles, Japan and the Pacific Rim nations, as the Lord showed us in the dreams before He brought us out to Hopiland.

We've begun to see this dream come true, now, as our team has been able to minister to the tribal peoples of Philippines. It really showed us that our job is not just here in Arizona, but to encourage other tribes.

Our students range in age from 19 to 60 years. Their nationalities are Samoan-American, Irish, Micronesian, European-American and Cherokee.

We have such exciting reports from two of our young staff gals, Charity and Danielle who wrote wonderful accounts of what the Lord had done in these islands. It is so amazing to be able to raise up workers! I want you to see what the Lord can do through these young people when you release them. It is not to say that we do not need the older generation, as we need all three—Abraham, Isaac and Jacob generations—to help bring completeness, wisdom and an adventure spirit in the body of Christ. We must let the young people rise to the occasion.

It takes great wisdom to know when to release a young leader and when to have faith in them to go do their own exploits. This is a delicate matter, in that sometimes it can be disastrous, when they have the fear of men while they are leading others on outreach. However, as much as possible, we find we need to release our young leaders within Youth With a Mission. Young people are looking for adventure. It is fantastic when they can show their own generation what a full and meaningful life is all about.

Charity reports, "I was blown away"

We are in the Philippine Islands! Our week in Abra was awesome. We had a really good time with the youth. All of us taught on different subjects, and we were able to help them prepare presentations for their outreach. We did some teaching on using creative arts and culture, so it was really cool to see them put that into practice. One evening AJ, our Samoan student, taught the Father Heart of God, and had us make up dramas to illustrate it. It was amazing what they came up with, and I was blown away at what good actors they were.

They really got the vision of using their cultural dances, as well. We were all learning how to do them, which was a blast. I personally felt like a duck when I was trying to do it, but they looked incredibly graceful. We taught them a few Island songs, and we have been using songs that they taught us for our kids' programs since then. The last night there we had a commissioning for their two youth outreach teams going out to different tribes and for our team continuing on to Palawan. It was a really powerful night. I was so blessed to see all those young people so sincere and growing in their faith being released into their giftings and ministry.

We had a twelve-hour bus ride to Manila that Monday. At least the seats were soft and it was air-conditioned. We stayed at a YWAM ministry house in Manila overnight. There is one lady doing ministry in a red-light district there to the bar girls. She is also the Director of another YWAM base a couple hours away that does the same kind of ministry. She herself was a prostitute and came to Jesus because of a German missionary. She is an incredible woman, and does amazing work there. A few of us got to go out with her and take food to the little girls who are selling themselves just so they can get enough to eat. It had a real impact on all of us. We will also be staying there the night before we fly home and will get to spend a whole day there.

We flew to Palawan on Tuesday. The next morning we got up at three a.m. to catch the early morning bus out to the tribe, which was about ten hours of really bad roads on a really hard seat (but, honestly, it wasn't too bad). We got there and our schedule wasn't quite what we expected. They had us doing a lot of stuff in the village with kids, and very little in the tribe. I really spent some time praying about why we were there. We had flown halfway across the world, and then flown to this island, and ridden a bus way out into the jungle, and I was wondering why.

The leaders came to us the first morning, though, and said they had sensed our heart for the tribe, and that they were going to add quite a bit more ministry for us in that area. That afternoon was our global YWAM day of prayer, so we all got together for that. As we were doing intercession a bunch of stuff came up for the staff there. They were basically tired, burnt out, and discouraged for over ten years of work with little to no fruit among the tribe. We were able to really pray for them, we washed their feet, and I ended up giving quite a few massages.

We also felt we were to do some teaching for the staff about doing ministry to tribal people. So that evening Danielle shared for a couple hours on all the stuff we have learned over the years. Their eyes were totally opened to how they had been doing things, and they were all starting to get fresh vision and ideas for the ministry when they had been giving up. The next couple of days the Director would pray about where she needed to go to ask forgiveness. She would take a few of our team, who would go along and share about the Native Americans and bring a message of freedom in worship. It was really good.

One of the evenings we did a presentation of some of our dances, mostly cultural stuff, and some teaching on culture and worship. We had met some of the original believers from the tribe that afternoon. As we shared with them why we had come way out here, and that we wanted to ask forgiveness for them being told they couldn't be tribal to believe in Jesus. They were right away, like, we could do this one traditional dance the missionaries told us not to do. It was for the harvest, that's not evil. It was so innocent and sincere how easily they saw it. That night a couple ladies danced that dance, possibly for the first time for Christ, and one of the men brought an instrument they had been told not to use anymore and played and sang. It was so awesome.

On Sunday we went to an even more remote place to a house church. It was two hours of hiking through rice fields, through mud over our ankles and deeper, through rivers, across bamboo bridges. It was really fun, and we were joking about showing up to church after wading through rivers and being all muddy. On the way home we went to a deep place in the river and swam. The whole time there we did our showering and laundry in a creek, which was amazing. It was so refreshing, and good for the soul.

We also did three days of VBS with the kids there, which turned out really good. The students really stepped up and did most of the planning and leading of that. The third morning we were all eating breakfast, and some people brought up stuff they had gotten *during the night, dreams, words of the Lord, etc. We all felt like we needed to change our whole plan for the kids that day.*

We ended up teaching on identity. Sheila shared a quilt she had brought, I taught, and then we had a ministry time. It was like everything was set up for heaven to open on those kids. Jordan was playing a song called "I Have A Maker" in the background, as the kids asked God what lies they believed about themselves, and what He really thought of them, and the purposes that He had for their lives. I was standing up from leading, but the Holy Spirit just moved.

A lot of kids started crying, and there was a lot of deep stuff happening. I was basically at a loss for what to do. That is what I always long to see when we minister to children, and here it was happening before my eyes. We had our team and the staff there to start praying with kids individually. It was really powerful for me personally. As I prayed, words just came, encouragements, blessing, and the kids were really crying.

When we finally finished, we asked if the kids wanted to stay longer and talk and pray or go out and play, and they all stayed longer. We broke into small groups and a lot more good stuff happened. I had a group of the youngest kids, and they were all laying hands on and praying for each other. So anyway, it was really awesome. I felt like I was at Signs and Wonders camp, and I was really blessed that we were able to take that kind of ministry to the kids here. Although I really didn't feel like it was much of us. I mostly felt like I was just trying to keep up with the Holy Spirit and not get in His way.

So, yeah, we had a good time out there. We came back to the city on Monday and did a couple days of ministry at a dumpsite community here. Danielle and AJ also went to protocol, bringing gifts and greetings to honor, *the Chieftain of all of the tribes in the area we were at. He had been in the hospital here in Puerto when we went to his house out in the tribal area, so that was cool it worked out for us to visit him here. They had a really good time, and he said that YWAM could bring people to the tribes any time, and that they were the only ones who ever came with respect.*

This has been a really blessed time, and it was obvious that we were supposed to be here, and that it was perfect timing. We have just over a week left of the five week outreach, which is crazy to think about. We will spend Saturday doing ministry in Davao, and then Sunday head up to a tribe in the mountains. It is going to be a really busy week, with lots of physical work. We are praying that we finish strong. We also pray for our safety and a spiritual covering over the team. There is a lot happening on Mindanao Island, and we have felt very strongly that we need to be careful and really be prepared in every way.

Thanks so much for your prayers. Blessings!

Love, Charity

A Note from Danielle

Our time in Palawan has been amazing. I can say we definitely accomplished the work we desired to do here. The majority of the time was spent in Ransang and we worked with the YWAMers who are working with the tribal people. One night I was able to speak to the staff about bringing the gospel but leaving out the cultural baggage that we sometimes add naturally from our own outlook on life. This was a total enlightening teaching and the next few days we went to the tribes. We also were able to protocol the chief of the tribes and ask his forgiveness for the pain Westerners and Christians have caused his people.

One night in Ransang we had a cultural celebration, and some Christians came and danced a cultural dance that the church had forbidden them to dance, even though the meaning was to celebrate the harvest. Another man played their two-stringed instrument that was also not usually welcomed in the church. So please pray for the tribe, so they are free to choose the way to worship the true God and pray for the workers to go with sensitivity to the people and for perseverance . . .

Our team has experienced everything it seems—from sickness to money stolen—but we have not given up and pray that we would run this race set out for us and not give up till it is over. This is the final stretch, but pray that we would finish well.

Love, Danielle

Pacific Rim Outreach

He lays the beams of His upper chambers in their waters,
(Hawaii, Micronesian islands)
You have set a boundary [for the waters] that they cannot cross,
never again will they cover the earth.
(Ps. 104: 3, 9)

I truly believe we are a ragamuffin bunch of people, who are daring to step out to dream and do what we feel the Creator of the universe is calling us to do! As we prayed over the weeks, the DTS students and staff felt that we were supposed to go to the Micronesian islands and also Hawaii for our school outreach.

I thought to myself, "Oh, give me a break! Who in the world is going to believe that we are going to Hawaii to do an outreach?"

I wanted to tell Will and the students, "Excuse me, I know I am the one who taught on 'Hearing God's Voice,' but you could not have possibly heard from God to go to Hawaii. That is the place where people go for vacations, for goodness sake!"

It was that fear of men thing again. I hate that when I care more about what people think than what God thinks of me. I think we had a lot of nerve. But, more than that, our God can do whatever He wants. Once we stepped out, He helped us raise all the funds for us to go—even for two of our Hopi students who did not have any money to contribute. If you knew how much it costs for one person to go to Hawaii and then to Micronesia and back to the U.S., you would know what an amazing miracle this was. I tell you this, so that you may know that our God can do anything, if we just step out—no matter how impossible and ridiculous it may seem. You, too, can step out and do things which you never thought you could, with His provision and power!

Some think that we are really rich to have taken our DTS students to Hawaii. It is just amazing how low the airfare was at that time. It was around three hundred dollars for round trip tickets from Sky Harbor airport in Phoenix. I truly don't know how we were able to take Nita, our Hopi student and her two children, as well as other students and staff who felt they were supposed to join in this reconciliation act. We all felt like we won the lottery, when we finally booked all the tickets.

I did not know that there were so many Micronesian people living there. Since they resemble Hawaiians, one would have a hard time knowing they are not natives, unless one is familiar with the differences

The Lord showed Poli Otoko a picture of a woman who was repeatedly violated and could hardly stand. She was trying to pull herself up on her balcony. God showed Poli that it was his people, the Micronesians, who had violated her with their pride and arrogance as they grew in numbers in Hawaii, never honoring the original people there. He asked us and our DTS to come and join the Reconciliation Ceremony which took place in Hilo to help bring healing to this island.

We were honored to be a part of the reconciliation, to intercede as Poli and the others asked for forgiveness. Their people had never sought permission to come onto the islands, and they wanted to honor the Hawaiians.

The theme for this trip was "Easter then, Easter now." There was a line-up of all the different nationalities facing the Hawaiians. All of us in YWAM Tribal Winds DTS wore our national outfits.

I wore a beautiful silk *Hanbok* traditional Korean dress, which I had found at a Thrift store in Sedona. It was brand new, had never been worn and was just my size—had it been a couple of inches smaller it would have been too tight for me. It was a beautiful peach-colored dress and top with elegant Korean symbols and even came with a royal outer garment vest. This was a huge blessing to me, as this would have cost hundreds of dollars (some *Hanbok* even cost thousands of dollars in Korea). There was also a *Hanbok* for a six-foot tall male, which fit both Will and our son, John. It was as though the Lord had some couple who was exactly our size get the set made in Korea. Or perhaps, the set was given as a gift to this American couple, exactly our sizes, so that they could donate them to the Thrift shop on that very day that I was going down to Sedona. While I was looking around the store, they were hung behind the cash register and I was able to purchase them when I was done shopping at that precise moment. It may be egotism to think that God did all that just for me but what can I say? He loves me best. I am His favorite or I feel that way often anyways. Our God is so wonderful beyond words!

I'll never forget the spirit of repentance which came over me, as I presented our gifts before the Hawaiians who lined up inside of a courtyard of a Hawaiian Church. As I began to say something, no words came out and all I could do was simply stand there and weep. I realized that my people, the Koreans had never done the protocol with the original people of Hawaii. We had never asked for permission to come onto their island and brought no protocol gifts to honor them. It just seemed like such a horrendous responsibility. I realized I could not undo the wrongs of my people's generation past. I simply needed to do my small part right there and then. I was somehow able to express the repentance of my people and ask for their forgiveness, and now for their friendship. I do know that many so called acts of reconciliation have been done cheaply with no lasting effects on almost all the reservations.

Indeed, we went for our outreach to the island people in Hawaii (Hilo, Kona, Maui) and Micronesia (Pohnpei, Chukk). We went with our two Hopi and two white "bahana" DTS students. The second team stayed back in North America to do the Native American outreach. Imagine the drum beats and the Native American songs and sharing of stories of what the Lord had taught us, which we got to boast about on the islands for the glory of our Lord!

Protocol is very important to all people groups—but especially indigenous people. It is bringing gifts to honor those who are "gatekeepers" over a certain territory. We need to seek the blessing of those leaders within the land, just as Abraham recognized and honored Melchizedek, King of Salem with his offerings.

Protocol is also studying the culture of the people group where one would be visiting or living. Neglecting to study the culture, could cost your life—physically, if not for socially, one way or the other. This is a true story of Missionary Baker in Fiji. His abalone comb was missing out of his room one day. He later found it adorning the Chief's hair and reached over to take it. He did not know that was a crime deserving of death.

Missionary Baker was killed and boiled and eaten along with seven of his Fijian followers in 1867. The lack of protocol had not just taken his life, but the lives of the followers. The axe used to kill Baker is still displayed in the village of Nabutatau. In 2003, Baker's relatives visited the village for a traditional *matanigasau* reconciliation ceremony. This was offered in apology for the killing by descendants of Reverend Baker's slayer.

We had such welcome from so many of the Hawaiians. There was a protocol song to welcome us to a Hawaiian Church in Kohala. The Island Breeze Polynesian team also welcomed us with a song in Makapala, and we sang them a song. It was wonderful to do a presentation at Haili Congregational Church in

Hilo with the elementary school children and also at the Hawaiian Homestead church at another village.

Many of the Hawaiians cannot afford to live on the land of their own ancestors. This is adding insult to injury.

I did not know this, but the Hawaiian Islands were stolen from the indigenous people by greedy landowners and the US government. This disrespect undermined the later work of the American missionaries who had brought Hawaii's queen and most of her people to Jesus. After the island was stolen, many people fell back into the old oppressive legalistic *Kapu* religion.

Today there are only 30,000 Hawaiians. White Americans are hated by many, and Christianity is often seen (as with American Indians) as the white man's religion. Learning all of this has been very disheartening for us, once again.

It was amazing how we were provided for! We were given a sheep by the Trump family. Skip, our Hopi student, taught us how to butcher it. Elnora made Hopi stew and Hopi bread to present to the Hawaiians at the Kalapana Church for the Mother's Day service. We were also given a turkey and a portion of wild pig, which our friend caught. We have been able to visit Kamehameha School in Keau and so much more. We are truly grateful to Alexis Wilson and to Auntie Mary for helping us set all these things up around the islands. God seems to be building a network of relationships in the islands.

We had the most fantastic time in one of the most beautiful valleys we had ever seen in Kapalalau. Oliver and Auntie Val had us working in the taro patches! Taro is the Hawaiian's prized ancient food source. Now we understand how much work it takes to grow them! I felt like a wine presser, with bare feet, knee high deep in the mud. Our job was to weed and to clean (getting totally filthy muddy for a few days) and then to plant taros. It was all good! It was so good to see how Hawaiian taro is raised and then cooked—just like the Hopi staple food, *sumuviki*, which has a similar taste. We are so grateful to Kahu Honalei and his family, who so richly blessed us by being with us and providing all the vehicles and so much more! It was almost embarrassing to be loved on so much.

These islands may be considered a "paradise", but it was not, by any means, a vacation for us as leaders. There was constant low-grade warfare on many levels. Sometimes, I could very well be done doing outreaches (in spite of all the blessings), as these many weeks can be exhausting with steady drippings of murmuring and moving from place to place every couple or a few days. Often, I forget where I am sleeping. Jesus often did not know where to lay his head either as he traveled with his disciples. And yet, I am reminded that the Lord is so faithful to give us one victory after another. Will and I will do this until the Lord tells us to stop. (Will is turning 60 this year.) How good our Lord is!

It is such an amazing thing to be called by God to go completely to the other side of this earth to be among, not the desert people, but with the Micronesian islanders this time.

Poli wore a suit and necktie on the islands, as that was what was needed in order to have a voice. Someday there will be a time when men will be heard—even without the suit and neckties in hundred degree temperatures and nearly one-hundred percent humidity. I don't know how to deal with some of these matters in their culture. Timing is everything sometimes. I must be patient. I cannot demand that, just because I am there that they must change their culture.

Someone had to speak up about the feet-binding matter of the girls in China. Tiny feet were deemed beautiful and the feet-binding was so much a part of the culture, that no one bothered to challenge it—even when some women could not even walk with deformed bones of their bound feet in their childhood. It was an atrocity to the female gender.

Someone else had to say something. It was Gladys Aylward, a missionary from England who spoke up. Yes, timing is everything.

She first had to earn the trust of the Chinese people and the higher officials. When the right time came, she was able to boldly speak up, and the ancient law was changed.

The Micronesian islands are where colonialism took place by the Spanish, Germans, Japanese, and now by the Americans. It is also a place where hospitality is overwhelming, beyond what we could have imagined.

Micronesia has as many islands, as Michigan has thousands of lakes. It is such an eerie feeling to swim with large 6-8 foot sharks at Shark Island. Alas it is where the sharks often congregate! This island is also known as "Ephraim's island," for it was given to Ephraim (Poli's son) by his grandfather. We were told by the diving boat owner that these sharks never bite people. But it was eerie, nevertheless, as they kept circling with their slick bodies, only fifteen to twenty feet below me. At one point, there were eight sharks swimming in our vicinity. That was crazy!

Hopi painting of a turtle at the Watch Tower, Grand Canyon.
It was surreal to swim with the sea turtles in Hawaii.
America was referred to as the "Turtle Island" by the
Native American tribes.

Chapter 9

Centipedes & the Sting of Death

    I felt something wiggle underneath my fingers and quickly moved my hand off the chair. There fell on the floor the biggest armored Centipede I had ever seen—about 8 inches long! It is so good to be secure in the safety of our Lord. Today, as I was talking to the students in our Retreat Center, I reached over to a floral chair next to me. Our Blackfeet friend Herman scooped it up in a cup and placed it outdoors. I hear that the centipedes can really sting badly, and I know that they are very tough to kill, as once I tried to kill one with a broom stick handle and only found it to keep twisting and writhing under my feet like some dying monster. I should not have done it, as I didn't know then to do as Herman did. This is not the first time we have had centipedes in our home in Flagstaff as well as on the Hopi reservation. It just comes with living in the desert.

    When Will was changing our light bulb in our living room, on our first week at our home in Hopiland, a small scorpion jumped off of the light cover onto the floor. These small straw-colored scorpions sting the worst, but the Lord watches over us and commands His angels to protect us while we are asleep. We cannot worry about poisonous things or the terror by night, but trust that we are in the shadow of His wings always. We could take all the precautions to protect ourselves from every single possible thing but we cannot protect ourselves 24 hours a day, as we need sleep. When it is time for us to go, it is time for us to go, and no amount of worrying is going to help or bring us a longer life.

Our good Hopi friend just had a second bad car accident. However, there was not a scratch on her car, nor was anyone behind her when it spun around. She had three flat tires. When her brothers showed up and said, "This is because you go to church and to YWAM," she only rejoiced saying, "No, the Lord protected me. And look, He sent me three angels, one on each of my tires," as she pointed to all her brothers working on her tires.

Nita's car finally died and Marjorie had her truck stolen. What is beautiful is that none of them are shrinking back from the Lord, but loving God all the more. We must continue to pray for protection and provision.

Another good Hopi friend is back in jail. We had so much hope for him to do youth ministries in Hopiland. Another Hopi lady who had received the Lord in jail and had come to YWAM often, from the village of Old Orabi, has just been found murdered a couple of weeks ago. Our friend, Skip, after being baptized a few months ago, recently had a minor heart attack. And some of our other believers in Hopiland are still very much struggling in their walk with God. So we continue to need your prayers, as we cannot do this alone, since it is sometimes so sad and discouraging still.

I found sometimes, it is simply better to let someone go to learn their own lessons of life. If you try to catch them, you can push them away further. It is like dropping a bobbin of thread. The more you pull the thread the further the bobbin unwinds away from you. I just let the bobbin drop so I know exactly where it lands. I can then pick it back up and get to work again. This same principle may apply to our children and friends.

It is so frustrating when we cannot help our friends who need help, because they do not want our help. We have a friend who comes and works once in a while around the Retreat Center ground. He has been recently living out on the streets. I asked him whether he would like to stay for our DTS, and help us with the maintenance, so that he could get strong in the Lord. He did not want our help. I would have begged him to stay for the school, but I knew that nothing I was going to say would persuade him. Later he ended up going back to jail. It would have been so good for him. My heart ached and I just wanted to cry. This must be how God feels, when we are determined to go our own ways.

> *Be of good courage, and He shall strengthen your heart;*
> *Wait, I say, on the Lord. (Psalm 27:14)*

We are thankful that we have these things that break down.

- ** YWAM's fifteen passenger van was broken. Now it works well, with a new water pump and radiator. We are thankful that we have a fifteen passenger van for YWAM!
- ** Our bookkeeping computer in our office crashed, so we couldn't print any receipts. Now it is replaced and the data has been saved. We are thankful that we have printers and computers!
- ** Our own house sewer line broke, so we had to bring in a backhoe to dig a six-foot deep by 20 foot long trench. Now the toilet does not over-flow. (Our son-in-law, Tim, gave us his hours on the backhoe).
We are thankful that we have running water and toilets! (Our staff, David Youngburg has not had running water at our old house in Kykotsmovi for over two months because of frozen pipes.)
- ** Our dishwasher was broken, but now it is fixed. We are thankful that we have a dishwasher!
- ** Four of our Retreat Center skylights are cracked, and one broke through completely from all the snow this winter. We now have that one replaced, as well as new domes for free for the cracked ones. We are thankful that we have skylights!
- ** Our towels in the bathroom are often filthy. But we have a washing machine that works! I am thankful that I have a husband who thinks I'm beautiful and that he is not afraid to work hard and get dirty.

What more can I ask for in my life? Well, a working washing machine and a dryer, and an Office Administrator would be nice. But, oh, I don't want to end up with nothing for wanting more all the time like the fisher man's wife whose appetite was insatiable. The story is that a fisher man caught a magic fish who told him that many of his wishes would be granted if the fisherman lets him go back into the water. The poor fisherman went back to his wife who had nothing, and asked what she wanted. She asked for one wish, and another and another until she was very wealthy. But, she was still greedy and told her husband to go back to ask for one more wish. The fisherman sadly went to ask the magic fish, but when he came back home, he found his wife sitting in their poor original hut. That would be a bummer.

Have you ever felt secure in the certainty that all that is wrong the Lord can set right? I am sensing this calmness, as I ask for not only the big things but little signs of love. I am asking the Lord to never let me judge. I recognize that the hearts of men are so delicate and so complex, that only the Maker can know them.

One person said that we are a laughing stock in Hopiland. I wanted to say something to defend ourselves. It is okay because I know we are doing what the Lord is requiring of us. There is a gentling which the Lord is doing in us. Even in a deep sense of loss, there is such a great peace in my heart. The Lord is indeed in control and it is good to just keep quiet sometimes.

Will and I have now have been in full-time ministry together for 27 years in 2006. There is not much we have not experienced as leaders. However, it is getting easier to be calm in the midst of the storm, now, when the attacks come. It is not to say that we are perfect by any means, but we are secure in knowing that God has chosen us to come to Arizona. He has given us a vision for both YWAM Hopiland and Flagstaff, and HE will accomplish what He has started with us. We did not wish for this position. On the contrary, I often wished that the Lord had chosen someone else. But He chose us, Will and I, who are both fatherless. (Will lost his father at age five; I lost mine by refusal.) How good it is to know that our God is much more intimate than any earthly fathers! Psalms 146:9 says that God relieves the fatherless. He is my Father and I go running to Him for advice. I can pour out my heart to Him as my children do with us. He lets me rest on His shoulders.

I was sarcastic when I said to one of our staff, "Try being in full time ministry for thirty years." We were going through some hard times with a DTS student. It is exhausting for the other students and staff to have these students who are not team players. It is amazing how people like this can turn things around so they become the victims. We become the villains who had abused them when everyone else had to suffer because of their uncooperative and selfish behaviors.

I had to repent because I made ministry sound undesirable and miserable. The Lord had to remind me what a glorious thing it is to be walking with the Creator of the universe and to be in full time ministry.

I wonder why it is that we sometimes cry at the movies. I choked and cried when *Babe*, the little pig completed his task by herding the sheep and the crowd got up and cheered like crazy. It was just a silly movie about a silly pig. I cried when the boxer in *Cinderella Man* won and everyone stood and cheered and roared. Our hearts are moved to tears when we see the cheering for the champions. I believe we are moved because we want to see ourselves in those people. I think this is God. He is cheering for us every time when we listen to his voice and do that small or big thing which touches His heart. We are the champions then.

"I am proud of you," I heard the Lord gently say to my heart one day. Hope is such a wonderful thing. I found hope in these kind words of my Father. He is not so proud of me because I am perfect, but simply for choosing Him that day and because of my desire to be in this process of walking with Him on this earth. He is proud of us every time we get back on our feet and not quit. Our own failures and shame and hopelessness may be great, but the grace of the hope we have in Christ is far greater! We can do this! We can live one day at a time, because we have a very good and loving Father who is rooting for us and proud of us! He is for us. Being a proud parent, His heart beats with love's strong current, as we choose Him this day!

The Sting of Death

Having been missing all night, a little girl's body was found in a sitting position in an abandoned refrigerator at Hotevilla Gospel Church. The Sacred Word says that each one of our days is numbered, and it was time for her to go home. This would have happened on this day somewhere else, no matter what, and I believe it was Satan's intention to bring shame to the Church.

We are all grieving deeply inside. However, our eight-year-old friend is in heaven! Women are not allowed at the gravesite at traditional Hopi burials, but a few of us were invited to come and sing some of her favorite songs. Yes, indeed, to some of these Hopi men, these four songs, "Our God Is an Awesome God," "This Is the Day That the Lord Has Made," "There's Power in the Blood" and "Lord, I lift your name on High" were new songs. The music lifted their spirits, as they were burying her little body.

O sing to the Lord a new song, Sing to the Lord all the earth!
Declare His glory among the nations,
His wonders among peoples! (Psalms 96:1 & 3)

We were amazed at how many people showed up at our YWAM facility the evening of the day when her body was found. The faith we witnessed would have been impossible ten years ago. So many Hopi people were singing many joyful songs, including, "Amazing Grace." They prayed over the little girl's mom, our dear friend, who was weeping on the floor. The people sang, "Yes, it was grace that brought you safe thus far, and grace, your fears relieved. How precious did that grace appear, and grace will lead you home." We, as outsiders, did not have to pray, for they were praying for one another. They were standing up and testifying, saying that their people do not understand why they are joyful, but that they want their loved ones to know this same joy in Christ.

When just a few of us from YWAM went out to where her body was found, so that we could worship and cleanse that area from any spirits which may try to hinder, we were surprised to find that many other Hopis also came, and worshipped the Lord with us. We called that site not a wicked place, but a holy place, where a child was taken to be in the arms of our loving Savior. What Satan meant for evil, the Lord is using for good! The Hopi nation is seeing the joy in the lives of the believers, in spite of this horrendous ordeal, which could have brought so many accusations (this is definitely out there, too) and harm. The Lord is winning, indeed!

Yes, there is a sting in death, but truly, this sting is so temporary, compared to what comfort and peace the Lord has offered to all of us here. It hurts like mad; my stomach and heart feels like it is going to rip at times. I cannot stop the waves of tears and emotions of losing such a beautiful little princess in our midst, who always smiled so wistfully. I do not believe our God is intimidated by our questioning Him. As I wept on the floor in our bedroom, holding onto my bedpost, I cried out to Him and asked where He was when this little girl was crying for her mommy in that box.

He asked me where I was when His only Son was dying on the cross. He gently told me that He was there with her comforting and holding her. I had just bought a small turquoise ring for her pinky finger, a few weeks back. I did not know that she would wear the ring to her grave.

I think this note which our 22-year-old staff gal, Danielle, wrote is an important thing to consider:

We were invited to the graveside to sing. An uncle is a believer; he helped dig the grave and he poured oil around her grave in prayer. After we left, Charity, Millie and I walked to the house to be 'purified.' Anyone who was at the graveside needed to be cleansed. They wash with cedar water and then let the smoke of cedar wash over them. I know a lot of the Christians shake their heads at this act. But as we walked over, I prayed, "Lord will this cause the believers to be angry?" But I felt strongly, "They are already saved; show the people (the family of non believers) you respect them. I didn't come for the healthy." On the day I found her, I felt like I needed to purify to symbolize what I know Christ has already done. It was good to wash the cedar water over me and think, this is the blood of Christ purifying me; and then to stand in the smoke and think, this is the breath of God breathing over me. After, I had done that I felt lighter, the burden was lightened.

A Hopi painting inside the Watch Tower at Grand Canyon

Chapter 10

Hardly a Dull moment

Chin hair is a disgusting thing on a woman. I must be getting old. You can tell when you start getting hairs on your chin. Some of my Hopi friends are relentless in making fun of me. I suppose this is their way of telling me that they love me in a teasing way. But it is okay, because I can dish it out back on them just as anyone of them can. After fifteen years of associating with the Hopis, we have been able to really get close to some of them to the point where they can treat me with utter mercilessness and with an almost embarrassing honesty and actions.

I suppose that it would be helpful to give an example of their taunting way of loving me. Annetta (we call her Nita) Koruh is my Hopi sister, a mighty and almost a fearless warrior, or at least it seems that way to me. She has a pretty daughter, Kayla, who was recently the runner-up for home-coming queen at Hopi High School. Kayla was also a long distance runner, who won a State championship with the Hopi High girls' cross country team in 2010.

It was Kayla who found my long hair on my chin—mind you, not even a black one, but a white one! Not just once, but twice! I don't want to admit that I am getting old, although it is a noble thing. Will's mom says that all her life she heard old age being called the "golden years." "Golden years, my foot," she says, "It is more like the pewter years!"

I knew an old lady, named Beatrice, who used to come and visit us very often, sometimes three to four times a day. She lived in a pretty shabby nursing home around the corner from our ministry place, called the "Winter House," in downtown Santa Barbara, when Will and I were first married. I was in my early twenties in full-time ministry and trying to raise our baby, Clover. Once when she knocked for the fifth time, I opened the door to politely say that we could not have her come in at that moment. She gave a kind nod of her head and said, "Oh, I see. You are comforting each other." I did not even think she even knew what that meant.

I was horrified to see a long chin hair on Beatrice every time she came over. She used to write prose for a greeting card company. She also had a bit of a mustache like the circus ladies with a beard you see in the movies. Although Beatrice was something of a genius, she was a chain smoker, who dripped her cigarette ash on our entire floor. It was amazing that she didn't burn down our apartment. Also spit often came straight out of her mouth, as though targeting the face of her listeners. She almost always drooled. I must say, quite frankly, she was not someone I wanted to emulate as a lady in any shape or manner at all.

So, no wonder I was horrified when Kayla not only found my long chin hair, which looked like Beatrice's chin hair, but tried to pull it out in front of some others. She had no mercy at all, to try to spare my reputation of pretending to be elegant like Princess Grace of Monaco. Princess Grace would never have had a chin hair, and if she did, she would never be seen in public with it.

Nita joined right in and grabbed and pinched that disgusting hair, and yanked it out of my chin. It hurt and I screamed. They both thought that was really funny, and I didn't know whether I quite liked the idea that they were having so much fun at my expense.

To be fair, I should mention that Kayla—being no respecter of persons—also jerked out one of Will's overly long, out of place, eye brow hairs, to his great dismay. He told me later he was grateful that she hadn't gone hunting miscreant nose hairs.

I guess I am mentioning this, because I am just thankful that I have some Native sisters who consider themselves so close to me that they could do something like this and get away with it. If this is the cross one must bear in order to be among my Native American brothers and sisters, it is a small price to pay. Besides, I also love giving them a hard time, simply because I like to.

Some of the Hopi men love to sing a silly song about Will which they made up when they went down the San Juan River on the Utah/Arizona border. They would sing this mock powwow song over and over again like it is going out of style. The song goes, "Is it a bird? No!!! Is it a plane? No!!! Etc . . . Oh, my gosh, it's Y-WUM Will!" (It is supposed to be YWAM—pronounced Y-Wham but they always say Y-Wum) Yes, one can still hear the echoes of these Hopi men singing in these canyons if you listen very carefully.

One ought to go down the San Juan River, as it is a Wild West adventure for sure. Down at the river's end, where the rafters have to get out before the waterfall, it becomes like a Lewis & Clark Expedition. The guys have to get out and pull the eight-man rafts and gear boats over the sand bars and beaches sometimes for miles. From a distance, it is like watching a man walking on water. We try to avoid those grueling low-water conditions.

It is absolutely beautiful to go down the San Juan River on our eight-man rafts and two-man kayaks. The canyons are streaks of brick red color and layers upon layers of other geometric rocks. These cathedral-like walls are so amazing, and sometimes climbed by the big horn desert sheep. It is definitely the wild Southwest country, and so worth seeing!

I came into SEA & SUMMIT Expeditions in 1976 as a young eighteen-year-old, to be trained to work with youth-at-risk in the Sierra Nevada Mountains of California. These were some of the most challenging and frightening experiences of my life. I had nightmares of falling off the rocks the first few weeks at Chimney Rock Base Camp. We did activities like rock climbing, rappelling and the rope bridge in our base camp in Sequoia National Forest.

We worked with the at-risk girls and boys in the back country in the High Sierra Mountains.

We had to climb a major peak on the Great Western Divide and hike rigorous trails in order to sign into a log book, which the rangers leave on top of the mountain in a metal box. We made all the kids do a "solo" time alone by a stream or a lake somewhere with only a sleeping bag and a Bible and no food for three days. They were given an emergency whistle, and we the staff were spread apart not too far from the kids somewhere where we could not be seen. Some years later, we allowed one granola bar, each, per day. They could eat any berries which they might find within their assigned boundaries. We had heavy packs at the beginning of each expedition, with the equivalent of thirty meals for almost a dozen people for ten days. My backpack was once sixty-five pounds or more, especially after Will had to leave much food and gear behind to hike out quickly to call a ranger for a helicopter evacuation of one of our participants.

I was overwhelmed with God's wondrous presence in these incredibly beautiful High Sierra lakes, thousand foot white granite cliffs, beautiful valleys and wild flower meadows. I have only known one true city slicker, Doug Giordani, who could hardly see the beauty of that place and was miserable in the Sierras.

I believe I felt the most beautiful I ever had at any time in my life. One cannot explain the beauty of these mountains, after a hair washing and the gentle breeze which caresses you all over like the loving arms of a mother with a child. Most importantly, the Lord drew me closer to Him as His daughter, touching my heart in the deepest places.

Sea & Summit Expeditions was not only used to dramatically transform many people's lives, but also my own. I was the one who benefited most, more than any of the youth at risk. I came in as a frumpy, out-of-shape adolescent. We all had to climb the rope every morning at our Chimney Rock Base Camp. By the end of the summer I was able to do over fifty men's pushups, as I lost so much weight after a full summer of hiking. I would not have believed it, if someone had told me at the beginning of my involvement, that I would someday be one of the directors of this ministry.

Today we have all sorts of outdoor adventure gear. We also have a ropes course—the tool which so dramatically taught me how to trust God and other people. It is an incredible means for teaching trust, courage and teamwork. We are praying and waiting on God to revive this wonderful ministry, as we need the staff people who will do more of these outreaches with Native peoples of Arizona and North America.

Will once told me that he plans on exploring, not just the canyons, but all the galaxies someday. I believe that we are not going to just sit around and play harps for eternity, when we get to heaven. Once in the 1980's, Will and I were hiking in a valley of the High Sierra mountains. On either side, there were breathtakingly beautiful white, rocky mountains like angels' wings. I was in such awe of the beauty of that place!

I was also curious as to what kind of lakes and towering peaks might be on the other side of the mountains. I said to Will that I wish I had a small rocket pack, so that I could fly and explore all the other parts of the Sierras easily, and see all the wild flowers.

Will said, "I think that God has assignments for us to do when we get to heaven. All that we are learning on this planet earth is preparing us for those adventures and battles to be had! Would you like to come with me someday?"

This one question boggled my mind so much that I could not even think for some moments. No, I don't think we will be sitting around playing harps. Somehow I believe that every time we say "yes" to God with our actions on this planet earth, no matter how small, that it is preparing us for the assignments and the battles we may have to fight in all the galaxies. Wow, what mysteries we will discover after we are done on this earth!

There is hardly a dull moment here at our Flagstaff base and at our home. There is always someone knocking or calling and everyone is always lined up to use the computers in our office. In the last months, we have had visitors from as far as Japan, Holland, France, and Sweden, as well as many who are representing the other branches of YWAM.

I wonder how many others in YWAM feel so without privacy. And yet, I cannot help but to trust that the Lord had a special plan for our lives to be surrounded by such people who are so eager to serve God and I am sure that I would not change this life for anyone else's. But even so, I do hope that I would soon get a bit of a fence around our home so that there would be some boundaries that would be healthy for Will and I, as the Leaders.

We have seven DTS students in Hopiland. We also have three part time students, who are male inmates from Hopi Jail. The meals are always served to twenty people or more, with speakers, guests, students, and staff. At the opening feast night of our school, Ruby and Nita welcomed our new students in their full regalia, singing a basket dance song. Jon Lansa, our Hopi friend, also came to welcome the students that evening and as our speaker that week.

Then, there was Ernie, our local musician friend, who brought many different types of flutes that he had made: such as a bamboo one, a fired clay turtle flute and an award winning carved wooden one, which had a snorting white horse head at one end and a black hoof at the mouth piece. He also had a double flute and one with a carved Eagle's head. He let all the students try playing them. We had a great jam session! It is truly an amazing thing to be able to have a Discipleship Training School right here in the most ancient land of North America. We are so grateful that the Lord has opened the door for us to come in.

There's a thin blanket of white snow all over Hopiland this morning. We're taking our speaker of this week, Fern Noble, into Flagstaff to the airport today. Even with all the snow flurries and the ceremonies going on, many Hopis showed up to hear how "worldly sorrow" only leads to death and "Godly sorrow" brings repentance and joy. The veils of shame were removed from the faces of the Hopi ladies and our DTS (Discipleship Training School) students. Joy in their hearts was restored.

DTS outreach this year turned out to be very fruitful. We believe that God is expanding our boundaries with churches, tribes, and people. It was good to build a deck for "Saul and Martha" and to work for "Juanita" and go out to her field and plant on the Jemez Pueblo Reservation.

We also were invited to the Feast Day on the San Felipe Reservation in New Mexico. It was an amazing thing to watch several hundred Corn Dancers and yet another several hundred waiting to come into the plaza for the next round. We found out that they have the dance only once a year, whereas, the Hopi have dances all throughout the ceremonial cycle of the year. The ladies wore the same dress and belts as the Hopi ladies and danced bare-footed with two pine tree sprigs in their hands. These are largely closed pueblos, in that they are very resistant to outside Christian influences. On our last day in Jemez, two of our people were stopped while walking a dirt road near the village. They were asked if they had permission to be there in the pueblo. These are sovereign Nations and we can understand their hostility against Christianity because of our disrespectful history in their lands.

Approximately twenty Maori Christian young people came to Hopiland to stay for a week at our YWAM facility. They will share their own culture and dances. They will also share a "Drug Free" presentation in Hopi schools and communities and at the Hopi Civic Center. December is a "quiet" month when there is to be no drumming, stomping or dancing in Hopiland, out of respect for the Earth. However, we are praying that we would have permission for these young people from New Zealand to be able to glorify God even in the month of December with their dances and songs to Jesus.

Jonathon Maracle is from the Mohawk nation. His father was an honored elder, who followed Jesus while simultaneously respecting his Mohawk heritage. Jonathon was a prodigal rock-and-roller, who left his Christian family to follow the god of worldly success. When he found that the lifestyle was killing him and that the music industry had no use for his Native identity, he finally called on Jesus. After coming here into our State, he wrote a song, called "Arizona Sky." We have traveled halfway around the world, and I have not seen any sky elsewhere as beautiful as here.

Jonathan Maracle and Cheryl Bear Barnetson both came out for a concert sponsored by Reztoration Ministry. Cheryl and Randy Barnetson are from British Columbia, where they ran an inner city ministry and a Native Christian Bible school. Both the Barnetsons and Jonathon are people that God is sovereignly using for His purpose of calling out the lost sheep of Native North America and beyond.

At the Red Wave First Nations Celebration and at the all-night prayer time on the Navajo reservation, there were only eleven people remaining to pray by 3:30 AM out of about a hundred people who started out praying. I was told that nine out of those eleven were from Hopiland. There are many times I have been discouraged working in Hopiland, and yet when I hear something like this, I know that the Lord is at work. These are the Gideons who can fight the battle!

It was also good to have Frank & Sonya Naia, our previous YWAM President, speak at Hotevilla Gospel Church and also at YWAM. We fellowshipped for several days and visited the Grand Canyon together. All the deep and beautiful colors of the red and brown stone walls, in the winter light and snow, were the most excellent hues that I had ever seen. Oh, how great and awesome our Creator is! At the IMAX Theatre in Grand Canyon was the first time I saw the film about John Wesley Powell's first full Colorado River Expedition.

It was wonderful when Hopi CPS (Child Protective Services) called YWAM to ask whether we would help with their children by having Emergency Foster care at our YWAM base. Our staff ladies (Charity, Sheila, and Danielle), after fasting and praying, believed that they were not to come up with new programs of their own. God was saying they should apply themselves to existing programs. Our staff ladies would be able to accommodate children for a week at a time and get to know the community much more through their families. We just got two teenage girls. One fourteen-year-old is eight months pregnant.

Four YWAM girls who are interested in scouting out the Zuni Indian Reservation are now here with us. The Zunis are a closely related tribe to the Hopis, with similar dances and ceremonies. There are twenty pueblo Native American tribes in the US, who live in stone homes, like the Jews in Israel. Hopis are the largest of these tribes. Only the Hopis live in Arizona; the other nineteen smaller tribes are in New Mexico. Outsiders cannot enter to live on these reservations without a special permit.

We just returned from a conference with our team of eleven from Hopiland. George and Lisa Otis, Jr. with the *Sentinel Group* (Transformation videos), had invited us to come to join them at the "Healing the Land Conference." Our hearts were excited, as we read the note they sent us to tell us of the mighty move of God in the nation of Fiji and the surrounding island nations. The Otis wrote to us saying, "We know that it is God's intention to give the host people of our own nation a leadership role in leading us back to Him and into a time of healing."

We had presented a dance and a song from Hopiland and were surprised to find that there was a standing ovation—not to us but to our Lord, who gave all of us in Hopiland a small beginning. Nita presented, on the stage, what looks like the *Morning Sun* basket to George and Lisa. It was an unfinished Hopi woven plaque, and she told them that someday, when they come to film the transformation video in Hopiland, the basket will be finished.

Great Eagle Rising

After coming back from Fort Worth, we have found out that someone had said that Ruby and Nita had done a Hopi Butterfly Dance at the Conference, which should have been done only in their Plazas. They did not do the Butterfly Dance. They did, however, do a simple dance which was choreographed to Tom Bee's song which says, "Today, an Indian boy/girl has been born and he/she will love the Lord in all his/her ways." It is a beautiful simple dance that declares that the Native American children will come to know and serve the Lord.

The dance was done in their Hopi outfits, for they see no shame in wearing their traditional clothes to honor Jesus. They did sing a "Basket Song" in their Hopi language that teaches the children how to live and have a good and long life.

This is a delicate matter, as some believe that what was done in the kivas should only be done down in there. How we need prayers for our sisters and brothers in Christ in Hopiland to do what the Lord requires—even though it may rock the boat, as Jesus did with the Pharisees and His disciples.

There is a flurry of activities and people getting in touch with us from literally around the world. We have been blessed to have some other ministries, such as Campus Crusade for Christ, Wycliffe Bible Translators and Inter Varsity writing or coming to visit us.

If we can all be humble and know that we are each responsible for a small portion of what God is doing on this earth, we can work together with Christ as our Commander. We are glad to be a part of this work which the Lord established here among so many Native American tribes in Arizona.

Our three staff ladies are doing Emergency Foster care. They now have five children, ages one through eleven (all from the same mom) for several weeks. May the Lord touch these children's lives and their mom also! This is a very good opportunity to show them the love of Christ!

Today our DTS was supposed to leave for Hopiland to plant corn in a field for an older couple, but instead we will be going up to the terrace garden in Bacavi village to clean up the spring and the garden area.

*As they pass through the valley of Baca,
They make it a spring.
(Psalm 84:6)*

Sexual Abuse Awareness event at the Hopi Civic Center
DTS & our Hopi friends, 2013

Chapter 11

Forgiveness

Will had a lot of nerve before we got married. He always says that he is the will of God. His name is Will after all. I had to forgive him for a lot of things. One evening, as we were walking in the moonlit night on the beach below Shoreline Park in Santa Barbara, he said he realized he was never going to have blond and blue-eyed kids. Will's mom calls him "My blue-eyed baby." In his mind he already knew that I was going to consent to his proposal and had already consummated our marriage. He had not yet asked me. He always says, "Where there is a will, there is a way." It is good to assure someone when there may be any doubt because this is also love.

It is not like I was desperate. One of my girl friends at Fullerton Junior College in California said that she thought I was going out with the best looking guy on the whole campus. People assumed things. I was not even going out with anyone. She said when he walks across campus it is like seeing a tall, dark and handsome prince walking by.

I am sure most all the girls have some grand idea that all the boys were crazy about them or write a book claiming it. What is a nice thing about getting older is that you can say anything you want, thirty, forty, fifty years later. What's anyone going to say? That you are lying? They won't because you would be considered an elder by that time. They think you are telling the truth.

True Confessions of a Missionary

When another male friend came over to pick me up once, the commotion from my roommates was so great that I thought a rock star or the President of the United States was coming to our apartment. Apparently, he was the most popular guy at my roommate's high school in Orange County where she attended. Every time we went out, he would use a coupon, like to Sizzlers or some other restaurant. Somehow it used to make me feel cheap when he was only trying to be wise with his money. I mean what difference did it make if he used coupons or not since I would have ordered what I wanted to eat either way? We would have made good missionaries together, if we had married. He died in the U.S. Air force while flying a plane as a test pilot. He did come to visit Will and me and saw our baby daughter, Clover, in Santa Barbara before he died. His mother called to let us know that he had been killed. His wife wrote afterwards, saying how Craig had treasured our friendship so much and talked about us. I cried and cried. I had to let Will know that I was not sorry I had not married Craig—just in case he was wondering.

I think boys were silly then. They seemed to like girls who were out-going and talked about things—sometimes imaginative things—because they are bored. I don't think these boys were strong enough to handle me. I would have been the boss. Even when I treated them like my own brothers, they misunderstood and thought things. Betty Hartley was right. It must have been that slinky cotton dress. They would tell me that they had been thinking some such thoughts for a long time, and I could not have been more shocked several times. I was very naïve. I thought they hung around with me because I was funny and made them laugh a lot. One must be really careful with some boys.

One should never go with someone because she feels sorry for him. He will eventually get over it. I felt sorry for one guy who called and sounded very serious about taking me out on a date. His parents had a house on a hill in Fullerton. He didn't even have the decency to take me out to a nice restaurant. I let him take me out to McDonald's, as I did not want him to say that I took advantage of him by having him take me out to some fancy place. But he really should have insisted. It was a bummer, because I had to talk the whole time. I am glad I am not married to someone like that. John Wayne is okay, but after awhile, a girl wants someone who says a little more than, "Yep" all the time.

I was not even pretty. I used to have some people tell me I looked like Yoko Ono. I like the Beetles, but I could not stand the girls who went berserk about them like they were some gods or something. I did not know enough about their personal lives to know that John Lennon was married to a Japanese hippie-looking lady named Yoko. I was also a hippie wanna-be in the seventies with my long, wild hairdo. I told Will that one guy came running across my college campus lawn and had asked me whether anyone had told me I looked like Yoko Ono. I told him, "Yes, many times." I thought this guy was going to hurt me or something, because he came running so fast. I was startled and almost told him that he was dim-witted for scaring me like that. I thought Will would be impressed with this that I looked like some famous rock star's wife. Will told me that was not a compliment, as Yoko was not very pretty at all.

Sometimes, Will really knows how to pop my bubbles. I had to forgive him for that too. But, he redeemed himself by saying that he thought I was way prettier than Yoko. I think you are okay. The Creator loves you more than you'd ever know!

Marriage is like the sun. You can't live without its heat as our whole planet will freeze to death. You are in the dark and can't see a thing at night unless you have an artificial light. However, the sun can be a real pain. It gets so hot that we end up sweating like a hog. When it gets in your eyes while you're driving, you can't see a thing and you have to squint like you're eating sour lemon because you are blinded by it.

I couldn't believe the response Will gave me one day during our engagement. We had just gone on a double date. He knew something was wrong and kept urging me to speak to him about what was bothering me. I didn't want to talk about it, because I did not want to hurt his feelings. He is really good about drawing me out, even when I don't want him to. At his persistent urging, I finally told him that I felt I was marrying him simply because I felt he was a man of God but that I was not attracted to him. He asked for it and now he had it. It all came out.

I was such a pain! He quietly responded, saying that although he was attracted to me physically, he was more attracted to me spiritually and in other ways. He didn't miss a beat! He told me that he believed that I would learn eventually to be attracted to him in the future. It was pretty amazing the confidence he had in himself. If it was the other way, I would have told him that he should have never asked me out in the first place. I would have wanted to scratch his eyes out, for my ego would have been deeply hurt, and I would have cried myself to sleep that night. I don't know whether I could have responded gently and confidently as he had. I think it is God's love, which so confidently woos us and loves us unconditionally when we are being brats like Scarlett O'Hara.

I have learned that forgiving someone is not just talk but taking actions. One can think about forgiving someone until they have constipation, but if one does not put it into action, their prayers will often prove to be nothing.

Before Will and I got married, I found out that he had been involved in other relationships. I almost broke off the engagement three days before the wedding. We were sitting at our counselor, Jerry's office, where we had gone through our pre-marital counseling classes. I told Jerry that something had just happened and I didn't know whether I could go on with the wedding. I knew that Will was now a godly man, but that I didn't know whether I was the right woman for him. I told Jerry that I felt so trapped, as Will's mom had already flown in from the east coast and the other family members were flying in that very day. I was crying a bucketful. I thought someone else would be able to accept his past and love him better than me, as though I was being a saint.

Jerry gave me the best advice. He told me that I was not trapped and that I could still cancel the wedding. He told me that when the guests come and see the "wedding cancelled" sign, they would go home disappointed but that they would still live. But was I going to regret my decision for the rest of my life? Will said later that was the hardest pill to swallow, as he sat there quietly with his arm around me, his fiancée. I remember changing my position and sitting up proper and straight, because I had just realized that I had received this grand revelation that there was still a way out. I was like a bird set free from her cage which did not know whether to fly or where, as the vast sky was opened to her in every direction. It was then that I knew I was going to overcome this feeling of betrayal and learn to forgive Will.

    I know this sounds really extreme, but I don't believe in kissing a guy until the engagement of one's marriage. I made up my mind that I would save it only for that one guy whom the Lord would have me spend the rest of my life with. I had only been kissed once before. It happened so fast, while he was saying good night to me at my door, that I could not stop him. In my opinion, that kiss did not count. I stayed awake that night, because I liked it and realized how dangerous kissing was. If just a moment of a kiss could stir such emotions in me, what would it do to anyone when the kiss is prolonged? Will used to be quite frustrated, when he tried to kiss me before our engagement and I used to turn my face quickly away from him before he could reach my lips. I should have made him wait until our wedding night. I don't want to judge anyone else for their standards, but I personally wanted a man who also had waited for me. Was that too much to ask?

    This revelation came to me after I once bit inside of my mouth during my teen years. I got a big open sore after I had chomped down on my own flesh somehow. In stretching out my bottom lip to see the open sore, it suddenly occurred to me that my lips were an extension of the inside of myself and that my lips were to be saved only for the man I was to marry.

    I thought once we had our wedding, everything would be okay. When I realized that the deep intimacy which should have been saved for the wedding bed had already been given to another, I hated Will more than I hated anyone. In the same way, Amnon hated

Tamar once he had her. II Samuel 13:15 says, "Amnon hated her exceedingly so that the hatred with which he hated her was greater than the love with which he loved her. And Amnon said to her, 'Arise, be gone!'"

I tried to comfort myself with psychology, saying that his past should not matter one bit. But his past mattered deeply to me. Will asked me why I would want to dredge up the things which had been flushed down the toilet. I am sure that pride, self-righteousness, bitterness and self pity were involved. I could not help myself. I was hurting so much, that I wanted to hurt him just as badly. Will knows how hard I tried, and he says that the first ten years of our marriage was bliss for him. So, I know that I tried to be kind to him, even though I couldn't forgive him.

Will said to me that he would have never slept with anyone else, if he had only known how much pain and grief this would bring to his bride someday. It was like when he said to me during my most painful moments of labor with our first daughter, Clover that he wished he could take away my pain. He could not.

I am so glad that I had godly people to counsel me. I went and saw Betty Hartley in Yorba Linda, California. She asked me whether I had considered II Corinthians 2:7-8. Paul had written to the Corinthian church in the first letter to discipline and purge from the church the man who was sinning with his father's wife. The church of Corinth had disciplined the man so harshly that Paul was now saying, "So that on the contrary, you ought rather to *forgive* and *comfort* and *reaffirm* your love to him, lest perhaps such a one be swallowed up with too much sorrow" (emphasis added).

I understood about forgiving someone, but I didn't understand about comforting Will, when I felt I was the one wronged. I should have been the one to be comforted. The Word of God doesn't say that we only do things which make sense to us. I had to simply obey the Lord and take actions to comfort Will and to do what the Word of God said. I did not want him to be swallowed up with too much sorrow, as Paul said. I noticed the lines on his forehead, and I realized that he had paid a price for his past. I tried to comfort him the best I could. I whispered to him while he was sleeping that I was sorry that I was making him sad with my reactions and asked him to forgive me. I began to reaffirm my love to him in words and actions. This is what brought about the healing of my heart and, ultimately, the healing of our marriage. Forgiveness is not just words; one must act on those commands which the Lord requires of us.

I believe that this is a huge battle in Hopiland. There is so much unforgiveness among families, churches, tribe, clan leaders and others. I asked the Lord to start with me to love the others who may disagree or even hate us.

Forgiving Myself

I did not like myself. I wanted to be like someone else. Once, I ran into my bedroom and cried during my younger days. I was approached by some physical fitness guy, who had spotted me during my college track class. He tested me and told me I was the strongest gal he had ever met in his whole life. I am not exaggerating; that is what he said. He was probably in his mid-thirties, and he wanted me to help him start a fitness center like Jack La Laine. When I got home, my parents were watching an old movie with Elizabeth Taylor, looking so gorgeous and feminine.

It made me sick to see someone so beautiful like that, and I ran to my bedroom and sobbed on my bed. I was thinking why someone else has to look that gorgeous when I felt so muscular compared to her tiny figure. At least, if someone else wasn't so strikingly beautiful, I would not feel so ordinary.

Soon after this experience, "The Bionic Woman" and "Wonder Woman" weekly series came on T.V., with top ratings. This thrilled me to pieces, as I could much more relate with these ladies, who were not such sissies.

I am glad that I don't think like that anymore. Most of the time, I find that I like myself. I like being strong, which enables me to do gardening and other physical work around our ministry center. I don't feel in the least "less feminine" for my physical strength, as when I saw Liz with her tiny waist long ago. It helps for a missionary to be strong, as the mission fields are neither for the faint-hearted nor the weak.

As I am getting older with grown kids, I can't help but think about being a grandma someday. I don't think I want to be an old fat grandma who bakes all-American apple pies for the grandchildren, even though that is the kind of a grandma I would have preferred for myself. Even if I become a grandma, I think I would like to look fit and trim. But, I cannot stand those movie stars who look so fake with their countless plastic surgeries. One ought to at least look their age a little bit. Before, I used to think, "What is a good figure if one cannot show it off? I think this was Scarlett O'Hara talking. But now, I see that everyone's genes are made differently, as some people could eat half the amount I would normally eat and still look obese. So it is not so much about the figure, but I do want to be healthy, when and if I am ever in my eighties. I don't want to ever retire; I want to keep working for the Lord.

I don't want to romanticize everything of the past. It is sort of like how people talk about dead people at funerals. All of a sudden the dead become the heroes and the saints. Everything gets flowery about them even though they may only have been a normal person or even a bit dull. I don't know why we can't say these nice things while people are still alive. I saw some old folks do that and they seem to get worse as they get older, repeating the same stories over and over again. I used to visit convalescent homes, when in High School, and deliver books to the shut-ins and they used to tell me the same old story a hundred times. I wanted to scream and tell them that I heard it a gazillion times but I sat and smiled the whole time because God wanted me to be nice.

Then again, what is the harm in romanticizing the past? If I get real old and I had so much time on my hands and I could not really go to too many places and not many come to visit me, I would want to tell the same stories to whomever I could hold captive for as long as I could and make it as interesting as I can. This world can be so dreary at times. I am glad that heaven will have so much more interesting things to talk about for eternity. I will be sitting there talking with an old friend from earth and see something magnificent happen before our eyes and we will talk about it for a couple of years. We will have some more friends show up and see some other fantastic thing happen in the galaxies and we will all gasp and talk about it for ten years and no one would interrupt one another as we will have all the time in the world.

Denise Austin's fat burning work-out with low and slow and continuous movement, coupled with muscle toning is good to do. I realize this is also spiritual, in that our minds, bodies and spirits are meant to function together to glorify our God. When I was an avid exerciser in my thirties, I would have found this routine hardly worth doing, as it was too easy. But in my early fifties, I found myself moaning and sweating. I am writing this in hope that we would make a fresh new attempt to honor God by eating right, exercising and drinking more water. It is good to keep physically fit, as it helps us to be healthier to do the Lord's work and we want to be all that we can be on this planet earth.

It is a strange thing how people fall in love. I am glad that Will and I married. Sometimes, you never expect certain people to come together, and some people have said that about us. It is like Shakespeare's "Midnight summer's Dream." One minute one could be madly in love with someone; the next minute one could detest that person, like a poisoned arrow had gone inside of one's heart. Then you fall in love with someone you never had expected to be in love with.

It took awhile for the scales to fall off of Will's eyes. He must have been a little dull in his head or something. Otherwise, he is incredibly smart. I am glad that it was not some Cupid who shot an arrow of love into Will's heart, but our loving God who put us together.

Most human beings want the forbidden things which they cannot have. We think how stupid it is that Adam and Eve ate the forbidden fruit, but we do it all the time. It is like Asians wanting to have blue eyes and blond hair or white Europeans wanting to be dark and tanned. It is like the white explorers finding "Shangri-La" full of beautiful Asians and not their own white skin people with the round eyes in the *Lost Horizon*. We think something else other than who we are is more exotic.

My dad once asked me whether I would like to have eye surgery to make my eyes more European, as many of the Koreans and the Japanese girls are having these days. I don't know how the surgery is done these days. In the past, the incisions were made over the eyes and a piece of thin plastic like material was inserted so that the eye lids would fold back to make bigger, rounder eyes. Sometimes cheap surgeries are done by an inexperienced doctor and the patients cannot even close their eyes all the way when they go to sleep as the eye lids have been stretched or cut too far back.

I can't stand plastic objects. There is something very unnatural about them. When Tupperware became so big, I did not want any plastic around my home. Give me a glass rather than a plastic cup any day! I do admit they last forever. Plastic dish wares last forever unless you melt them somehow. I guess that is why they put something like plastic in our bodies; these implants will be there long after we have died. I told my dad I was happy with my sexy oriental eyes. It is a good thing that he told me once that the happiest day of his life was when I was born or I would have felt terribly insecure. French fries are not French fries if they are round in shape. I want to be who I am and not try to be something else.

It was later that I realized that I liked Will's slim face, like Ashley in *Gone with the Wind*. I used to not like my round face but I like it now. I also liked his nose. But then, I liked Ringo Starr's big nose, too. If one cannot have a nice aristocratic pointy nose like Will, it would be nice to have a distinct big nose like Ringo.

Great Eagle Rising

It was partly the love letters from Will which I fell in love with. Love letters can be a powerful tool to bring two people together. I couldn't wait to check my mailbox every single day before I was engaged to Will. I was looking for those love letters. I realized that I missed his love letters when I got engaged and moved to Santa Barbara to be near Will and work alongside him in ministry. I pouted one day, telling Will that I missed his love letters. He drew me in his arms and asked whether I would rather have the love letters than the real him, who could tell me those things in person. I find that we as Christians are often looking for the love letters—the narcotic sense of feelings—rather than experiencing the true close walk with the Lord on a daily basis. I think we are often like this with God. We just like to read the Bible but never fully fall in love with Him.

The Toms family 2011
If there was no forgiveness in this marriage,
this family would not have been possible.

Chapter 12

Repent for our arrogant ways and Take a position of Humility

Our Hopi friends wonder why the Christians always want people to come into a church building, when they should be going out to reach the people as Jesus has done.

What does church look like in Hopi? Does it look like a building with a steeple, with a bell? Our friend was wrestling in her heart and praying as to whether she needed to go to a Sunday morning service at a church in her village or go and help cook with her mom who had so many guests to feed. It is traditional to feed all the guests who come into one's home during the dances. She felt led by the Lord to go and help her mom. So many people had come to eat that day and many more were still waiting outside. An elderly man walked in and began to freely share his testimony with all the traditional Hopis around the table. He shared of how he was healed of a sickness which he had for many years, when he was touched by the Lord's hand at a church gathering.

He said he tried all the Hopi ways but could not be healed. Now Jesus had healed him, and Jesus is real. Although there were some real traditional people who were not happy that day to hear this man share his story at the meal, no one could deny this elder in his eighties from proclaiming his faith out loud. And our friend was able to share her faith with the others there later, and comfort and pray with them. As it turned out, she was able to share with more of her people than if she had gone to a church service.

When she went back to her church the next Sunday, she was told by the pastor that she was in sin not to have attended the Sunday morning service, for it is idolatry that she was not willing to give up her culture. On the contrary, it is idolatry to hold onto our white man's religious ways where only Sundays are holy.

With people like the Hopis and other indigenous people, it may be much more effective to let the church happen in their own cultural setting, which is so natural for them—for example, around the dances and when preparing corn. We are looking forward to Hopi men and women telling stories of the Master of Life to their children and grandchildren in their plazas someday.

Nita was able to sit in front of the piles of corn with the other ladies and have church. One lady began to gossip about another person. Nita found herself mumbling "Let those without sin, cast the first stone." Another lady asked what that meant. So, Nita explained that, unless we are perfect ourselves—not having done anything wrong—that we should not speak about others. They agreed, and Nita was able to further share about other things which the Lord was teaching her. If this is not doing church, I do not know what is.

One of the problems that can occur in missions work is to send people like Nita off to lengthy Bible schools and such. Too often the Native believer becomes a convert to a way of life that does not help them upon returning to their people. They become used to all the material conveniences of the "White man's" world, and become more indoctrinated by denominational biases. Another consequence is that, upon returning, their people may not recognize them as one of their own. The end result is that the Native minister now has lost touch with his or her people and has less impact on them. Another problem can be that the student drops out of the school, because they feel so isolated and homesick, and they return home feeling like a failure.

Our goal with Nita has been to try to help her stay connected with her village, her simple means of employment and the no frills lifestyle of her people. We do not want her saddled with the problem of being identified with the stigma of being called a *missionary*.

It is not us but the Holy Spirit who is speaking to them to obey His voice. A Hopi Christian friend who has a big leadership position in one traditional village shared with us that she has not used the corn meal during a Ceremonial Dance this year for the first time ever. Many of our Christian "high churches" use incense, candles, rosary beads, etc. for their church services.

We have been asked to help with a church in the village of *Shongopovi* where there are more traditional ceremonies and dances held. It is the only place still holding the Snake Dance, where the priests go out and gather snakes, including many rattlesnakes, from the high desert places and dance in the plaza, praying for rain and blessings. We are asking the Lord for much wisdom, as not every need is God's will to be fulfilled. He may have a better plan or a better time.

We want to be sensitive to our Native American friends, who also have their symbolic items like feathers and cornmeal to use in their ceremonies. And yet, this lady sensed that the Holy Spirit was speaking to her not to do this. She had the responsibility to go up to each of the men who were dancing in the plaza and sprinkle cornmeal on them in front of all the crowd, as the Hopis have done for many centuries. However, she knew she needed to obey the voice of the Lord, no matter what her people may say afterwards. What was amazing was that not any of her grown adult children, nor any others, have asked why she did not do her role in this Dance in the normal way. She was certain that they knew that the Lord was with her and she wanted to please Him.

Why do we, as the Church, continue to argue about things which do not matter in Heaven's perspective? As long as we believe in the finished work of the Cross, why don't we link our arms together and go to the center of the field together? We ought to boast of our Father together.

Sometimes, I feel like I can hardly say anything these days. I can't say I am a "Christian," because there are so many wrong things which have been done in this name. It is definitely a word I would avoid using among the Native Americans. Of course, it is okay with those who are believers. "When in Rome, do as the Romans do." One could hardly say that they are a "fundamentalist," because this also has so many rules and regulations which one cannot buy into one hundred percent. The word, "evangelical," sounds like someone who is interested in getting many people to say the sinner's prayer, as though that is an end to itself.

It is like one has to be politically correct in everything. It is like some people get upset, if they are called "Black" instead of "Afro—American," or "Indian" instead of "Native American." I think it is all about trying to be sensitive. It is really presenting ourselves with words which draw all men to Christ and not erecting walls with words which may trigger negative reactions in people.

We have some Native American friends who love golfing. Should we criticize them, too? No one complains when Whites go golfing. If Native Americans are on skid row as drunks, people complain; when they work hard and spend their money on golfing, people are surprised. They are even told that they should use the money to help their people, rather than on golfing.

Money is to be spent sometimes for noble things and other times for just simply living. It is for each person to decide how to spend their money. How much is too extravagant to spend and how far can we go to be frugal? We could get really dysfunctional, to the point of not living at all. We might as well go live in a cave somewhere.

When Will brought me flower bouquets before we got married, I was happy. Once we got married, I felt our money could be spent on more practical things. When Mary poured the expensive perfume on the feet of Jesus, the disciples said that money could have been used for the poor. Life is not just about money, but love and beauty and intimacy.

I am convinced that the Church cannot be fully Christ-like in Hopiland, unless they are allowed to be who they are as Hopis. Perhaps, the White-looking Church may work in some other reservations, where they may have lost most of the culture due to history. However, White man's religion will not work on the Hopi reservation. We recognize that all stages of human growth can get messy. There are poopy diapers to be changed, burping the baby and cleaning up spit-up. And the babies don't always turn out to be clean-cut teen-agers without any problems.

We need to let Native American believers work this out for themselves, just as churches had to work through whether to have guitars, drum sets, speaking in tongues, etc. Is it bearing fruit? This is the question. Do they give their allegiance to the only Son of God? Do they love others and tell others of the origin of their joy, their peace and their love? Then, as much as it may bug us, we ought to bless them. So it is with our Native American people's spiritual walk.

It is not always as simple as creating a cookie-cutter Christianity, if we want to see the glory of God manifest in our generation through the indigenous people of our land. I am often in fear and trembling, as I wrestle with many of the issues concerning the Native American's culture in the context of following Christ. It is hard for us as outsiders to accurately determine which of the Hopi ways are godly and honoring to our Lord. Our Native friends tell us, "You deal with your sin-stained culture and we will deal with ours."

Yesterday, we had a young Hopi man, who had written many of the new songs for Jesus, in our home. He sang these songs, and we knew that God had indeed been in Hopiland. His version of the song, "This little light of mine, I'm going to let it shine, let it shine, let it shine, Yahweh, Yahweh, Yah!" is already being sung by many Native American Christians around this country.

It seems everyone wants to record our Hopi brother, who wrote so many songs. No one seems to be able to coordinate with him to do it, as he is going back and forth from the Hopi rez to Flagstaff. We really need prayer for these thirty-some songs to the Lord to be recorded, so they don't get lost. It was crushing to realize that he could not sing these songs to the Lord in any (perhaps, one) of the churches in Hopiland, as they do not believe that Native American drums can be used for the glory of God.

Another Hopi Christian was told to cut his long, black hair earlier this year. He was told that it was so the angels would not look upon him as a woman. Now he looks like a white man and has isolated himself from his traditional families. It is amazingly sad to see the White Church still desiring to control how the Native Americans should look, sing and eat. It is no wonder that progress is so painstakingly slow. What is even sadder is that the intentions of these missionaries are so well-meaning. Our hearts ache and we moan.

One day, we had a group of Christians who came and stayed at our retreat center. Some of them have been going into Hopiland to minister once in awhile. When I went into the retreat center to see how they were doing, I found all the ladies with head coverings. I rushed back to our house and told Will that I hope these people don't bring more legalism and law to the Hopi believers like the Pharisees. The Hopi people have too many duties within their culture already.

Will simply said, "What difference does that make? Do they love our Lord? As long as they love and serve Jesus, we need to love them." He was wondering why the head covering was bothering me so much. I wanted their faith to look just like mine. I wanted to demand that they drop the things which I may not approve, like I was some queen or something. Who do I think I am? As long as they love Christ, I need to bless those I will be spending eternity with. I think when we get to heaven we may be sorry how we wasted so much of our precious time, fighting each other over matters which mattered so little.

It is ironic that we, as missionaries, can tell the Hopis and the other indigenous peoples how to live. We have many gods of our own, for example—money, materialism, fame, etc. It is about time that we loose the bonds of our Native American believers and allow them to follow Christ in their unique cultures.

We are seeing reconciliations and many good things unfolding all around us. The things we could not possibly accomplish in our own power financially, physically and spiritually, are being done by His love and power alone. But these things are only secondary blessings, for the Lord Himself is our foremost and primary blessing. He alone is our great and exceeding reward and joy. It is not about how big of a ministry we have or even how many people we may reach, but it is about knowing His heart intimately and doing as He asks.

It has been our dream to see our Hopi Christian brothers and sisters going to the nations. Nita went to Israel to represent her nation at the *World Christian Gathering of Indigenous People*, to say that our Creator through His Son, Jesus, has come to her people and to the Native American nations! You couldn't stop Nita from giving her beautiful testimonies wherever she went! Nita often wore her Hopi *manta* and walked the streets in Jerusalem and the Holy Land. She has had so many opportunities to share Christ! Yes, we will see more and more Native Americans going out to represent the beauty and the wonders of our Lord Jesus!

It was so beautiful to see the progress of the Hopi believers praying for their own people last week at Hotevilla Gospel Church when we had our friends from CCNA (Coalition of Christian Native Americans) come to speak.

To hear the following sorts of prayers from new Hopi believers would have been almost impossible ten years ago.

- "We need to take up the mat and take up the responsibility. It is up to us, O Lord, to bring the change."
- "Our people are lost. We don't know how to love each other. There is no forgiveness, there is no love. It is up to us to get the message out to our people."
- "Our people are completely forgetting Jesus, forgetting God. We forget that the Holy Spirit is right here moving and available to us."
- "Oh, please forgive us" (over and over again).
- "We're sick from our own people persecuting us."
- "We're reaching out to you. We ask your Son, Jesus Christ, to come and help our people. We invite your Holy Spirit to come and help us."

The word of God says that, when His people humble themselves and pray, He will heal their land. I believe this is happening. Thank you, Father! How good He is!

Two times in recent weeks, we have had physical violence against our Hopi believers who come to YWAM. One friend was angrily confronted by his brother-in-law for being a follower of Christ and for getting baptized. There was a physical confrontation and after receiving the first punch, our friend knocked his brother-in-law down with one punch in self defense. Shortly after, his sisters asked this same friend to mentor his nephews in the Hopi way because the oldest brother was drinking and out of control. Our friend initially said, no, but then in prayer, he felt that Jesus would have him carry out this family responsibility.

Another friend of ours went up on top of First Mesa and was whipped violently by a kachina at the ceremonial dance. She felt that it was too much and went after the kachina and ripped some feathers off of his mask, saying that they should not treat the people this way. When they told her that she should never come up there again, since she is a Christian, she told them that she can be there, for that is also her village.

Many of our Hopi friends believe that they don't have to wear a tie and act European in order to follow Christ. On the contrary, they are finding that they should be where their people congregate—at Hopi dances, in the kivas, etc., so that they may be able to share the love of Christ.

In the village of Shongopavi, the police were called in by the village people and a major confrontation happened. An aggressive, legalistic Christian missionary and the Hopi man who held Christian meetings at his home were ushered out of the village. When an elderly Hopi woman tried to defend them, some others said, "Are you baptized also?" It appears that some of the village people would like all the new believers to get out—both those who are respectful and those who are less so.

Yes, as Dr. Billy Graham said in the 1970's, "The Greatest moments of Native history may lie ahead of us, if a great spiritual renewal and revival should take place. The Native American has been a sleeping giant. He is awakening! The original Americans could become the evangelists who will help win America for Christ. Remember these forgotten people." We personally believe the whole world will be impacted by Native believers, because people everywhere are fascinated by them, and they are welcomed where no White Christians are allowed.

Our Hopi brother, Skip, got baptized. It was a special time for us to share with him, many years after he got saved in jail. Will was asked by Abel, a Hopi/Navajo pastor, to speak and do the baptism with him at the church in Shongopavi. Will spoke about the necessity of humbly seeking *Sus Oqal Tutuyqawhqa* (the One Great God), and not letting religion get in the way. This Hopi word for God could have been used in the Hopi New Testament, but for whatever reason, it was rejected. The English word, "God" was used instead. People most benefit from hearing truth in their own heart language. After all, the word "God" in English is a Germanic transliteration of a tribal name for a lesser god.

When someone gets baptized, it seems that the people expect a lot more from that person. Recently, I had another believer tell me that "so-and-so" is not even a Christian, because he had fallen back into drinking. So we had a good conversation that, just because one obeys the Lord's command to be baptized that one will not become perfect overnight. We need to pray for one another, rather than pronouncing judgment against one another. This idea seemed very novel to this Hopi believer, but soon she accepted this and agreed.

About three weeks ago we hosted our first wedding at the Flagstaff base. Herman, *Blackfeet*, and Andrea, *Hopi*, came together in Jesus. It was really very beautiful to see the two of them in traditional garb committing themselves to each other in Him. When they sat down at their places of honor for the reception meal, we saw big beautiful snowflakes falling behind them through the tall vaulted ceiling windows of our center. A perfect conclusion for the desert born Hopi people. The next morning we did church together, about ten of us. Our native friends, with four generations represented, moved into a discussion of how to follow Jesus and be the Hopis, *people of peace*, God made them to be.

I learned that Tom and Huron Clause and Ray Smith from CHIEF ministries would be speaking at a church in Hopiland. I was thrilled when they accepted my spontaneous invitation to host them in our home for dinner. It was good to have fellowship together and find the common ground of our love of Jesus. The Word says, "Behold, how good and pleasant it is for brethren to dwell in unity" (Psalm 133:1). We did not speak of our differences or debate, but held hands at the end of the evening and prayed together. Tom blessed us and our ministry.

We are shooting ourselves in the foot, when we argue about minor things. We destroy the trust of our Hopi and other friends, when they see the Body of Christ divided. I believe that, as long as we have Christ as our common theme, we need to bless one another in our differences, so that we can have unity in our diversity. For example: Baptisms by emersion or sprinkling? Pianos, acoustic/electric guitars, or drums for worship services? Speaking in tongues or no tongues? Can we not see that Christ and His Church are so much bigger than our small, finite perceptions?

Will just finished five days of learning from Lyn Green, one of our YWAM International leaders. Will's greatest passion, besides God and diving in the sea, is to see the Native American nations rise up to be released into God's destiny at this time. He believes that this can only be done if we as the Western church and, as a nation, truly repent for our arrogant ways and take a position of humility. We need to seek God as to how we can respectfully reach these nations for Jesus. How can we come alongside as friends, partnering with Native Americans to expand the Kingdom of God out to the world?

One Hopi student was told that she must not have heard the right voice, when she heard from the Lord that she was to come and do a Discipleship Training School. She cried through our whole DTS saying, "Why is it that a white man is still telling us that he can hear God, but we can't? Why is it that everyone else seems to know my life plan but me?" She cried out to the Lord, asking Him to reveal His life plan for her.

Some believe that Native musical instruments—especially the Native American drums—but not Yamaha or bongo drums, are of the devil. We say that the instruments are not evil, but instead, can be turned to worship the Living God. The instruments of the people may best reach the people for Christ. Some believe that all Hopi ceremonies and dances are evil. We believe that it is for the Hopi Christians to decide. We recognize that "syncretism," the blending of two opposing belief systems, is counterproductive. However, we believe that the time has come for the Hopi and other Native American Christians to read their Bibles and hear the Holy Spirit for themselves—not for outsiders to control all their actions. We believe that, as we disciple the new believers, we also need to trust them to hear God for themselves.

I understand if we simply cannot worship with certain types of music because we can't stand that style. I cannot stand heavy metal or punk type music but that does not mean it is not giving honor to Christ. Some other young people may be able to worship the Lord much more that way than with some soft guitar or piano music. I don't understand it but I don't have to understand why this horrendous, ghastly sounding music makes them tick. So, let them bless His holy name in their own way.

Proverbs 20:25 says, "It is a snare for a man to devote rashly something as holy, and afterward to reconsider his vows." This goes for those in "contextual" and traditional views. For instance, I have heard from many Native American Christians that the drums are sacred. One can use the objects to do sacred ceremonies which honor the Lamb/ the Great Eagle. Who is to know which gift will be accepted by God?

One can really be enthusiastic for the wrong cause. It just makes me sick to think about how I grieved an old gentle lady teacher, when I was a teenager at Le Conte Jr. High in Hollywood. I was enrolled in an Ancient Greek Mythology class, where we had to read about all the Greek mythical figures and legends. I thought I was being a good Christian girl, but I was full of pride and ignorance. I thought God would be proud of me for speaking up and talking back to the teacher, saying we don't need to read about these false gods. It had nothing to do with false gods. These were just stories, which I could learn from. Every good thing comes from God. Sometimes, I think our religions are like this. Being so high and mighty, we may mean well, but we only end up making fools of ourselves.

I could not have been more adamant and enthusiastic, when I was once asked to sign a petition. After hearing the cause, I was so sold, that I ended up going around recruiting hundreds of signatures myself. That is until I heard the other side of the story and realized that I was on the wrong side of the petition. Proverbs 18:17 says, "The first to present his case seems right, till another comes forward and questions him." It also says that "There is a way that seems right to a man, but in the end it leads to death" (Proverbs 14:12 & 16:25).

I don't always see things clearly. As I get older, my 20/20 vision is getting dimmer. The other day, I thought I read "The Book of Virus" when it was really "The Book of Virtues." I think it is like that with the eyes of our hearts. We don't always see things clearly. We interpret things through our own lenses which have been distorted by our own prejudices.

Once I read on the wall of a restaurant which said, "I was so far behind I thought I was in front."

I went to Mexico twice while trying to come home to Arizona from California. Will says that I am directionally challenged. Some people are like that. They get all turned around and don't know what direction they are going. I forget where I was on the freeway but I thought if I went onto a freeway that goes east, I would be okay as I knew Arizona was not going west from California. I did not know though that I first needed to go north before going east. I really should have looked at a map or called Will when I was in doubt.

I was so surprised when I realized that I was in line going into Mexico at the border. The first time, there were not as many cars and I was able to find a spot to turn around. The second time, the lines were so packed that I had to go through the line into Mexico. I told the border patrol that I made a mistake and that I needed to go back to U.S. I was terrified that he was going to detain me as I had no passport. (We were once held almost an hour with Will and our three kids when we were coming back from Mexico, from a mission trip, because I didn't have my papers.) He did not ask any questions but simply gave me a way out to turn around. This truly was like repenting.

We went out to Hopiland thinking that we would be buried there. What we think is not what God thinks. We thought this is what God wanted. But we learned it is not best for the missionaries to hang around for any people group to be dependent on them. Our goal is to release and send than—not to keep the converts.

We need God's revival fire in our nation! Fire is such a needed thing on this earth. We cannot live without fire to cook, keep warm, etc. Fire can also consume a whole city, especially if there are strong winds. We need the wind of the Spirit of God. It is sometimes very hard for a novice to get a fire going. It has been difficult to get the fire started among the Native American nations. If we try to put too big of a log on top of a small fire, before it has sufficient time to get going, the fire can be put out. We have to be careful not to put unnecessary burdens on our Native peoples.

We are looking forward to the day when Native American Christians will spark a fire that will reach our whole nation.

We found out that it is never too late to repent and do the right thing. After sixteen years, we went to the village governor of Kykotsmovi and asked for forgiveness for never coming to the village elders to ask permission to enter this land. It is true that our house was opened up to us by the two daughters of the first Hopi Pastors Daniel and Amy Schirmer so we felt that was an invitation enough. We were also received at Hotevilla Gospel Church by Daniel and Uberta Quimayousi so we thought that was also serendipitous. We thought we did not need to do any more protocol but we were wrong.

As we've mentioned before, Protocol is very important to all people but especially indigenous people. It is bringing gifts to honor those who are "gatekeepers" over a certain territory. We felt it was important that we make it right even though it was very late in the game. We do not want to be perceived as thieves, bursting in where we are uninvited.

Many of our indigenous teacher friends have taught in our schools on this topic. Most recently Suuqiina showed us how Jesus in John 10 taught that Jesus chastised religious leaders who do not go through the proper door to gain influence over people.

We took a Pendleton blanket to our village governor, who said that he could not receive it for himself. He said that the blanket needed to go to the whole village. He said he would like to invite us to the village board meeting coming up and that he'd invite other elders to attend also.

This governor who we already had relationship with told us that we have been a mutual blessing to one another. He said that no one had ever come to do protocol as long as he could ever remember. He said the Hopis used to do this all the time and that they need to go back to doing it again.

The Lord went before us all the way. We already had our DTS students, staff and others doing 21 days of prayer and fasting. We were taking turns non-stop all throughout the day and through the night, banging on heaven's gates. We needed Him to come bring His kingdom and His healing to this land. We did not want to let Him go. There were people praying in the meeting room no matter when anyone walked in during those 21 days. We sensed that we were at a pivotal point once again in our time here in Hopiland.

Going before the whole village counsel three weeks later was nerve wracking. There were about ten board members plus the governor, lieutenant governor, another staff lady and several elders from the village. We realized that any one of them could ask us to leave and the others may follow suit. Then, we would have to leave. What is the use of asking for permission only to stay, if they tell you to go? We were trusting God that His will would be done, however it all turned out.

The governor introduced us and this matter, and he held up the big beautiful star design wool blanket we had previously given him. Then Will and I came forward. I moved off to the side and watched. Will began by saying, "Good evening, lolma. We are Will and Millie Toms of YWAM Tribal Winds. My full name is William Alan Toms. I was born in Jamaica, New York, to William Albert Toms and . . . ." He told how he came west to serve in the US Navy and go to Vietnam. And briefly he spoke of how we met, married and ran a Christian discipleship house for young adults who were struggling to find their way and how we ran an outdoor adventure program for youth at risk, etc. "In 1994 through '96 Creator gave us dreams and visions regarding indigenous peoples of the Pacific Rim and then He led us to come out to this land to be friends to the Hopi people." Will continued to tell of our history of living and serving on Hopi. He told about our getting our home and the "old NPC building" opening up to us through Marvin, a Hopi friend. He spoke of our work in the villages for the past sixteen years. Around this point Will apologized to the people for not having protocoled them before now. He went on to ask for their permission and blessing for us and our co-workers to serve them through Tribal Winds.

The first person to respond was Marion, a Christ following elder. She spoke strongly in Hopi for several minutes. Then one by one the board members all spoke and officially welcomed us after sixteen years! We know that the Lord was merciful and that He was triumphant. He kept those people out who should not have been there at the meeting and kept the mouths closed who should not have spoken. He also quieted the dogs which were fighting outside and causing a real disturbance during the meeting. Finally, our students and staff were able to gift all the leaders. The Lord even restored a relationship with one elder who always seemed to have been against us in the past. That night we praised Jesus for His victory in Hopiland.

Chapter 13

Dragonflies and Roses

Culture is like dragonflies with multi-iridescent colors of the rainbow! I don't know why we insist on having just one color of dragonflies. When I was a little girl growing up in South Korea, my family lived in Tae-nung province in Seoul. My father was a major in the army, and that was where all the officers' families lived.

It was a beautiful place, where my mother had a corn field out in the back of our house. I remember there were many dragonflies, which came to rest on top of these corn stalks. I would ever so gingerly walk toward them while they were resting. I don't know how they didn't see the little girl's hand coming ever so closely over them as they gently flapped their wings, but I was a very talented child. I would catch them when their wings folded on top and met together and touched each other into one wing like a high tower. I would run back to the house with my trophy and release it into my room. Then I'd run back and forth from the corn field, until my room was swirling with colorful dragonflies.

The rainbow colors of their iridescent bodies and their transparent wings were mesmerizing and wondrous to me as a little child. If only I could capture this little Asian girl in a painting, sitting on the floor in the corner of her room, gazing up at all the multicolored dragonflies as though if she was in a magical world!

I believe we cannot fully see the beauty of God in the Native American world, if we try to make them white. This would be to ask

God to turn all the multi-faceted colors of the dragonflies into just one gray color. How would our world be with just one color of roses, one color of tulips, one color of butterflies, one color of grass, one color of frogs, one color of rocks, one color of hummingbirds, one color of apples, one color of fish, one color of shells, one color of lilies, one color of moss, one color of lichen, one color of orchids, one color of mistletoe, one color of fungi, one color of everything? Our world would be as dismal and grim as the grave.

I am so in love with our magnificent God, who is so breathtakingly glorious in His artistry and creation! He is fantastic in everything He does!

For six years of my life, I did art every single day except on weekends. I was an art major, while attending Le Conte Junior High School and Hollywood High School. Somehow I never felt good enough, even when I was given an Artist of the Year award during my senior year. In fact, I couldn't believe that I deserved the award. My problem was that I compared myself to others. I saw some other art which other students had done, which was amazing! I don't know how it was that I was favored. In my heart, I even quietly disrespected my teacher who gave me the award.

I think sometimes it is not so much how good one's art or a book is that matters, but rather how one is able to commune and socialize with others. I am looking forward to heaven, where I would not ever feel inadequate.

In heaven, my palette would have an array of millions of colors. The palette would change color, as I think it in my mind. I would have a perfect mind to create and splash the galaxies, which would be my whole canvas.

Somehow, God would have some kind of an order, so that all these trillions of artists since the beginning of time would not splash on each other's canvases and cancel each other out with their wild imagination. Perhaps it would be a madness of creativity throughout the galaxies, but no one would care, because all would be harmonious with no vein of competiveness and jealousy. There would be a display of visions and pictures and paintings, which would be never-ending.

There would be no judging of which art is the best, but all of the human race would genuinely gasp in delight at every piece of work, as they go by because everything would be splendid beyond any words. Even the creatures in heaven would look in amazement at what these artists have done and will do.

Okay, I was talking about culture. Culture is not everything; it must be based in love. Some of our Native American friends have told us that they are invisible and have no voice, because no one sees them in the cities and no one cares to listen to them. However, this does not make it right to reciprocate this same behavior that has been done to them. We are for them and not against them. I recognize that I do not have the right to demand from the Native Americans to be warmly greeted or even be recognized. Their culture may say that it is good to be stoic and silent. However, when being stoic and silent is simply rude and not Christ-like, it may need to be evaluated and not defended. We have too much to do together and we cannot afford to hurt each other.

Sometimes the Native Americans can be rude. Recently, I was at a Native American conference where we were to divide into smaller groups. We were instructed to go into different rooms to discuss various topics. We found two men, both Native American Christian leaders, already sitting and talking by themselves when we entered into our designated room. Three of us were completely ignored, like we did not even exist. They went on talking by themselves, until I quietly interrupted after about ten to fifteen minutes, whether we should start the group discussion.

In Korean culture, women were not allowed to touch men's hands, unless it was their own husbands. In the 70's and 80's, at Korean-owned stores in Los Angeles, cashiers would only put the change on the counter, rather than into the customers' extended hands. This cultural behavior, which was completely accepted and valued back in Korea, was now bringing tension and division in this new American world. Some of the Afro-Americans, especially, felt that the Koreans had taken over their city and that they were being treated as though their hands were dirty.

After the famous L.A. riot, in which many Korean stores were ransacked and burned by the Afro-Americans, the Korean elders recognized that they needed to teach these new Korean immigrants that the old culture was no longer acceptable. I admit that I used to be afraid to go into any of the Korean restaurants, because of the rude behavior of the servers. Perhaps it was my own imagination, but I thought it was because of our mixed marriage. The servers sure seemed to treat the others sitting at the tables next to us much better. I also used to detest the ways in which the women were treated by the men in Korea long ago. However, I saw that—as Christ came into my homeland—God began to transform not just the hearts but their manners, within our culture.

Once in England, while attending the London Symphony, I watched a young, budding violinist play a solo. He moved so gracefully, as he played his heart out. But when the performance was done, the English audience sat very properly, stiff as a board, and applauded quite unenthusiastically. I just wanted to get up and scream and shout, "Bravo!" It was as though they were all England's royal family wannabees. I realized, however, that this was not my country and that I could not demand that the English be more encouraging to this young man with an enthusiastic applause. I wanted them to act like a bunch of Americans at a football or ice hockey game. In this case, with this performance, there was no harm done other than lacking enthusiasm, at least to MY standard. It was not rude. I simply had to adjust and respect their culture.

I was very pleasantly surprised and pleased to have been treated so kindly by many of the Korean pastors in Los Angeles, when I went out to seek their help regarding our YWAM work. Many of them told me that they had already been praying for Native Americans.

True Confessions of a Missionary

I never forgot one experience in which I met with a senior pastor of a Korean mega-church in Los Angeles, along with his staff at a Korean restaurant. "Nang-Myun," cold rice noodle, was ordered for me by the pastor. I rolled up the noodles like I usually do with spaghetti, as I was uncomfortable slurping the noodles and making lots of noise like the Koreans do. I had forgotten that it is not rude for the Koreans to do this, but I just cannot make myself do it, or I don't want to.

When I am eating with a whole bunch of Koreans, there is a chorus of noises. Well, I should have done what was being done by these Koreans, for I found myself with a big clump of very rubbery, stringy cold noodles stuffed in my mouth like a squirrel with two fat cheeks, and also noodles hanging out of my mouth! I could not swallow for fear of choking, because that would be like trying to swallow a whole bunch of marshmallows. I could not slurp, as I already had a mouthful, nor spit out the noodles, for that would not be lady-like.

It was truly one of those most embarrassing moments of my life! This senior pastor raised his hand gently and signaled for the waitress. He asked her to bring a pair of scissors for him. Then he took the scissors and proceeded to cut the noodles below my mouth, as I was still trying to chew. I was very much moved by this kind act of this gentle Korean pastor. In the past, I do not believe that a Korean male leader would have even met with me—let alone a senior pastor—to sit down and listen to me. I found this simple experience to be almost profound, because I saw that the "Work of the Cross" had indeed changed my nation and the Korean culture.

Chapter 14

Clash of Two Cultures

It seems that there is a clash of two cultures, no matter where we may look—between males and females, between the different generations, between nationalities, etc.

We need to use the language that people are familiar with. The Bible says, "Cleanse us with hyssop." What does hyssop mean to a nation where there is no such plant? Would it be proper to say to cleanse us with cedar? The Hopis use cedar to cleanse themselves and to cleanse their homes by burning cedar and letting the smoke rise from it. A picture of a sheep is perfect for the Navajos and the Irish, who have many sheep in the desert or on the rolling grass hills. But what does "A sheep that was slain" mean when a person may not have a clue what a sheep looks like? Would it be proper to translate that to "an eagle that was slain"? The Native tribes understand the "eagle that was slain," while a turtle would be more appropriate on the islands.

My mom used to repeatedly say to people, "Oh, my grandkids are so lousy." What she really meant was that our kids are loud. What she meant to say and what she said were two completely different things. If I was not there to tell the others what she really meant, people might have thought that she did not love her grandchildren.

One of our DTS students said something sweet to me one day. I said, "You just want to earn more banana points." I went back to teaching, but the students were giggling and disturbing the class.

I finally stopped and asked what in the world was going on. Finally Nate said, "You mean 'brownie' points, not banana points." I said that bananas are healthier than brownies. We all had a hearty laugh together. Some cultures don't have brownies but bananas.

I get a lot of the American clichés all mixed up. I used to say things like, "A chicken without a neck" instead of "Chicken with its head cut off." I used to also say "You can't get turnips out of water" instead of "You can't get blood out of turnips." Anyways, what are chickens or turnips, if a nation does not have those things?

The Christians don't understand why the Native American Indians put out food for their ancestors. This action could be seen as these people worshipping their ancestors. However, they say, "You leave flowers at the grave site which your ancestors cannot smell. We leave food which our ancestors cannot eat. What difference is there?"

Language is different from culture to culture. Language is culture.

Navajos have a tonal language. Most of the Navajo churches have hymnals, which had been translated from our own beloved hymns in the American language. What is amazing is that, when the hymns are sung in the Navajo language, it is not understandable. This is because these melodies change their language. In order for traditional Navajos to understand what is being sung, someone would have to read all the words out of the hymnals first. The words need to be chanted in order to be understood.

There is a Navajo elder who now chants all the Bible scriptures. All the words can be understood perfectly by every Navajo. What is so sad is that he is accused by some other Christians of being a heretic and as someone who is not even a Christian. Most of the Navajo churches say that they should sing the European hymns in order to be a Christian. They say that all the chanting is evil because the medicine men used that style to worship other idols or in peyote church. To say that the Navajo language cannot be sung in a chanting way would be to send them back to the Indian boarding schools, where the children's mouths were washed with soap whenever they spoke their own language.

I have a good Navajo friend. Mary is a Navajo elder who lives right on the other side of our Hopi village, in Hard Rock on the Din'e reservation. She was born and raised there, when there were no paved roads to Flagstaff and only horse carriages. Mary comes into Hopiland weekly in her traditional Navajo skirt and blouse to get her mail at the Kykotsmovi Post Office. She is a widow now and herds her sheep like many other Din'e. When we lived in Hopiland, Mary often visited our home and had tea with us.

Out of her different colored sheep, she spins the black and white wool, and weaves these Navajo rugs. She also uses red and gray naturally dyed wool. It takes many precious hours in her hogan (Navajo octagon shape home) to make one rug. At most trading posts, one would be able to find a small rug, the size of 30 by 24 inches, usually for $300-600. However, one can get it much more reasonably, directly from the maker, cutting out the middleman.

There have been four generations since the Navajo nation was founded in 1868. The Bible says that curses last for four generations but blessings for a thousand generations. It is time for blessings for the Navajo nation! They are the newest comer to North America among the Natives. The Hopis are the oldest. They have the oldest continually dwelt settlement in all of North America, contested by only one other place. The first and the last of the bookends are right next to each other in Arizona.

I had a young Navajo girl who came to me crying. She said she could not forgive the Hopis because her grandparents' graves are in Hopiland. I could not tell her that the land had belonged to Hopi before her people ever came into this region as the Hopi are the oldest tribe. Land disputes between the Navajos and the Hopis have been mostly settled. There were only seven Navajo families who lived on the disputed border line but it seemed like so many more people as one family represents all their extended families. It became such a big issue that people from Europe and other countries came taking sides. It is really a hard thing as the lines were drawn by our U.S. government a couple of different times. It is somewhat like the Israel and Palestinian land disputes.

It also has been around four generations since the Cherokee "Trail of Tears" which occurred between 1831 and 1839 when they were moved by the U.S. government. The curses last only four generations so it is now also the time of blessings for the Cherokees and the other nations! The Trail of Tears was not only called by that name because of the Cherokees and the other Natives who cried, but because so many white settlers cried, when they watched this forced march.

We have a friend who did the Sundance. He had his back pierced and dragged a buffalo skull behind him with a leather thong. Many Christians are against the Sundance because Jesus paid the price, therefore, we don't need to do things like that to ourselves. But this friend is honored among many traditional Indians because he has done the Sundance. He is invited to many places where no one else may be able to enter and speak as a follower of Jesus. It is hard to know what is right. Everyone needs to make their own decisions in the fear of the Lord.

There are differences between the Native American tribes themselves. The Chumash lived in different bands all over central California, but we did not even know how to go over to befriend them, as the Lord had not shown us the love for these original people when we were back in California.

I met a Chumash woman who is now dancing her dance at the powwows. She was told by her white parents that she was white. But she could not be fooled as she looked at her dark brown skin and she knew she was not white. She found out that she was adopted and discovered her Chumash roots. It is a real bummer when someone asks you to believe what is so blatantly false, because it makes you to be a fool to believe a lie. She began to learn the language and dances and songs. Now she is teaching not just her children, but many other Chumash people to dance their dance. When she danced, she almost ran, clacking her two sticks. For me it is both a primitive and a beautiful thing to watch.

She began to attend the powwows even though she was told that was not the Chumash way. She wanted to fellowship with the other tribes so that they can all see what her people were about. Her grandfather started going to the powwows, also, but he no longer goes anymore. He was dishonored by some of the other Native American tribal people who told him he could not do some of the Chumash practices at those powwows.

In the Chumash nation, owls are not looked down upon as a messenger of a bad omen, as they are in some other tribes. They wear owl feathers to dance. They also do the bear and sword fish dance as they are coastal sea people. But he was told that he had to take the owl feathers off. He was also told that he had to wear moccasins. The Chumash did not wear shoes. So it is not just the white people telling the Natives how to do things, but the Natives telling other Natives how to do things.

Where we have come from influences who we are. We are told that in the Amazon, for an Indian woman being topless is perfectly okay. We heard a story that some missionaries had some churches send boxes of bras for the Indian ladies. They found out that the only ladies who wore the bras were the ones who were prostitutes. They wore the bras because they were doing better business with the bras.

I find that some Native Americans like to spend all their money in the stores as soon as they have it. It is a true biblical example of not worrying about tomorrow as there is enough to be concerned about today. They are generous. They don't think about tomorrow. What about the biblical principal of a godly person who "leaves an inheritance for his children"? Does this mean money and houses and stocks only?

The Bible talks of a woman who "seeks wool and flax, and willingly works with her hands." The Hopi ladies definitely do that, as they are basket and plaque makers. (Plaques are tightly woven plates made of rabbit brush). But one cannot buy a field, unless one saves the money. They mostly do not know how to do this, because money wasn't a traditional aspect of their culture. They are generous, especially if someone needs something. They are very quick to buy for their loved ones and often for any needy person.

This is troublesome to outsiders, who perceive their conditions to be poor in some areas of Hopi. The outward appearances of their houses are not as important to the Natives as to Europeans. This is also another cultural difference between Europeans and Natives.

In Asian cultures, when someone offers food, one is supposed to politely refuse, giving some kind of an excuse. They are to say that they had already eaten or that they are not really hungry. Perhaps this started during the wars, when food was scarce and it was polite to refuse in order to save face for the host. However, the host will always insist, offering the food once again to the guest saying, "Are you sure? You should at least try some." This dialog will go back and forth a few times, until there is sufficient time for the guest to finally accept. This sort of stuff can drive someone crazy. Some like to say things just once, and act as though the world is going to end, if they have to repeat themselves. Perhaps they think that their pride is at stake, and they do not feel heard.

It seems to me that my Asian culture has found a deep root in some of my dealings with people. If I see that there may not be enough of something, I politely make excuses to let someone else have it, even though I may want the last bite. When someone refuses something I may offer, I often ask once more to make sure that the person is not just trying to be polite by refusing. However, I found that some people get upset when a question is asked the second time. Some people do not like me to ask more than once, although I only mean to be polite.

In South Korea, where I grew up as a child, I would often hear my name being called rather loudly by my mother, grandmother or friends, "Mee-Dee yah!" (Hey, Millie!) We did not have cell phones then, and it was rather an affectionate thing to call someone in a crowd or out on the streets. However, here one may be horrified to be called this way (like my daughter), as she may feel that she is being treated like a child. On the other hand, all I may desire is to show my affection. I care about her and love her and don't want her to miss out on something which I think may be special. What we may think is love may be an offense to someone else. However hard as we may try, there seems to be no way of completely getting around this.

It is hard for faint hearted or sensitive people to hang around Indian people, because they really like to joke around. It seems like they are being terrible to each other, but it is more like they are giving hugs to each other. They say things like "So-and-so likes his ladies like his fry-bread—round, brown and greasy." We don't understand it. Sometimes there seems to be a fine line between this cultural matter of joking and what the Bible calls letting unwholesome words come out of our mouths. Proverbs 26:18, 19 says that a madman who throws firebrands, arrows, and death is the man who deceives his neighbor and says, "I was only joking." Sarcasm in Greek means to cut or slash something. So when we are sarcastic, we are cutting or slashing someone. This is where it gets hard. It gets awkward when you desire to be their friends, but don't agree with their ways.

Once at a conference, a Native American Christian leader was dividing the audience into small discussion groups. He said, "All the Natives on this side and all the white oppressors on that side." Even though this was meant to be a joke, it was not funny at all to the missionaries who were there. In fact, it was very painful. We talked to our friend about it and told him we did not find that humorous. He did not agree. We want to honor the culture but not when it is contrary to the Word of God.

Snail jokes are great if you have to cut down anything. You can't really hurt their feelings no matter what you say about them. Snail jokes are not against any gender or the blonds or any race or religion. It is a great way to joke and not hurt anyone. Did you ever hear the "escargot" joke? Or about a family who was having a Christmas meal and found a snail knocking at the door? How about the snail that got a ride on top of a turtle? You have not lived until you heard these snail jokes.

Then there is the drug culture. I had a neighbor in Santa Barbara with whom I often shared about Jesus. A landscaper friend had just brought some left-over sod and laid it down in our yard. It was only a narrow strip about 4 feet wide and 20ft. long (We had picnics on that small lawn with our friends!) inside our fenced-in yard at our apartment complex. I was so excited about my lawn that, as soon as I saw my neighbor, I asked her whether she would like to come and see my grass. She looked really puzzled and paused for awhile. Then, she finally answered, "Okay, I'll come and see." So I ushered her through our small apartment, and out to our tiny patio and finally to my new grass lawn.

She started to laugh hilariously for some moments as if she could hardly contain herself. I think I make a lot of people laugh. Finally, when she was able to stop laughing, she said, "I thought when you said, 'grass,' you meant marijuana." She simply did not understand why her Christian neighbor, who had been witnessing to her, was now trying to offer her marijuana. This is a great example of a miscommunication problem. This incident was not even about male-female, nationality, or social class differences. There are thousands of other cultures within the human race which we do not even think about!

I had never been in a drug culture myself. I got sick like a dog for three whole days after smoking four to five cigarettes a very long time ago. It was right after I had broken off with that tall, dark and handsome guy in college. It came to a point where either I needed to marry him or break up. He was not interested in knowing Christ or desiring a deep spiritual walk. This was very important to me. He was very kind to me, but you don't marry a guy just because he is kind. I had many dreams. I wanted a lover who would pray with me about everything. I wanted our children to go to church, as we held their hands between us. I wanted us to be in the service of the Lord all the days of our lives together. I wanted my husband to lead me to the mission fields.

As good looking and kind as he was, he was not the one! Even so, I felt dreadful that I had to break up with him as he was such a good and faithful friend to me for several years. I was bummed out and for the first time in my life, I decided to go across from my apartment and buy a pack of Virginia Slims. I closed my curtains and sat down. I held the cigarette between my fingers trying to look cool like Madame Bovary. I sat in every position possible trying to look slick. I could not believe how badly my head hurt the next few days. If I could have chopped off my head, I would have. Looking back, I am grateful that I did not get hooked. It was simply God's mercy.

I was like some dumb kids who smoke under the bleachers in high school. They think they are so cool, standing or sitting there, puffing smoke out through their mouth and nose. I did not even know how to inhale, let alone blow through my nose. They squint their eyes and try to look cool like James Dean (who is dead, by the way). No one else thinks that they are cool, except themselves. In fact, everyone else thinks they are idiots to let their lungs get all black, like the coal we used in our wood-burning stove. They are only going to die with lung cancer later, like the Marlboro man in the cigarette commercials, who looked so grand on the billboards.

It is mind-boggling how many people come into a ministry and think they have better ideas and ways. It is like coming out to the Wild West, plowing the hard field and building a ranch from scratch. Some others come along after you are already exhausted. The ranch houses and barns have been built; trees and flowers have been planted. They move into one of the houses and say how it could have been built better. They also go around to the other workers complaining. Some come with their own agendas and want the ranch to finance their dreams. They don't understand that there are mortgages, utilities and other bills which someone else has to pay to keep the ranch going.

You get some people like Korah, who opposed Moses and Aaron (Numbers 16). You get some like Absolom who wanted his father King David's crown. There are those like Ananias and

Sapphira who had no fear of the Lord (Acts 5). You also get people like Aaron and Miriam, who were anointed people who still spoke against Moses out of jealousy (Numbers 12). They said, "Has the Lord spoken only through Moses? Hasn't the Lord also spoken through us?" We had a staff who said to us, "We are tired of being the tail and not the head." The wife said to me, "When you walk into a room, I feel like I disappear." There was a jealousy and bitterness which I could not do anything about. I could not help walking into a room and I could not help what she felt. I confess I have been jealous also when I see other YWAM bases getting bigger. But, I don't know what they all have to go through with bigger numbers. We saw that when someone is jealous, they start accusing you. You get enough accusations that you start accusing yourself and each other as a couple.

I was once in the prayer room at IHOP (International House of Prayer) in Kansas City. A new set of worship leaders went onto the stage. A young man on the keyboard was rather distracted. It seemed that there was a mistake that was made, because this young man quickly turned his head to his band members. He did this a few times to make it very obvious that they were doing it all wrong. It brought attention to himself. The rest of the band quietly ignored him and continued to usher us into the throne room. I had to close my eyes not to be distracted by this young man. Some things are worth quietly ignoring.

The ones that I can't stand are the kind of people who have the *spirit of Uriah Heep*. Uriah was a character in Charles Dickens' story, *David Copperfield*. He always used to say, "I am your *umble* (humble) servant". He was a slime of a guy, who had a greedy agenda of his own for money and position. I can handle someone cussing straight at me or even throwing something at me. But I can't stand those who have this Uriah spirit.

Sometimes, it is better not to confess too much. It is like when my arms get scratched up badly by the thorny branches. I could bring attention to myself as soon as I am with people by saying, "I got these scratches from gardening" or let them think what they want. There are people who want to know and have an opinion about everything. They may ask, "Did a cat claw you?" And then, you could say, "No, I don't even have a cat." If the person asks what happened, you could casually say, "Curiosity killed the cat." That would not be nice. The person may go crazy and walk away huffing and puffing. I really would not egg them on unless they are my good friends and I want to irritate them. If they are my good friends, they would laugh with me.

It is not always profitable to bring attention to the bad areas of yourself or your ministry. Believe me; the others will do it for you. Be quiet and let them think you are okay or pretty cool.

Being a leader is such a delicate thing. It is like playing a game of chess. When you have an ungodly person who is bringing discord and discontentment in the ministry, a leader may have to go out and put out the small fires by saying something before the fire or the poison spreads too far to recover. This is not fun. It is like putting the lid on the frying pan of fire by giving the other side of the story. Take the air/fuel out by bringing truth. It is not the glory of God to let the wild fire of discord and rumors devour the things of God which the Lord has established and which you have worked so hard for. However, sometimes it is the glory of God to ignore certain matters by just letting it go. It is a delicate dance.

Often, I feel that Will and I are not fit to be leaders. Sometimes I really hate being a leader. I am so sick of it all, at times, that I want to wave a white flag.

Once, back in Santa Barbara, I shut all the doors and windows and closed all the curtains in our apartment and shut myself in for three days. I couldn't take it anymore. I was just tired of ministry. But then I got up after three days and opened the windows and the curtains and came back to life. I had to keep on getting back up and doing the best I could. We cannot ever quit.

As a leader, you can hardly say anything because everyone else thinks they have better ideas. Can you imagine what would have happened when Joshua told people to march around the walls of Jericho for six days if everyone said that they should go march for three or five days, or around other cities. On the seventh day when Joshua commanded the Israelites to march around seven times and to blow their horns and shout, if people all said that they should rather get on their knees and pray and not shout but sing a soft hymn. I wonder whether the walls of Jericho would have fallen. These Israelites might have called Joshua a controlling leader. Nehemiah was probably called a controlling leader for calling people to come to rebuild the walls, Moses also for calling the solemn assemblies.

I don't want to be like Moses, who hit the rock and caused God's anger. He just got tired of all the people complaining. Because he got impatient and lost his temper, Moses did not get to go into the promise land.

I have been a Miriam myself. The Lord was good, because I didn't get leprosy like her when I should have.

Once I thought I should pack up and leave the reservation while Will had gone out for awhile. This was when I still had my own Grand Caravan. When I tried to get my bottom off the couch, I sensed the Lord was saying, "Millie, don't you dare get off that couch!" His voice was stern. I knew if I got up, I was packing.

I was on the edge of that seat, trying so hard to control myself with all my might. When I tried once again to wiggle my bottom even a little bit, I knew that the Holy Spirit was saying once again, "No! Don't you dare! Don't do it, Millie, don't! Don't you dare get up!" Again and again I heard His voice at my slightest movement. His tender voice won in my heart that day. If I had left, the enemy would have had a good old field day. He would have won, throwing mud at our God's face, as we would be another set of leaders who failed. We would have brought shame and disappointment to our children, staff and students, and so many others.

It is no wonder there are so many divorces with those in full time ministries. There are many challenges when couples are both fully involved in a ministry together and working side by side. There can also be a danger when just one is fully engaged in a ministry, and the other is not. I have seen ministers leave their partners to join another with whom they think they could do more ministries with. They don't understand that being in ministry together will prove to present other challenges. You really need to stand in the gap in prayers for those who are leaders and pastors so that they don't collapse and fall.

I could have married an African young man who asked me to marry him in college. He really thought we would make a good couple. He said that he will be the next Chief in his village and that I would be his first wife. He said I would always have the best of everything and be honored.

I told him "No thank you." I was thinking more like "Over my dead body!"

I could just imagine myself old someday with him taking a wife who is half my age. I did not want to be in the same predicament as Anne Boleyn and Queen Catherine Howard, who were wives of King Henry the Eighth of England. He had six wives. Both of these wives were beheaded by order of their own husband. Who wants to be the royal wife, only to have her head get chopped off? That would not be fun.

Who cares about the honor of being the first wife and having all the good stuff, when you cannot have a husband who would treasure you as his only bride and loves you, as Christ loved the church? I wanted more for my life.

I invited him and some of the other international students to Bob and Betty Hartley's home for a Gospel presentation. This young Chief stood up and screamed and ranted in the middle of the presentation, saying that he did not agree with the message. His friend stood up and profusely apologized for his behavior. I might have done the same thing if he had taken me to another religious presentation. It would have never worked.

146

When we had the Broken Walls Band with Jonathan Maracle come to Hopiland, we had a dilemma. Will wanted some Hopi Christian brothers to do the first entry song at the Hopi Cultural Center. I disagreed. I felt that if they were going to do an honor song to God to begin the whole event, they needed to have a lifestyle that was honoring to the Lord. These kinds of things can drive a couple apart, when they each have strong convictions.

Some of the men were deliberately living a lifestyle which broke God's heart. They said they knew that they were doing wrong, but choosing to continue in that path. I felt it would be hypocritical to let them sing a praise song to God. "No way," I said. But Will made it sound like he had mercy and I did not. It had nothing to do with mercy in my opinion. Of course, we need to have mercy but not when they are being looked up to do the opening song for our Lord Jesus. I thought I was going to get in trouble by one of our Native American brothers for my opinion, because I found the majority of them to be soft on discipline.

Our Native American speaker for our DTS said that they must have a clean heart to be able to drum for their ceremonies or at the gatherings. This is also true in Hopiland. He said that they have had to stop the songs at times, as bad things would happen at certain gatherings. For instance, some people would get hurt while they were dancing, and eagle feathers kept falling off of people's regalia. This is not a good thing, as everything has to be done right. When a feather falls on the ground, one has to go make amends by going to the arena director and the elders. They have to sprinkle some tobacco (it is a symbolic practice) over where the feather fell. So they would stop and ask who may be the culprit of this bad omen. In one instance, they found a drummer/singer who had hidden some alcohol. He was sipping it like water while drumming. Once he was ushered out, everything went smoothly from then on.

Chapter 15

The Koreans are crazy in good and bad ways!

I think Koreans are like Asian Jews. They are everywhere! They have been persecuted and attacked by so many other nations, but they just would not die. One Japanese Emperor asked why it was that he could conquer half of the world but not the tiny neighboring nation of Korea. The Koreans thrive and set up K-towns (Korean town) everywhere they go. Kykotsmovi village in Hopiland is also called K-town, because a lot of people cannot pronounce it.

The Koreans have the most fantastic sword, drum, ribbon, and exotic fan dances. I have not yet seen other dances that are more enchanting, except maybe the Native American ribbon or jingle dance. I am not saying that because that is my country. We just have the most amazing dances. That's all.

I think sometimes that Koreans are crazy in a good way. But, other times, I find the Koreans to be crazy in some not so good ways. I am including myself in this statement. People ask me about the Koreans who were taken prisoners by the Taliban in Afghanistan in the nineties. I cannot judge for sure, as I do not know the circumstances in which they were captured. But it seems that they were praying loudly inside a building. I know that it is common Korean style to pray by shouting out their prayers all at once, like a chorus. I wonder whether our God would have responded to their prayers just as powerfully, even if they had prayed in whispers.

I also know that our God has greatly blessed my nation to be one of the greatest missionary sending nations. The Lord spoke in my heart before we came out to Hopiland that, "Your people will be a part of this adventure." And we were so blessed to have had so many wonderful Korean teams. However, once in awhile, it appears that my people have zeal without wisdom and restraint. Proverbs 19:2 says, "It is not good to have zeal without knowledge, nor to be hasty and miss the way."

When we first moved into the Hopi Indian reservation, we had a Korean team come to do ministry. We did an orientation time to tell them that we can get kicked out of this land, as the Hopis have a very strong belief system, and we are trying to live among the people and not flaunt ourselves as missionaries. We asked them not to do any overt evangelism or other actions which might jeopardize our stay there, for they would be gone in a week, while we would be left behind to reap any of their actions.

We drove to different villages, so that they could pray as we toured around. We then stopped at the Hopi Cultural Center, so they could check out all the different venders who were selling their pottery, jewelry and carved Kachinas dolls. I went inside to use the restroom and was delayed, because I ran into a Hopi friend. When I came out, I found that the team had made a big circle at the front entrance of Hopi Cultural Center, praying loudly and singing. This action may have seemed a highly spiritual thing to do, but it was inconsiderate to those who were hosting them and who had asked them not to be too overt.

We also had another situation where we let a Korean team stay in our home while we were away. When we came back, we saw that they had erected a huge cross in front of our home. In a land where there were only 1% believers at that time (There are many more believers today!) and where most of the people were hostile to Christianity, it was not helpful to our trust-building process. It could have jeopardized our stay in Hopiland.

I have heard that more Koreans are willing to be "martyrs," saying that they desire now to go to Afghanistan and die. I believe that we should perhaps not call "martyrdom" what may have been "zeal without knowledge." Wisdom may have saved the lives of those who were killed by the Taliban, as well as kept the doors open for others to be able to quietly share God's love in that nation. Perhaps we should CONSIDER and learn from these sorts of experiences, for I am concerned that if we cannot learn from these experiences that we will not learn at all. May the Lord have mercy on us and show us all how to do this better, for I know I have certainly made mistakes of my own and am in no place to judge anyone.

Greed can kill you. An example is what happened to my family during the Korean War. My grandparents told my mother and her older brother to start heading to South Korea, as the communists were moving in very quickly. The whole of North Korea was in a panic with all the roads inundated with fleeing citizens like a million ants. As soon as my mom and uncle crossed what is now the 38th parallel which divides North and South Korea, the border was closed.

My mom had told me that her father was a mayor of one town in North Korea. He and my grandmother were well off and wanted to pack more stuff. My grandparents should have left all their stuff behind. They probably lost all their possessions to Kim-Il-Song anyway. He was the puppet dictator who was put in by the Communists. We have never been able to communicate with my grandparents, to write or call, as the Communists would not allow it. It is the few top Communist regime leaders who are evil, not the people of North Korea.

We must not confuse that because they are just normal people, it is just that they got stuck in a time capsule. My grandparents are probably dead by now, as they would be around a hundred years old if they were still living. This is not possible, because North Korea is one of the few places on earth where people are still starving. It became the most depressed country with the nutrition factor so bad, that it is the only country where the present generation of young people is smaller than the previous generation.

All that is to say that greed can literally kill you. If my grandparents had simply left their stuff and come down with their children to the south, they could have seen their grand children and their great-grandchildren in America.

We should leave behind our earthly treasures in order to enter into an eternal mind set! We must leave North Korea (Egypt)—let's do it!

So my great-aunt in South Korea became my grandma instead. She was rich and I had to be with her, because my mom could not afford to keep me. I would have preferred to be with my mom, as I think that is every girl's dream to be with her mother. That is why it was sad that we were all separated.

I heard from another relative that my grandma's husband once was the third richest man in Korea during the war. I don't know how anyone would know whether someone was the first or second or third richest person in the country at that time. They didn't have all the modern computer technology to know everyone's bank accounts, like we do these days. But that is what this relative said. At any rate, she must have been quite wealthy until her husband left her to live in Japan and began living with a Japanese woman. How sad is that, when he had a good loving wife and three daughters?

My grandmother lived once in a white European house that looked like a castle from far away among all the thousands of Korean houses. The house even had a European balcony with decorative columns and European heaters in the hallway. She had a pet dog which was all white with beautiful fluffy tail. No one I knew as a child had a pet dog in their home in Korea. The Koreans ate dogs; I was told that the mutts were the best tasting ones. One time I had to fight off some girls who made fun of me, calling me the "rich girl," and would not let me pass to get to the gate to my grandmother's house. They always used to play in front of my grandmother's house.

One girl grabbed me and tried to trip me to get me on the ground. With arms locked together, I would not go down. Many kids were cheering for her, but not me.

It was so unfair. They didn't even know how poor I felt inside. My own mom couldn't even keep me, and they lived with their moms. I would have liked to have been their friend. My grandma was very upset over this.

My grandmother did not take anything well when it had something bad to do with me. She really loved me, as I was her first grandchild. I heard that I was an ugly child. My grandmother overheard a couple of teenagers, saying that they had come to see me because I had a rare and pretty name (Mee-lee or Mee-Dee). But they thought I was quite ugly. When she heard this, my grandmother chased them away down the road with a laundry bat, screaming and ranting that they were not so pretty themselves.

My family was separated into four different directions when my dad was studying in the U.S. This is very common among the Koreans where families are separated in order for one to get a higher education. Daniel (Seh-Hoon) was the blessed one, who got to stay with our mom. My youngest brother, David Oliver, had to live with my paternal grandparents in Taegu.

My father who was a major in the army, chose not to stay in Korea because he had seen too much corruption in the government. He was offered a very good position in Korea. His friend, who took a job which was a lower position than what my father was offered, became rich. He owned many apartments in Seoul. My mom and two brothers ended up living in a small side of their house after my father came to the U.S. I am glad that my dad did not take that job. Money is not everything. There is so much more.

David Oliver (Jung-Hoon) was an exceptionally cute baby. I used to sit and just stare at him. One day I could not stand it that he was so adorable. When he was sleeping, I gently grabbed his bare foot and bit it. I don't think it really hurt, because I didn't even bite that hard. I think he was mad, because he was rudely awakened. He wailed like the world was ending. My mother came rushing in and gave me a smack, but I was glad I did it. He changed his name to Oliver, like Oliver Twist. His real name is David, like King David. He became a professional personal trainer.

I think a child is blessed, when he or she is able to live with his/her parents and siblings, even if they are not rich or perfect. Once I was so envious of seeing two siblings arguing at my friend's house, that I felt tears stinging my eyes. Even the sound of them quarreling was like music to my ears, because at least they were together as a family under one roof. So I made a vow then that someday, when I grew up and had a family, we would never separate for education or wealth or anything else. We would stay together, no matter what.

Koreans can eat a lot and hardly get fat. My motto was, "Eat like a horse and act like a lady." When I married Will I couldn't stand girls who picked at their food and ate like birds. By the way, I don't know who ever came up with that term, "ate like birds" (meaning they ate very little). Obviously whoever came up with this saying never had a pet bird. We had parakeets, love birds and finches, and they all ate a lot. I let our kids have all sorts of animals and birds, because I was not allowed to have any as a child.

In fact, once I killed a small finch because I didn't feed it for a couple of days. It was an accident. I didn't know the bird seeds were only shelled seeds, which were all empty. I found the poor little finch inside its feeder and I cried, because I felt like a murderer. We never had another bird after that. If that finch was a cat or a dog or some other thing, it would have lived, even if it didn't eat for a few days. So nobody can tell me that birds don't eat a lot. They need to eat constantly to flap those wings, which take a lot of energy to fly. Alas, we should not use a bird as an example for someone who eats very little, as it just does not make any sense to say that.

Koreans eat a lot of "Kimchi." (A traditional fermented pickled cabbage) Red chili pepper and lots of garlic is used in all Kimchi varieties. When I was a little girl in Korea, the ladies came and helped by getting together to help make Kimchi. A truck load of cabbages were dumped at my mother's place. All the other ladies showed up and they chopped all the cabbages and put red pepper and salted them all day as they chatted together. When the day was done, we had many big clay jars which were filled and put in the ground. We had no refrigeration then. These jars of Kimchi would ferment and carry us through the winter.

I think it is because of this dish that Koreans did not get the bird disease when there was a huge epidemic in the nineties in China. Even though many Chinese died from this bird flu, not one single Korean died in the province where Koreans lived.

I knew something was up when I could not keep this motto for the first time in my life. I could not eat anything at a Chinese restaurant in Lompoc, California. Will and I had finished our follow-up visit with one of our Sea & Summit girls and he had taken me out to eat. I could not swallow anything. I was in love.

I have kept that motto, "Eat like a horse and act like a lady," to this day. However, it is getting harder to keep a good figure as I get older, whatever that means. You have to remember that my people almost starved to death during the Korean War. But, of course, that would be like saying that a woman needs to eat for two people, thirty years after she had her baby. It is like telling your children that they have to finish what is left on their plates, because there are people in China who are starving.

When I was fifteen, I woke up one night at 2:00 AM and wrote an Easter play. I showed this play to a Korean pastor. He got excited and said that we must put the play on at Easter time.

However, a different pastor believed I was lying and didn't believe I wrote the play. He asked me why I had lied. I told him I had not. He told me that everyone wants to be somebody and that I must have said I wrote the play when I did not. He said it was okay to confess so that I could be clean. I told him that I really did write the Easter play. He got exasperated, when he could not get me to say that I had lied. Finally, he was angry (and he never got angry as he was a very quiet man), and told me to recite the play. I recited almost a whole page of the play, for I could see the play in my head, just as the Lord had inspired me. This pastor cried in the end, after he realized he had made a terrible mistake and repented.

He may have thought I did not fit the ideal image of what a Korean girl was supposed to be. I don't know whether this would have happened, if I was an intelligent young Korean man. It left a deep wounding in my heart that this quiet man, whom I had trusted so much, did not trust me. When I think of him now, my heart is filled with love for him. I know he was so good and faithful to pick me and my two younger brothers up every Sunday for church. I love him, even though he could not believe that I could be a writer.

I was not like the other girls, like Tanya or Eun-Hi, who were so quiet, petite and smart. I used to feel really bad that I was so different. One time, I even decided that I was not going to talk for three whole days, except to say "yes" or "no," so as not to be rude to any questions someone may ask of me. I was so miserable that I was terribly grumpy. I will never try that again.

The Lord clearly showed me that was not who He wanted me to be. I was beautiful, just as the red rose was, rather than white lilies. The play did go on at the Easter Morning service at Baldwin Hills Baptist Church that year in the mid-seventies. I got to direct the 35-minute production. It brought the young and the old performing together, and the congregation was blessed tremendously!

Koreans, by the way, are an ancient people group. Not as ancient as the Aborigines of Australia, perhaps, but still ancient. A gene study was done recently, which showed that the Koreans are a more ancient group than the Japanese. I always had the impression that the Japanese were more ancient, I don't know why. What significance could this have in our being? I don't know that either. Does this fact somehow, if it is a fact at all, make the Koreans more superior? There is a huge history between our two nations, and I must admit that I used to have a cultural bias toward the Japanese.

However, the feeling in my heart about being connected to an ancient people is wonderful for me, because I also love antiques.

Being in America is great, because there is no baggage about your family line. One can have a fresh new start. In Korea, they check out your family lines before you can get married to their son or daughter. I did not think that I had a good heritage so I did not know whether anyone would want me for a daughter-in-law. I was glad that I married a white man who did not care about that. Will just loved me for who I was. But it tormented me somewhere deep inside that I was not good enough. Perhaps it was because I thought we had a bad temper in our family line, and everyone else had perfect families. I realized later that what temper we saw in our family was nothing compared to so many others.

I had a bad temper once (okay, more than once) back in Santa Barbara. Our children were bickering and fighting ever since they got back from school that day. I told them to stop but they didn't listen. They made me so mad. Finally, I told them to go to bed. I told them that I was so mad at them that I would not come up to pray for them. I heard the kids crying in their beds. I think they left their doors open on purpose so I could hear. The Lord was nudging in my heart to go up and pray and give them a good night kiss. But I kept my temper. It was the first time I had ever refused to do the bed-time prayer for them. I think John was in second grade. John began sobbing really hard. But, I still didn't go up. Finally, when I changed my mind and went up-stairs, I saw that they had all cried themselves to sleep with their tear-stained faces. It broke their hearts that their mom would not pray a prayer of blessing over them before they went to sleep.

My heart broke. I felt so mad at myself that I didn't even make it all the way downstairs. I sat on the stairs and wept. I was so sorry. And then I had a temper again. I told the Lord, "This is all Your fault! I can't help it if I am this way that you put me in a family line with bad tempers. I can't help it if my father, grandfather and his father all had a bad temper. God, didn't you hear the saying that blood is thicker than water?" I sat and sobbed for awhile longer until

I ran out of tears. When I finally calmed down, I heard the Lord say in my heart, "Millie, you are no longer in your earthly family line. I have brought you into the family line of my only Son who purchased you. You are now in His most royal blood line!" After that, I knew I could never blame my earthly blood line when I had a temper as I knew I needed to be like Jesus instead.

But this is the ploy of the enemy to make all of us feel inadequate. Several years ago I went to visit my homeland for the first time in over thirty years. An uncle on my mother's side had done extensive studies on family names. He spread out a large drawing of his family tree. He looked at my mom and said, "You know, the Eehns are from the king's line." He was a distant in-law so he had nothing to gain by saying this.

I couldn't believe what I was hearing. "Oh give me a break," I thought to myself. *Who knows what that means? Who knows how many wives the king could have had?* Actually, I think they had one wife and other concubines. But, I don't know everything, that's for sure.

I did not want to live in some delusion like someone who claims to be some princess from Africa or a prince from Hawaii. And I don't know how many times I heard some people say that their grandmother was some Native American princess. I thought to myself, "Wow, I know a lot of descendents of Chiefs."

And yet, I found myself realizing that I had believed in a lie for a very long time. I was from a noble blood line after all. Why did I choose to believe that I was from some unworthy, cursed blood line? I could have just as well believed that I was from a very good blood line. I believed the worst, rather than best.

It would not have mattered one way or the other. I was from a King's line, because I knew I had been adopted into the family of the Most High King of the universe. It was such a lie of the enemy and I believed it for so long.

I am like an AIDs patient who had been HIV infected and was soon to die. Unless the patient gets new blood transfusions or HIV medicine, he/she will die. Jesus paid the price on the cross and gave His blood for me. In fact, I need His blood transfusion every single day. He is my ultimate medicine! I live because His blood has cleansed me and given me a new life.

Once, I read a story of an eaglet which was stolen from the mother's nest and put into a hen's nest. The eaglet grew up with all the other chickens and pecked on the ground for its food. One day it saw a great bird in the sky. It was the noblest bird it had ever seen and thought how grand it would be to be such a bird of nobility. But it never learned to fly and died never knowing who he really was.

It is the opposite story of Hans Christian Anderson's swan story. An ugly duckling finds his true identity.

It is amazing how we can believe the lies of the enemy. We can live our whole life not knowing the truth of who we really are, just like this eaglet that never learned to fly. I want to find my true identity, because of the Great Eagle rising within me every single day of my life. I want to learn to fly.

There was once a Korean man who came to the U.S. on a ship, as this was the main way of transportation then. He saw everyone going into the cafeteria to sit for a banquet at every meal. Sometimes, he used to look into the banquet room and grieve in his heart that he did not have the finances to eat all those mountain heaps of various foods. He was so envious of all those others who were wealthy enough to afford to eat in there every single day.

He ate his stale crackers and the other things he brought from his country because he could not afford to buy these meals. The day before the ship was to land at the end of a few months, he decided to beg the captain for just one meal in the banquet room. He mustered all his nerve and went and asked the Captain. He sheepishly asked whether he could sit to enjoy all the scrumptious food just once before the ship docked.

True Confessions of a Missionary

The captain could hardly talk, as he was in such a shock. Finally, he told this man, "What do you mean? Didn't you know that all the meals were included with your ticket which you purchased?'

This man went away and wept bitterly. How bitterly sad it is that so many of us don't partake of what our Heavenly Father has given us for this life here on earth!

No teeth showing here!
The Koreans did not smile (like the stoic Native Americans)
at the weddings long ago.
Mom & dad's wedding, 1955
Mom in her traditional Korean dress but with a western lace veil-
(The East meets West)

Chapter 16

A Garden Near the Mountain

I correlate all my gardening experiences with what we experience in our ministry among the Hopis and others. This past winter was so fierce that I am amazed that anything in my garden could have survived.

There are signs of life everywhere! Along with all the indigenous plants and trees, it is always good to have some fresh new colors in the garden. Gail, Erin and Shannon Callaway just planted all the pansies for me in our hanging baskets and in the pots outside for Clover's wedding reception.

Pansies are one of the most resilient flowers in the garden. They will survive the freeze, wind and the lack of water. However, it bothers me when people use the expression "pansy" to speak of weakness, e.g. "He's a pansy."

Dianthus (in the carnation family) are also remarkably resilient, as they come bouncing back after the winter snow melts away. But, of course, it does not sound right to say, "Oh, he is such a Dianthus."

It is like the song called, "Standing on the corner of Winslow, Arizona" by the Eagles. The song was really written inside of a café in Flagstaff, but the singer changed the word to Winslow because it sounded better than, "Standing on the corner of Flagstaff." That would be hard to sing. People say things because it sounds better, even though it may not make sense.

It is like calling Hwy 89 in Sedona, "Stage Coach Road." It just sounds romantic and nice to call it by that name even though there were no stage coaches on that old highway.

I planted many trees—apple, cherry, almond, pear, plum, nectarine, etc. and many flowers. Only the apple and the almond tree have survived the winter. Our new fence has provided a boundary and shelter from the strong winds. The garden has archways and pathways. Will made small gates out of an old bed post, which I painted with welcome signs, scriptures and flowers.

I don't think Jesus ever gardened. Sometimes, I wonder whether I should quit gardening since Jesus did not. But then, Jesus never decorated His house as He did not have a house of His own. Jesus did not raise children either but that does not mean none of us should marry and have children. All that we do on this earth—gardening, raising our children, decorating should be kingdom work. It is not less spiritual.

I so miss my apple tree, which I planted many years ago in Hopiland. It had grown tall enough for me to have my garden chair underneath it, where I was able to meet my Lord early every morning. When the spring came, after six months of freezing cold weather and snow in Flagstaff, I felt desperate to have a spot of my own in the garden to meet my Lord.

I sense that the Lord cares about the garden, for it restores my soul. I planted blue grama grass seeds, not kentucky blue grass, (which should be outlawed around here, since water is at a premium in this Southwest region).

One of the saddest things about living in Flagstaff is that one cannot see flowers blooming for many months out of the year. The Lord is requiring of me to bloom in the dead of winter in my challenging life of ministry—just like the glorious white flowering Christmas cactus on my kitchen window sill!

All my flowers and the trees outside looked dead as a door-knob at the end of winter. Yet this is such a beautiful picture of resurrection life, for it will be all the more glorious when I see life come back to all the trees and indigenous plants when spring arrives!

Some of our Hopi friends have fallen away from Jesus, and their faith looks so dead. But we know they can come back to life again! We know that the seed of His resurrection power is within them and there is still a hope!

> *Hope in the Lord! For with the Lord,*
> *There is mercy and loving kindness,*
> *And with Him is plenteous redemption.*
> *(Psalm 130:7)*

I never knew that growing grass from seed was so very difficult. One never knows which areas will grow. The winds, the birds and the hot sun have taken away much of the seed which I planted, even with top soil and mulch to cover it. I must have spread the seeds five times or more in some sections where it was bare. Yet, I am determined to have just these two patches of green lawn on this planet earth. I pray all the time for the Lord to bless the land, as I pray for the Lord to bless the Hopis and the other Native peoples of the earth. I recognized that this is a partnership between the Lord and me. I planted the seeds in the ground and watered them, but it is the Lord who brings the harvest.

C.S. Lewis once wrote, that even a single blade of grass in heaven would be so unique and sharp that it could almost cut your feet. But of course it won't. All creation will be redeemed back to its perfect order as it was before Adam and Eve's sin. We will see all creation through our redeemed and perfect eyes.

When blue grama grass did not grow fast enough in my garden, I got impatient and decided to fill in the bare spots with some golf course grass which was left here by the previous owners. Soon I realized that I had a mess! I had an Ishmael along with an Isaac! Blue grama stayed low and wispy and tan-colored much longer after the winter. Mean while, the golf course blades were thick and tall and green, and needed lots of water. Now I was on my knees, working just as hard to pull out the golf course grass, as I was in my madness to plant and plug and water.

I wonder whether it is wrong that I did not like blue grama grass. Yes, it is the indigenous grass for the southwest region, but I cannot help it if I like seeing green grass.

Is it a sin not to like blue grama? I don't have to like everything about every culture.

Just because I like items from Talbots, Jones, Banana Republic and Lands'End, does not mean I have to like *everything* from these stores. Some things just don't fit right no matter what stores they come from. I have found some articles with these labels at the thrift stores through the years. Once I find good things, I keep them for a long time. That is why I have so many clothes. It is not so much that I look for these labels for the sake of labels. One could have the label of some fancy store, but who cares? Some stores simply seem to have good designers. I don't know why people get rid of these classy, quality items. Maybe they gained some weight or something.

I don't have to like everything about this indigenous grass, either. It is a warm region grass and turns yellow as soon as the weather gets cold (which is six months out of the year). I finally ended up going to a local nursery in town and reseeded with the mixture of several different kinds of grass, which brought a perfect solution of indigenous and green together. Just like a mixed marriage like Will's and mine.

I think my garden in heaven will have lots of climbing roses, as I have not yet been successful growing these in Flagstaff. Or perhaps, the most beautiful roses will be like filthy rags, in comparison to what we find in heaven. I often see myself walking in a garden with my Lord. Sometimes I see the most beautiful rolling green hills. I am certain that our lawn, which I toiled so hard over, is rather pathetic in comparison to the lush, green, grassy hills in heaven.

We get huge tumbleweeds in our yard during windy days. Sometimes one can see a whole bunch of them rolling around outside like fast beach balls.

It is like watching some cool cowboy movies. You know, the ones with those elongated whistle sounds that follow that deep male voice singing "rolling, rolling, rolling . . ." They were in movies like *The Good, The Bad and The Ugly*, starring Clint Eastwood. I believe that was the first movie my father took my brothers and I to see when we first came to the U.S. It was a great American experience.

I used to get really bothered by these ugly dead plants which would pile up in my garden. Some of them are as big as the house. It is no use to toss these tumbleweeds over the fence hoping they would roll away to someone else's yard. It is like casting the bread into the water as they always come back. Sometimes, I feel like God punished me when I didn't care about my neighbors but only cared about myself by bringing even more tumbleweeds into my yard. Now I stack them up and crush them under my feet and put them near my compost pile. Once, I collected more than one hundred tumbleweeds around our house after a very strong wind. This is the cost of living in the wild high desert.

But I did find one good use for these dead plants. It is not easy to start fire from scratch for those who are novices. Tumbleweeds are great fire starters! These tumbleweeds are a gift from the Lord for those who do not want to use kerosene. It is like making lemonade out of lemons.

Sometimes, I toss the tumbleweeds over the fence. There is too much inside of our yard. I was hoping that the winds would carry them far away. But, they would most likely end up at YWAM or at our daughter, Clover's place down the road. It is like throwing your trash in someone else's yard. On the other hand, maybe I could justify it by saying I am blessing them with a fire starter tool. One can justify almost anything.

I cut myself a lot when I am gardening. If you don't have a band-aid, you could super-glue your cut back together. Camille Nordwall told me that it really works. Super glue came about during Vietnam as a means of quickly closing wounds on the front lines where troops were under fire and had no time to bandage wounds in a more traditional manner. It saved many lives.

I go to many stores where they have plants and gardening tools. Once I purchased a green plant bucket with wheels. I was going to return it to the store when the bottom cracked. But, it was my fault in that I threw a heavy piece of coal into it. I sensed that the Lord was not pleased that I blamed the product in order to get another one or get my money back. That would be dishonest.

When the Lord brought us from Hopiland to here, where the soil is rocky and full of cinders from the volcanic mountains around us, I had to start all over again to cultivate a new garden. It is not for us to question where God sends us. We only need to count it a *privilege* and an honor to do anything in His name for His kingdom.

We can see the snow up on the mountains from our base in Flagstaff. And yet it was only this past week, that we just had the most brilliant autumn days in this railroad mountain town. The aspen leaves in the shape of Chinese lanterns and maple trees had turned bright yellow and red on our conference ground. It truly is a wonder to go up to Lockett Meadow and see the colorful palette, which our Lord used to paint the mountainside! The colors of the sky, the meadows, and the trees are as different as listening to classical, country, or a jazz music. Oh, our God is magnificent!

Many aspens and purple locust trees have been planted in our garden. Hanging baskets of flowers have been placed around the retreat center. Free river stones were donated by *Tirzah* Salon in Flagstaff and have been placed around the indigenous flowers and plants. The Lord has certainly given us a beautiful place indeed. It is a perfect place to wait on Him.

Weeds are like our sins. They are so easy to pull out when they are small, but so much harder to take out when the roots have been deeply established in the ground and have spread to so many other areas. I stand in awe of our Lord Jesus this day. I make my boast in Jesus, because He is gracious to gently show us our sins!

One must be careful what kind of weeds we bring into this country, no matter how pretty they may appear. One mature salt cedar which is not native to southwest transpires 200 gallons of water a day into the atmosphere. That water is no longer available in the soil for native plants and animals, or to help fill southwest aquifers for human uses. I think the white church who are not natives can also do much damage. Sometimes they suck the life out of the cultural soil of native believers.

Sometimes, I have wanted to quit this work, in my longing to be loved by other human beings who want to put me in a box. If one wants to have an easy and carefree life, one should not get into a Christian ministry, especially in the Native American field. It would be so fabulous to have everyone love and adore you. And then, I realize how Jesus was not loved by everyone at all, but rather, crucified. I press into the heart of Jesus and realize that we cannot be less than who we are.

The other day, I was sitting in a disarray of my garden. It was in disarray because I was too tired to take care of it. "What is the use of my gardening? Who cares anyway," I thought to myself. I felt sick inside to look at my unsuccessful lawn and garden. I seem to have more questions than answers. Did I fertilize too much? Did I use too much insecticide? Did I not give it enough water?

Did I water too much? I see the workers at some nurseries over watering their flowers and trees. The trees have been watered to death like some children and spouses who have been too spoiled to be able to live or be good to anyone.

No matter how much I tend my garden, it would never be as beautiful as God's natural gardens. I realize how insignificant my small garden is with an artificial electric fountain when I see the waterfalls and the meadows and all the wild flowers up in the mountains.

As I sat quietly reading the Word and praying, I heard the Lord gently urging me to get up and pick up the pruning scissors and cut one branch off of an aspen tree. I did, and then I cut another and another, as I went around my whole garden. As I tended my garden once again, the Lord showed me that there were many trees, plants and flowers which are still living. He cares! He cares to walk the garden with me.

All one's work can be in vain if one leaves the garden to someone else who does not have the desire to take care of it. The garden had already mostly gone to pot by the time our staff family arrived at our old house. It was heart breaking to find out that my garden in Hopiland had been plowed over with nothing left in it. They were afraid of the snakes. It was not their fault. They were city folks and did not know how to live in this desert place. It was not their cup of tea. We raised our three kids here too. I figure if we're going to get bit by a snake and die, we're going to die and no use worrying about it. We could take out all the bushes in Arizona, and could get bit in California and die.

Almost ten years of work had disintegrated almost overnight. All the Irises which would have given such vibrant colors in the summer were all taken out. It would have taken just a small amount of water to bring them back to life. Some of the churches were a part of helping tear apart what had been done. What used to be a garden with beautiful winding paths and a campfire area, divided by indigenous bushes like a botanical garden, had completely turned into a desolate field. A beautiful flower garden inside of the front gated area is also all gone.

This is a painful reality of what can happen in ministries.

How many times have we missed watching the sunset because of being so busy? As our lives are so brief on this earth that I try to ask everyone to stop whatever they are doing for a few minutes, so they can sit and watch the sunset every evening with me in our swing chair on our front deck. We have watched some spectacular Arizona sunsets! It is not like on the east coast where there are so many towering trees that one cannot see the open skies. Everything is wide open here in the high desert country. It is worth making a bit of a fool of oneself to cause others to enjoy the magnificence of what the Lord has given us on this beautiful planet earth, don't you think? It is especially nice with a cup of tea.

The thick green grass in our yard is growing so fast that we have to mow almost twice a week! When I was little, only the very rich people had grass in their yards in Korea. I am rich!

This can be a problem when the grass grows too fast as it is a man's job to mow the lawn. The more you water the lawn, the more you have to mow. There is a reaction to every action. When I was younger, I saw many ladies mowing their lawn one Saturday morning. I wondered where all their lazy husbands were and promised myself that when I get married that would be the job of the man of the house. I found out that it is not necessarily that a man is lazy when the lawn does not get mowed, but that it is not their priority no matter how much a woman thinks that is a man's job and tries to convince him that it is.

And yes, "Aslan" (The lion in the Narnia books by C.S. Lewis) is on the move in this region and spring has arrived! There is no doubt that the coldness of hearts are being thawed, and many sleeping giants are being awakened, just as the green buds are sprouting from all the trees.

True Confessions of a Missionary

There is an accusing voice in my mind that tells me I am never praying enough. As the spring has come and it is now warmer weather, I find myself going out to work in my garden very early in the morning. Sometimes I feel a tremendous guilt that I should be going into the prayer room first for several hours, or else the Lord will not hear me. Has my garden become an idol? I asked the Lord.

I asked Him whether it was okay to garden before the winds, which so often come later in the mornings in Flagstaff. He spoke in my heart saying, "Millie, do you think I am so legalistic that I would not love you, if you went to work in your garden? Do you not think that I could enjoy your presence with me just as much later? Or do you think that I am such a hard task master that I insist that you must meet with me first, so that you are in the hot sun and strong mountain winds later?" I realized His tender love for me.

He then asked me, "Would You be willing to leave your home and your garden, if I called you to go to the Amazon or anywhere else?"

"Yes, Lord. I believe I am willing. Help me Lord to always love you." That is all He needed to hear from me.

Other times, the Lord asked me to sit with Him first. He knew what interruptions I would have later.

Like Peter who dropped his fishing net to follow Jesus, I want to be able to drop my nets at any minute, because He is the most beautiful thing in my life. I realized that He was more interested in my heart and not the Law.

Flagstaff is the worst place to live if you want an English garden. I cannot help it if I happen to love roses. But if you want to see cascading, climbing roses, forget it! Not here in this mountain/high desert town. It really stinks to have your garden totally go to pot for six months out of the year, as this town is almost 7,000 feet high.

One can't ever have pomegranate or orange trees, as they all die. Winter just takes over and devours them with death. I am amazed that anything survives after the cruel winter. I mean it truly is a miracle to see these trees sprouting in the spring! However, if one is satisfied and has surrendered to not having any flowers, other than the Christmas cactus on your dining table, it is quite a quaint pretty town.

Forget about the roses. Give me evergreen trees. I've come to love the evergreen needles of the Blue Spruce and the pine cones of Ponderosa trees. I want to be steady like these evergreens, even in all the harsh winters of wind and blizzards. I want to stay steady and firm even in times of persecutions and trials.

Flagstaff is ranked eighth in US cities with the most snow in the country. But it is also the sixth sunniest city in the country, as well.

Our big peach tree right next to our retreat center in Flagstaff, which never bore any fruit, had almost a hundred sweet peaches this year. We believe this is prophetic of the fruit which we're about to see out in Hopiland. This peach tree was here six years ago, when we first came to check out the land. We have been here four years and there was never even one peach on it until now. We were able to pick and eat and give some to our friends. A Hopi friend who is here with us for the school also told us that the irises which he took from our garden in Kykotsmovi have spread so much in his garden that he has been able to dig some up and give them out to some others. This is the kind of multiplication we want to see happen spiritually in Hopiland.

My garden is very important in my life. I would not be able to have a garden if it was not for God's gift of a little stray puppy. All the wild rabbits in this region would gobble them up as soon as anything got planted.

Did you know how fast rabbits can reproduce? They are continually fertile. They have seven baby bunnies on average, and it only takes one month of gestation for the bunnies to be born. Two rabbits will reproduce to four hundred seventy six million rabbits in three years!

After losing Daisy to vicious wild dogs or coyotes out on the reservation, I felt that I would wait for the Lord to bring me a dog, rather than going out to get one somewhere. It was a gentle surprise when a black, blue heeler puppy followed some of our YWAM girls onto our property. These girls named it "Zoey" (Zoe means "life" in Greek). I had to bribe Zoey with some bacon, as she was so afraid of human beings at first, that she would not come closer than twenty yards away. I fell in love with this one-year-old stray puppy and adopted it. She did not bark for almost a year. She acted like she had been abused, because she cringed every time she began to yelp. But now she barks all the time, whenever anyone comes to our door. I feel safe when Will is gone, because she is around.

I took Zoey to get all her shots and a red heart name tag. She slept in our bedroom in her own bed in the cold winter evenings. When warm spring weather came, she went chasing after the rabbits and brought me offerings of dead bunnies and jack rabbit parts, such as a skull. Will nick-named her "the Black Bullet." She has such an incredible speed when going after wild rabbits.

One day, I complained to the Lord of all the carnage Zoey was leaving for me in front of our home and the office. I was disgusted to see all the fresh red meat, bones and guts.

The Lord gently spoke to my heart, "Millie, did you not pray to Me about the rabbits which were eating all your flowers in your garden?"

I smiled and apologized to God, realizing that Zoey was an answer to my prayer. Even then, I asked the Lord whether He could fix it so I don't have to see all those bones. Zoey stopped bringing them, except for a few occasions. It was really sad the other day when she had a cute, fluffy baby cottontail in her mouth, as her tail was wagging and following behind Will.

Our staff, Eric and Laura, doted on Zoey much more than I ever could, for I am not a natural animal lover. They gave her treats every day. It seemed Zoey was no longer our pet alone. She was over at their place much more than at our home. It irritated me that someone else could act like they had a claim on our pet, and I felt that they tried to steal her affection. I wanted Zoey to be ours alone.

I believe this is how some of the pastors and the ministry leaders sometimes may feel—the people they disciple are like their pets. Sometimes we may get jealous when some others want to "steal" the lives of those whom we have loved and doted on. Yes, it is good for one to have a more focused discipling relationship for a season. But for the long run of their Christian life, how much better it is when one is supported by so many others. I think it best if we can release as much as possible.

Two doves made their home in my garden early in the spring. They never left, even when the autumn leaves began to fall as the cold season was moving in. We are seeing hawks and eagles around our property also.

This life on earth is strange thing; it is full of mystery of goodness of our Lord. There is a secret garden in each of us. It is our Great Shepherd who unlocks the gate (if we allow Him) and He comes in to cultivate and heal the soil of our garden in our hearts. It is indeed a mystery to me that He comes to take us away with Him to His garden, His chambers! He takes us away to talk and laugh and share the deepest longing of His heart. When we're feeling not so good about ourselves, He calls us "a rose of Sharon" and "a lily among thorns". Yes, indeed there are thorns all around us- the thorns of this fallen world, the thorns we have allowed, the thorns of the others which prick us. But He, our Shepherd, is like an apple tree among the trees of the forest. (Song of Solomon 2:3) How I delight to sit in His shade!

He is saying to us this day, "Arise, my darling, my beautiful one, and come with me." (Song of Solomon 2:10) Let us run away with Him this day and sit in His shade in the secret garden which He has set out for us to rest. Yes, He restores our souls. He guides us in the path of righteousness for His name's sake (Ps. 23:3) In all of our business, those most important voice we need to hear is His voice. He is saying to us, "You who dwell in the gardens, with friends in attendance, let Me hear your voice!" He desires to hear our voice- this is a mystery! Let us respond and say as the beloved said in Song of Solomon 8: 14- "Come away, my lover, and be like a gazelle or like a young stag on the spice laden mountains!" (Oh, by the way, this verse was on Will's and my wedding invitation card in 1980) Yes, my dear friend, come away with the Great Shepherd! He is wild and beautiful!

Chapter 17

Our Lives on this Earth, Such a Mystery to Me

The first thing I heard the Lord say in my heart when I woke up one morning was, "You have done six Discipleship Training Schools in a row. This is the seventh; it is the sabbatical one." So we obeyed the Lord and cancelled that upcoming DTS.

We believe that the Lord would have us be still and know that He is holy at this time. We sense that He is saying that we have plowed for twelve years in Hopiland and trained others to work among the Native Americans. In the last six years more than 70% of our DTS graduates are working among indigenous people. We have prayed and worked among the Hopi and other tribes, and we have seen many victories. However, we have not seen a great breakthrough. We believe that the Lord would now have us sit and simply be in intercession so that He may do it!

But how does one tell, as a ministry, that they're going to sit and do nothing for a year? One must heed the voice of the Lord, no matter how it may appear to others. It was amazing how we were able to pay all the monthly bills. We found our God was faithful to provide for our ministry. In fact, He had provided more than ever and began unfolding the things we had been searching for for many years.

Often I could not sleep, because I could not wait to wake up to walk over to the retreat center to meet with my wonderful Friend, my Savior. Sometimes He and I would sit and simply smile together. Other times we would weep and travail together.

Sometimes He asked me to fast from coffee, meat, dessert or watching a video, etc. One morning it was okay to have my first black cup of tea with milk and sugar. But when I was ready to make my second cup of tea, I sensed in my spirit that He was asking me to forego the sugar. It is different day by day, week to week, but all I want to do is to please Him. He said that His sheep will hear His voice. All I know is that I was made to love Him and to be loved by Him. All I want to do is to hear His voice and obey His every whisper, as I know this makes a difference in eternity with Him.

It seemed at times that I felt worse and more desperate and wretched, the deeper I went with the Lord during these prayer times. I was so painfully aware of even the smallest of all my selfishness, greed or double-mindedness, that I felt more miserable than ever. I realized that these prayer times, done in pride or self-effort, are also "all vanity and chasing and striving after the wind."

The staff at Hopiland is also gathering to pray almost daily. We sense that this is a very special time! As I have spent more concentrated time in prayers, I am so aware of those who are praying for us and with us!

I cannot understand how God has loved us from endless ages! But He does. He still loves us deeper and more beautifully than we can even began to fathom. During this time of prayer, I often see myself walking with Him in a garden. I can see that we are not in a hurry; we are tarrying together, as we talk and listen to one another. He is indeed so beautiful! It is our one hope to see Him and to honor Him. We desire to please Him on this planet earth. He will guide and lead us—that is our comfort.

We do not ever have to be disappointed and become bitter, if any of these secondary blessings are delayed, when we truly know that God alone is our great and exceeding reward. What an amazing thing that we can come near to His heart as His sons and daughters, to hear His whispers of love and to share even in His burdens. The angels can only get near to His throne as His messengers. What an awesome thing not to come to him as beggars, but as His beloved! What comes to my mind is how "John the Beloved" rested his head on Jesus' breast. Oh how beautiful He is—so worthy of our praise and worship indeed!

One day while I was sitting at His feet, I sensed that He was so near to me. He showed me how His grace had followed me for so many years of my life, and then I saw a video clip of my life flash in front of me. One picture came up over and over again of a small three-year-old boy. I hadn't thought of him in over thirty years. This was during the time I was sixteen and teaching Sunday school at a Church in Los Angeles. Sometimes I sat alone with just him. God spoke to my heart, "Millie that was precious to My heart!"

That one small boy who I thought was of so little significance who was so important to Him. This was so precious and brought Him joy! It was not all the big things I thought I had done. I do not want to do things to impress others anymore. I cried out to the Lord and asked Him to help me do the things which bring joy to His heart.

Sitting at the feet of Jesus and knowing that I am a treasure in His heart is just astonishing to me! It has been a very good year to cancel DTS, and to meditate and receive teams. We have many jobs done around the base and have seen things get accomplished which were not even in the picture at the beginning of the year. It has been wonderful to be able to sit and simply watch God work so many miracles!

I had written a journal for each of our children during their first year of life. It was more of a letter to them, so they could get to know me if I should die early. I was not trying to be morbid, but one does not know when we will leave this earth. I wanted them each to know how much I love them. One day I wrote to our son, John: "As I had you in my arms after nursing you and seeing how beautiful you are, I caught the splendid moment of joy. It was as though I held it still and realized 'Ah, this is joy!'" I cherished the moments of seeing their first tooth, their first step, their first book, etc.

I know now that my Heavenly Father treasures the moments of our own spiritual growth as well. I could see Him rooting for me saying, "Atta girl! That's my girl!" Sometimes I loved our children so much that it was unreal! I think sitting at the feet of Jesus is unreal. It is like those simple, splendid, cherished moments of joy!

I remember when Will looked at me across a very crowded room. We had much company that day and I could only see him way on the other side of the room. I saw him look at me and it was as though we were the only ones in that room. He winked at me. With that one glance and that one wink of his eye, I knew without a doubt what he was saying to me. He was proud of me and saying that I was the most beautiful woman in the world to him. I think my love with the Lord is just like that.

One good thing about Will is that he always tells me I am beautiful, even when I can't stand to look at myself in the mirror. You can forgive a man almost anything when he says things like that.

Jesus has truly ravished my heart. I cried once when I read in the Song of Solomon 4:9, "You have ravished my heart with one look of your eyes." It absolutely floored me to think that I was that beautiful to Him. In our wedding invitation cards we wrote: "Make haste, my beloved, and be like a gazelle on the mountains of spices!" (Song of Solomon 8:14).

I don't know whether you ever went to a dance where the boys pick a girl to dance or visa versa. I did when I was in Jr. High School. Those were awkward moments. All the girls standing on one side hoping some boy, any boy who stood on the other side, would come and pick you to dance. Only a few boys had the nerve to actually pick a girl and dance. So the whole big gymnasium floor had a few couples dancing during the lunch hour. It is such a beautiful picture when the Bible says that He sings over us. Not only that, He wants to dance with us. He came across the gymnasium floor of the universe and He has stretched out his hand. He is asking us to dance this day, every day! He is not shy.

It is just like our God to lavish us with the things which we like. I thought at one point that I had way too many English tea pots (my hobby). Will told me that I had too many tea pots. These tea cups and tea pots do not just sit pretty in my cupboard. They get used for special occasions—like Mother-Daughter Tea parties, Valentine's day, Christmas and other events, to bring the ladies together to know that our Father thinks that they are very special.

Just when I had said to the Lord that I do not need any more tea pots, a friend Carol, who is a registered nurse in Flagstaff called. She said that she wanted to bring a missionary from the Philippines to visit me. I simply could not believe that they came and brought me another tea pot which was made in England! I like English tea pots the best! This Filipino missionary said that the Lord spoke to her to buy me the tea pot! Now imagine that! She had never even met me and didn't even know that I collected them. I don't understand God at all sometimes.

There are waves upon waves of people and friends, churches and groups who are coming here to YWAM Tribalwinds in Flagstaff. It is exhilarating and exhausting all at the same time, and yet we find that this, too, is of God. We sense the urging from the Lord to spend time with some teams. Some others we do not see even if they are staying right next door at the conference center. We do not have enough energy, nor the guidance from the Lord to spend time with every single person who comes to our base. There are so many things we long to do, but *we wait upon Him.*

Will just ran the "Tewanima" 10K race in the village of Shungopovi and came in second for his age group. Running in Hopiland is a cultural way to pray. For Will, it is also a way to continue to build relations with the Hopi people, especially with the men.

Our lives seem to be full of travels, and we are rarely alone. I asked Will whether he thought we would ever travel without having a van full of people when we are seventy years old. He said, only if we buy a motorcycle for two. We should be like the Leffews.

Mike and Jeanie Leffew are a couple who both have Harley motorcycles. Once when we were having dinner over at their place, I told Mike that I felt the Harley bikes were overrated. He ushered me and Charity Thiessen, our beautiful blonde staff gal, over to their garage. I saw the most stunning and shiny bike I ever saw in my whole life. Then Mike started and revved the engine. I could not believe the powerful sound. It floored me. I was so impressed that my beautiful slanted eyes were opened round like the full moon in the sky. My mouth swung open involuntarily for some moments like my friend's had, after I said I liked Scarlett O'Hara. Jeanie is something else. Mike and Jeanie both have a backhoe and a dump truck. I don't know any other lady who owns her own dump truck. They saved us a lot of money and our backs by dumping many loads of firewood logs for our ministry.

It was such a joy to hear that our daughter, Naphtali, had just passed the Arizona Teacher's exam. She has decided to teach at Hopi Mission School in January for $20 a day. She has always wanted to be in full-time ministry. She taught fourth grade there where her little brother, John, went into the sixth grade when we first moved to Hopiland.

Another year, our son John also worked full-time doing youth ministries in Hopi. Then 22 years old, John lived by himself at our old house in Kykotsmovi. This worried me sometimes. It was such a big house and can get quite lonely. I was proud of him that he could do this. No one really appreciated what Johnny did. Everyone is disposable on the reservation.

Perhaps, this is how the Hopis deal with their pain of all the people coming through and having to love them only to say "bye" so soon. I think it is a matter of protection for one's heart. Will used to be gone a long time on expeditions when we were first married. I did not miss him and I used to think something was wrong with me, until two or three days prior to his return. Will says he used to forget the names of the kids after being on summer expeditions and they were about to all go home. He realized that he would be a basket case if his heart was ripped out every time he had to say "bye" to every single kid. Perhaps, it was God's grace to spare us so that we can continue to work with people.

Johnny was interviewed by Harvard and urged to attend there with a scholarship. You should not pray about going to such a place, right? But he said he would pray about it. He said that he heard from the Lord that he was not to go to Harvard but to Wheaton College. That is where Billy Graham graduated from. That is not why he went there. After having been accepted and attending Wheaton College with a scholarship, he felt the Lord was calling him to come back to Hopiland for a full year to serve. He had seen too many of the Hopi youth who had back-slid from the Lord when he came back each summer to serve in Hopiland. John was asked to speak at the Hopi Mission School for their first chapel.

It has not been easy for John. He called one day saying that a young fifteen-year-old Hopi boy had been accidentally shot and killed. John sounded very sad on the phone, as this boy had attended the youth group many times. All we could do was pray together on the phone for the families.

Will and I also pray with our eldest daughter, Clover, who is in social work with the CPS and adoption programs. Sometimes she is so sad with all that she has seen with the foster kids who wish desperately to be adopted so they can belong to a family. We are so grateful that we can pray together as a family!

Four of our YWAM young staff had been shot by a gunman who came into the YWAM Denver (Arvada) base. We have been shaken by this, as we are all family in this mission. It felt as though we had lost one of our young staff girls here. We pray for the families of these staff and the gunman and his family also. Long ago, missionaries took their belongings in their coffins, for their lives were at stake when going to a mission field. Perhaps this is what is required, once again, to be in the mission field right here in North America. These deaths make all the difficulties and problems in our lives seem trivial.

I just did not want to be in ministry anymore the other week, after having had to confront a young staff person. I felt so awful.

After I had been in a low-grade depressed state for a couple of days, the Lord gently asked me, "Why are you down cast? Do you have any sin which you need to tell me?" I answered, "No."

He asked me again, "Would you have confronted that situation any differently, if you had to do it again?" Again my answer was, "No Lord. I honestly don't know what I could have done differently. I believe I listened to you and did what was required."

"Then," He said, "Get up and keep on doing what is required of you."

For almost ten years, when we lived in Hopiland, I remember asking the Lord, "How did you get me out here?" And I am still amazed as to how He brought us into the circle of our Native American brothers and sisters who are chanting and dancing to the Creator in such colorful ways.

One day, all I wanted was for Will and me to just turn right around and go back to Flagstaff. We'd had an awful argument, and there was no use pretending anything else. It was all I could do, sitting there in our car, not to sob. Will had gone into our YWAM building in Kykotsmovi to tell our speaker and our staff that we were turning around and going home. I don't know whether it was ever his intention to turn around. I think he knew that the Hopi ladies were going to come out to me.

Four of the Native ladies came out from our YWAM building to our car and opened the door and took turns holding me in their arms. We all cried together. I had been able to comfort these same ladies in the past, but now they were comforting me with the words with which I had comforted them before. How I love the Lord for He has given us victory!

Our friend talked about his daughter, who had such bad asthma that she had to have a breather and all sorts of medication. They learned later that their daughter wanted to have a cat, but was afraid as all their cats had either been attacked or died somehow. They decided to deal with this fear head on by getting her a cat, because he believed that asthma stems from fear. A friend found a hissing alley cat which their daughter tamed and loved. She no longer had any asthma.

A friend has a son who has Tourette's Syndrome. She says that this disease stems from fear also. He used to go into terrible fits of rage and anger. She had to grab him, while he was small, and hold him really tight. She said, "This anger is not okay; it is a sin. You need to repent and tell God you are sorry." Her son would resist and scream, "Why is it not okay? No, I don't want to say I am sorry." But, she was stronger. She would hold him in love in her arms, until he finally calmed down and repented.

He knew what the meaning of repent was, and he finally said, "Okay, I repent." She then would look at the calm boy and ask, "How are you now?" He looked at her with a new countenance and simply replied, "I love you, mom." She had to do this for six years regularly, until the time came when she rarely had this with her son. She was teaching him to circumcise his heart by having him repent daily of his anger. We all have things which we need to repent of. I realized that we all have to do this daily to also circumcise our hearts of the things which grieve our Maker's heart. We also need to be wrapped up in His arms when we have our fits, so that we can be calmed down and repent.

It is hard to know whether it is better to be a Mozart in life or Soliere. Does one live so wild at heart like Mozart did all his life—only to be buried in a pubic mass grave without even a tomb stone to be remembered? Or does one live conservatively in the king's court, like Soliere did as the king's musician only to realize later that his music and his life had amounted to mediocracy? Who is to say which one of us is more excellent in the Lord's eyes?

Will and I went to Colorado to spend several days with my family, who flew out from California for New Year's Eve. When it was time for us to come home, Will told me that we should pack and get out early. God spoke in my heart to listen to my husband and not try to stay there as long as I could that morning. After we had driven over Winter Park pass, we found out that there was an avalanche which had buried eight people in their cars, literally moments after we left that area, closing the highway for hours until the next day. How good it is of our Father to still speak in His soft voice to His children!

There is always something to do and people coming and going. YWAM has a saying that there is no distinction between what is secular and what is sacred, and that all we do (e.g. washing dishes, cleaning the toilet, praying, etc.) is holy, when it is done unto the Lord.

I catch myself more quickly, as I grow older, and realize that this work is not about us, but about Him! Instead of doubts and fear, the Lord reminds me that He is delighted with us, because we fear Him and because we are His children. Do missionaries worry about things, without having to worry about what people may say about them worrying?

"You know, I can speak through Balaam's ass," the Lord told me once when I was about to speak in front of 400 ladies at a women's retreat. I think I must have been feeling a little proud inside of my heart, even though I tried not to be. The Lord wanted to make sure that I knew that He could even use a donkey to talk, and that I should give the honor and glory only to Him.

I do understand that the Lord will finish the work which He has started with or without any of us. He reminded me that He was able to make Balaam's ass talk, and that it is no special thing for

God to use me or Will. Even the rocks will cry out to praise Him if we do not. We are only very grateful that we get to be here to watch Him in action!

Will and I were put on the schedule to speak at the Lydia Conference in Lame Deer, Montana. I asked, "Lord, who am I to speak in front of these mighty Lydia prayer intercessors and the people of this land?" I thought I was trying to be humble, but this time He said, "Millie, put away the false humility. I have given you and Will authority to speak my words through the Lydia Fellowship. Speak what I am telling you to say." The words to the Northern Cheyenne people were that the time has come for them to rise up and go to the nations! One minute, the Lord tells you not to be proud, as He can talk through a donkey. The next minute, He is telling you to put away false humility. But that is because He is God. We are truly thankful for the Lydia Fellowship inviting us.

I am always reminded by the Lord that I, as His daughter, need to have "a law of kindness" on my lips. "She opens her mouth in skillful and godly wisdom, and on her tongue is the law of kindness" (Proverbs 31:26). I need to remind myself that, although I don't feel that I could do another DTS, strength and dignity are my clothing, and my position is strong and secure in our Lord.

God showed us that we needed to have our main YWAM Tribal Winds base in Flagstaff, so we could do a variety of Schools, and outreaches to Natives in the cities. We needed a central office and also more housing available for the staff.

We looked at two separate properties. One was a retreat center, where we would be able to do our Discipleship Training Schools right away. It was situated on twelve acres on four parcels of land with a beautiful lodge, staff housing, a ranch house, and some land for future buildings. There was another eighty acres with a beautiful view of the San Francisco Peaks. We wanted to have great faith to move into things that seemed impossible at the moment.

True Confessions of a Missionary

Selling our house in Flagstaff, which I had loved, was a death of another dream. This was a very important step for us to complete the purchase of all 4 parcels. We, as YWAM, could not qualify to get the loan without Will and me personally buying one parcel.

We had purchased our house in Flagstaff after having sold our tiny condominium in Santa Barbara. Our girls were living in it while they were attending Northern Arizona University. They also had a few other roommates which helped us pay the mortgage while we were ministering in Hopiland.

I had told myself that if the Lord should ever release us from the reservation that I would live in that house. It was a "Leave it to Beaver" house in a pretty nice neighborhood. So when Will asked me to sell the house, I said, "No way!" But then he asked me to pray about it. I just hated that, because I knew what the Lord was going to say even before I prayed. He was having me release the house.

God has a way of changing our minds. He is so kind and patient and does not demand. I just love that about Him. I felt like I was turning into sweet Melanie instead of being a Scarlett O'Hara in the book, "Gone with the Wind".

Psalm 81:16 says, "He would have fed them also with the finest of wheat, and with honey from the rock I would have satisfied you." Now figure this out! Our God can provide honey from the rock! It does not matter if He put the honey bees there since He made the bees, or if He makes the honey come out of the rock like Moses hit the rock and the water gushed out.

We all walked around like we were in a dream the first time we saw the retreat center in Flagstaff. All of our mouths dropped open with God-fearing holy awe. It is so good to be in our beautiful mountain town of Flagstaff. It all seemed too good to be true and yet, this is our God who does things which seem so impossible. Now we have another chapter that lies ahead of us.

I love it when God speaks to us and changes the course of our lives. It is like re-directing potato chip bags to tear in a different direction when the bag keeps tearing downward and your entire potato chips spill out. The only way to stop the tear is to tear a bit more and re-direct the tear upward. Sometimes, we have to go deeper in order to find the solution or be healed.

Back when we were still living in Santa Barbara, I went away for three days to take time to pray. I felt that our marriage was in trouble, five years after we decided to come into YWAM. The support we had raised was not enough, and I was working full time to bring in the majority of our income. I felt that it was wrong that a wife should have to provide for the family. I had longed also to be in a full-time ministry (what was I thinking?), and I felt unloved as a bride—especially because my mother worked so hard much of her life to help support the family while my father continued his education. He also worked full time while going to school.

As I spent time with the Lord for three days, I did not hear anything from God the first couple of days. But on the third day He spoke three things to me. One was that "Will is doing exactly what he is supposed to be doing." The second was that I was doing exactly what I was supposed to be doing, and the third thing was that "Will is a man of God." I came back home changed like Moses down from the mountaintop.

My circumstances had not changed a bit, but I knew that we were in God's perfect will, and therefore our marriage was saved. It was soon after that the Lord began to call us to Hopiland. How grateful I am that He spoke and that Will and I have had such an amazing journey. How tragic it is that so many thousands of couples end in divorce, when the voice of God is just around the corner.

The "Wave" team was just here with us. When the team left, they drove off with my beautiful 1996 Grand Caravan, because one of their vans had died in Phoenix. The Lord had spoken to both Will's and my heart to give it to them. Well, actually it was Will who first had the idea that He heard from the Lord to give my car, not his, to the Wave team and asked me to pray about it. I hate that. I knew before I even prayed that the Lord was going to ask me to give it away.

It was one of the harder things I had ever done, because it was the prettiest and most reliable vehicle I ever had. We had driven so many ugly cars in our married life together, as they were donated to our ministry, and we could not afford anything better. One van was so ugly that it was called "Jonah", for it looked like something a whale had spit out.

Our kids were so embarrassed by our junky cars that they begged us not to park in front of their schools when we went to pick them up. I was so proud of my shiny maroon Grand Caravan! We were able to purchase it with a special gift from my sister-in-law, Kathryn. When we first bought the Caravan, I used to look out our windows often from our home in Kykotsmovi, because I could hardly believe that I could own such a new and a nice-looking car. Like Cinderella, I feared it may have turned into a pumpkin at midnight.

And I was so stupid in college that I turned down my only chance of a new car which my dad had offered to me. I think he thought he was being a good Korean father to buy me a new car, perhaps because he saw some of his friends doing it for their kids. Of course, we must keep up with the Kims (these are the most common names like the Joneses in America). But I thought I was really fine and independent and arrogant and told him that I did not need the new car and that I would purchase one myself, since I was working as a waitress. I was working a graveyard shift at Cindi's Restaurant and taking classes at Fullerton City College during the day, and later at Cal State, Fullerton.

My friend Jan had a father who had many broken-down cars in his driveway and in his backyard. He was always fixing old, junky cars. So I asked him whether he had a car to sell to me. Of course, he did. I bought an old, ugly small English Cortina (which they don't even make anymore), for around one hundred fifty dollars in 1977.

That car gave me so much grief, that I cried many times when it would not start for me to go to my class or work. What was the point of my arrogance anyway? Who in the world cared that I bought my own car? Did anyone think that I was more independent or noble, because I bought that cursed thing with my own cash? What was I thinking?

My younger brother, Daniel, was not so stupid. He was always smarter than me in school. One time he took the same class with the same teacher except another hour and got a better grade than me. I don't know how he does it as an Asian, but he does a great imitation of Elvis Presley, because he is good-looking. He lives in a big house in California with his wife, Kathryn. She has the most beautiful, big blue eyes and the kindest heart.

He accepted the offer of a brand new 1980 Datsun during his University days. Later my brother bought a brand new 1989 Toyota Corolla after he got married. It looked like a sports car, even though it wasn't, and had the front lights pop up like some cool race car. It was the kind of a car I would have asked from my dad while I was in college. After he got tired of it, he gave it to our daughter, Clover, when she went to college. Then she gave it to her younger sister, Naphtali, until she bought her own car. After that, it was given to our youngest son, John, until he went off to a full-time mission in South Asia in 2010. That car was called "the car that never dies." It was hit twice and declared "totaled," but it still just kept running. I think it never dies to remind me of my stupidity and arrogance and not to refuse what the Lord may be sending my way ever again.

As I was able to release my beautiful Grand Caravan, I realized that this freed me from my greed. It is a glorious thing. I see now that anything I may acquire the Lord may ask me to give away, and I want to be willing.

Chapter 18

Rising Up!

For almost a year, our Hopi friend, Nita, felt that she was to go to the high place in Hopiland to worship the Lord and make an altar as Gideon had done. It says in Judges 6:21, "Gideon built an altar to the Lord and called it 'the Lord is peace.'" And yet when she had talked to some of the other Hopi believers, it never seemed to work out. Then, the Lord showed her a picture of a White and Native hand, holding a Bible in a friendship symbol. So she knew now that she was to go up to a high place with a *pahana*. When she went down to YWAM, a Hopi ranger friend was there showing a map of Hopiland to Danielle. Now they knew where they were supposed to go to pray.

It was not an easy trek. Before she even went, there were many delays and hindrances. She knew that this was serious. When she was ready to climb up to the highest place, she got stuck, so she cried out to Danielle who was already at the top. But Danielle was not coming to her rescue, for she did not hear Nita because of the strong wind. Nita realized that the Lord was urging her to get up to the top on her own. Nita and Danielle sang and worshipped the Lord on top. They declared out loud, "The Lord is peace!" and built an altar for the Lord. The next week, she had her car window broken by a rock.

But, he who puts his trust in Me, shall possess the land,
And shall inherit My holy mountain
And one shall say, "Heap it up! Heap it up! Prepare the way,

> *Take the stumbling block out of the way of My people.*
> *For thus says the High and Lofty One who inhabits eternity,*
> *Whose name is Holy,*
> *"I dwell in the high and holy place, with him who has a contrite and humble spirit*
> *To revive the heart of the contrite ones.*
> *Isaiah 57:13-15*

Some other Hopi believers feel that they are supposed to go and do a cleansing prayer over the village of Owattavi. This was the place where the massacre of the Hopi believers took place almost 300 years ago. The chiefs of almost every village got together and made a pact to decimate the whole village of Owattavi. Some say not one survived in that village, while others report that only a few women were taken to other villages to work. Now it is a ghost town with not even a single dwelling—not even pottery was left behind, as everything was smashed to obliteration. It is a barren, forbidding place now, where only the winds and the coyotes visit. It is a fantastic thing when Hopis say that they heard from the Lord to go to these high places to bring God's peace once again.

There were two more baptisms in front of our YWAM center which borders the main highway. Angelina and Angelica, two beautiful girls with the noble blood of Hopi and the Santa Domingo tribe, got baptized by Will and our staff ladies. There had not been a baptism of eight and ten year olds here in Hopiland for a very long time! These two girls told their parents, Ernest & Marie, that this is what they really wanted. It was a beautiful reminder that our God is at work!

The Lord is continuing His beautiful work among the Hopi. I get so excited all the time about small movements forward. His grace seem so big to us. This is evident when you hear some of our Hopi friends sharing their testimonies among themselves. One lady said that her nephew was so drunk that no one in her family wanted him to come to their home for the feast during a dance. When he came to her asking for prayer, she invited him into her home and told him that all she had to offer him was to pray in Jesus' Name.

He accepted the prayer and then fell on the floor from his chair and threw up all over the floor. Then all the alcohol smell was gone and he was clean! He walked into his uncle's house for the feast and everyone was so surprised!

A few of the other ladies told of how they were invited to pray over someone's house, as their friend felt such darkness in her home. Her sister, who was into the powers of darkness was there. There was a power encounter that evening when these followers of Jesus prayed and played worship songs over this home. Finally, the lady who was doing dark things got up and left, and the house was cleansed of the evil presence. They are going and praying for one another and in each others' homes! God is most definitely at work in Hopiland!

*Then the seventy returned with joy, saying,
"Lord, even the demons are subject to us in Your name."
(Luke 10:17)*

Many of our Hopi friends are making some hard decisions with their Home Dance coming up. This is when the Kachinas go back to the San Francisco Peaks. We are on the threshold of something big happening. We have had a number of influential Hopi show up at our Flagstaff base, all like Nicodemus! They were attending a Hopi event at the Northern Arizona Museum this past weekend. They asked to come and stay here and talked to us, Will and I, late into the evening, asking many questions.

When we first arrived, the signs were posted at the entrance to almost every village warning outsiders not to take any photos, videos, make sketches, etc. There is now a sign that says, "Jesus is the answer!" when you first enter Hopiland in Kykotsmovi. A Hopi Christian man put the sign up several years ago. What is even more amazing is that sign has not been vandalized or torn down. I would have thought that a sign that says, "Jesus is the answer" would have been almost impossible when we first arrived.

Yes, we see the Hopis spreading the Good News to their own people and many who come to visit this land. Recently there was a big gathering to celebrate sobriety in Hopiland. Both Nita and her mom, Ruby, went, and found many guests who had come from far away. When many people went up to say how long they have been sober, Nita sensed no joy in that place. Everyone started out with their name and said, "I am an alcoholic." Nita and Ruby are the only two who did not say that, but instead said, ". . . and I give all the honor to Jesus Christ." Everyone else, except Nita and Ruby, got hugs and gifts that day, but they didn't care as they had the greatest gift already.

One man came up to us at a Hopi event at the Museum of Northern Arizona, and told us that he was at Hopi jail some years ago and used to come to our services. Now he is attending church all the time in Second Mesa. We are hearing of some other traditional Hopi men now attending the church and everyone is shocked to see them as they were the main ones in the kivas.

Satan would love to kill off every one of these Native American young men and ladies who have a calling in their lives. Another young Hopi man in his twenties said recently that he knew he had God's calling to do the Lord's work in this life. And this is why it was so sad to see him leave this earth early from too much alcohol. This is happening over and over again. I feel that the enemy wants to cut down these new believers at the roots before they can rise up.

Lift up your feet to the perpetual desolations.
The enemy has damaged everything in the sanctuary.
Your enemies roar in the midst of your meeting place;
They set up their banners for signs.
They seem like men who lift up axes among the thick trees.
(Psalms 74:3)

We are so encouraged to find that something beautiful is breaking out in Hopiland. Two Christian girls were asked to do the "Yotsiyom" (Praying for the Supai tribe) dance at two different villages. I could hardly contain my joy, as I was shown the videos of these two girls leaping (like the Apaches) and dancing in the plazas. Their joy was not like anything I had ever seen at any of the other Hopi plazas. They knew who they were dancing for—Jesus! What an awesome thing to see these two young ladies who have Him in their heart, dance with all their might! Nita believes that many of the Hopi dances are beautiful unto the Lord and that they should dance.

One young man who received Jesus at the jail many years ago says that he has refused his uncles to become a "One Horn" or a "Two Horn" kachina priest. He cried to the other Hopi Christians at YWAM saying how his people need this new "Path" following Jesus. It was an amazing sight to see these believers talking both in Hopi and in English, crying and praying together.

Today is the day of the "Home Dance" when all the girls who were married this year in the traditional Hopi way, will wear their robes and come into the plaza during the dance. These robes will be worn again when they die, and they will wear their wedding gown when they are buried. All the little boys will be given bows and arrows, and the girls will be given kachina dolls, which their uncles have carved out of cottonwood roots. Someday, we also will have a "Home Coming" day with our new robes in heaven!

A kachina came to our friend and said that he will dance no longer. This was very surprising news, because he had been a part of the kachina society. Another kachina in the same village had just given up his regalia and other dance items to his nephew, saying that he will no longer dance, and then he showed up in a church that Sunday. Yes, as I have mentioned, the Hopis have a prophecy that their religion will end and someday they will all enter the "Church," the body of believers in Christ.

More Hopi men are fainting during the dances, and others are choosing the Lord and getting baptized. One Hopi friend said that he knew that the Lord was telling him that he was not to be involved in this one Kachina dance. But he decided to do it anyway because of all the pressures from the other men. However, when he got all his regalia on, he got so sick that he could not climb up the ladder from the Kiva. The other men helped him but he fainted again when he got to the plaza. An ambulance had to be called in to take him to the hospital.

This is a difficult thing for any of us who are learning to walk out a new path with the Lord.

Another young man's mother called me from another village, saying that she had been praying for her son not to participate in the dances. However, he also decided to participate. The strange thing is that this young man also fainted and had to be taken back to the Kiva to rest. He came up to do the last dance, but once again, he fainted. I believe that the Lord is touching these men with His power, so they may learn to fear Him.

One young man told us last week that, when he went to Oklahoma, he got baptized. To be baptized used to mean that you are no longer a Hopi. But this is also changing! He asked the Lord whether he could be a Hopi and be a Christian. The Lord spoke to His heart to read the book of Esther. This was such an amazing thing for this young man had started reading the Bible only very recently. He would not have thought of the book of Esther on his own. It was there that he read the story of Haman who wanted to completely destroy the Jews and all their culture and their ways. Satan would love to destroy the Hopi and all the good that they have received from the Father. We only pray that the beautiful things of their culture will still remain to glorify God and that they will bring them to the other nations around the world.

So many Hopi men have died, some who are believers. I believe that the enemy would love to kill them all off before a huge Jesus movement breaks out in Hopiland.

According to the Lakota Sioux grandfather, in a movie called the "Dream Keepers," having an enemy gives men a chance to be warriors. When his grandson wanted to know why his dad had left, the grandfather said, "The question is not so much WHY he left, but

WHO will take his place, so that the enemy won't take us all down." When a Hopi believer falls, often another does not take his place. Rather they take many more with them back into a life of things worse than they had before. This can be very discouraging.

Awakening of the indigenous people is the divine dance which they will come into. "The first shall be last, the last shall be first." The indigenous people will lead the dance.

Hopi children are told not to point to any rainbows. They are told that they would lose their fingers. But, our friend still has all her fingers even though she pointed at the rainbows. The children are also told not to gaze at the clouds as they would get a sty in their eye. There is power in what people believe. She used to get a sty in her eye when she used to look at the clouds. She would have to go to her aunt and she would heal the eye with some ointment. But when she became a believer in Christ, she no longer believed that she would get a sty. She never did. She says that the truth will set her people free. The truth is that these are just superstitions. She could point and gaze all she wants as the Lord had created all these beautiful things.

Chapter 19

Polished Arrow

Polished Arrow is a short story that Will wrote to share with the elementary students at Hopi Mission School for their chapel.

I want to tell you a story about an Indian boy. His name, given to him when he was first presented to Creator as a baby, was Little Arrow. Later his name became Polished Arrow.

When Little Arrow was a young boy he loved to run and play with his friends. They scampered together, up and down the wooded slopes around his home. They climbed the rocky hills and made secret hideouts in the big red boulders.

One day when playing in one of his hideouts, Little Arrow found an old arrowhead. The stone head was big and almost perfect, except that the pointed tip was broken off. Quickly he ran to get the long stick he had been using as a play spear and tied the arrowhead on with yucca fiber. The rest of the day he played war, throwing his spear at all the bushes and trees that looked like terrible enemies.

When Little Arrow returned later that day, his mother smiled warmly and welcomed her brave young warrior back home. When Little Arrow's father, Yellow Hawk, saw him, his kindly face lit up. He immediately picked up the spear and closing one eye he looked sharply down the length of the shaft to see how straight it was. He said, "This spear is straight and strong. I am proud of you my son.

True Confessions of a Missionary

My prayer is that you too will grow straight and strong, keeping your eyes fixed sharply on the Creator, walking His good path."

Some years later, Little Arrow was bigger, getting stronger and learning to hunt with his dad when a great tragedy hit. An enemy war party raided their village and severely wounded his father, Yellow Hawk. Little Arrow and his mother were okay but his father died after only three days.

That was the beginning of a very hard time for Little Arrow. He sorely missed his father, and he would sometimes go up to the rock hideouts alone and cry, because he felt so sad.

Some time later, Little Arrow was getting angry with people around him. First, with his little sister and then with his mother. This scared him because he knew it was wrong. So during the night he began to call on Creator for help, wondering what sacrifice to make.

Late one night Little Arrow had a dream. He saw a big arrowhead with a broken tip that became whole and perfect. Then the Great Spirit said to him, "Little Arrow, you feel broken like this arrowhead since I took your father home to be with me. I tell you a great mystery; I too have been broken and suffered. I sacrificed my beloved son, Eagle Truth, to death.

He, like your father, suffered from his wounds and died. He, however, defeated the enemy of Death and like the Morning Star rose high again all the way to the heavens.

This chosen one who was broken from Me, like the arrowhead is the great sacrifice for your father, your people and all the peoples of my earth.

Now you must trust me through my son, Eagle Truth, Morningstar. The broken arrow is made whole again. Your new name is Polished Arrow.

I will be Father and Friend to you, teaching you to be straight and strong. I will protect you, your sister and mother. You must forgive all who have hurt you. You must trust Me and always be truthful with Me about all things.

You must learn My stories, speak to Me always. Most important you must be quiet and listen to me in order to walk My good Path. I love you and will always keep you in My quiver. And in the days to come, like your father, I will send you forth from my bow, for my good purposes.

Chapter 20

"Is It You, Jesus?"

We had to rake all the Aspen leaves and the long pine tree needles off of our grass to play a game of croquet with our Hopi friend. She brought her son and two of his friends to visit us from the reservation. She had received the Lord at Hopi Jail. This is the one whom the enemy could not take, as much as he tried! She had fallen off of the wagon and went back to drinking. She fell (or was pushed off) from the top of a mesa but she lived! It was a miracle that she was able to have a second chance in life to live for the Lord. She is still being healed from that fall, but when she visited us this week her joy was evident. She looked so beautiful and her face was radiant! Thank you, Jesus!

One of our other Hopi sisters was very much despondent one day, and the Lord led her to the top of "Pumpkin Seed Point" hill. She was not afraid of this place, which the Hopis believe is where "Wuti, a Woman warrior" is supposed to reside. She watched the clouds going by, as she cried out to God for help for her life. Then she saw a white butterfly come fluttering near her in the middle of this high desert.

"Oh, where did you come from?" she asked the butterfly. But she knew, for she felt the Lord's presence.

She cried out again, pouring out her heart to God. And this time, a small lizard came near (she is of the Lizard clan). She was relieved, for she knew that the Father had sent these little creatures to reassure her that everything was going to be okay. According to the Sacred Word the Holy Spirit alighted on Jesus as a dove, and sent a crow to feed Elisha.

The Lord had filled our YWAM facility with many Hopi friends who have attended some of our DTS classes. Some Hopis even took off from their work in order to hear some of our speakers. It is as though God is strategically picking out key leaders from almost every village. They are professionals in their fields and leaders in their villages, and they are telling others about how Christ has changed their lives.

I had been feeling discouraged, when two ladies from the Hopi Tribe stopped by. One of them was the Director of the Health Department. On the last day of "Wellness Week," they asked whether we would sing for an hour and a half at their final event at the tribal building. The Director said, "I have noticed that everyone who goes to your meeting seems to be happy and confident and sure of themselves." She had mentioned this to her mother. Her mother had also noticed the very same thing and told her that she should go to our meeting.

Yes, the people are watching. I told her it is not that the ladies are sure of themselves, but that they are sure of the Lord. He is changing them to believe the TRUTH about themselves, rather than believing the lies of the enemy. The enemy had tried to tell them they are of "no worth." The truth is that they are made beautifully and wonderfully by God. They can be forgiven through His Son and have a clean heart, starting anew every single day!

Wellness Week is a huge yearly event which packs out the Civic Center with many booths and presenters. We took the hand drums and sang the song, "Beautiful Great One" in Hopi, and other songs such as "Rise up, Rise up, Oh Men of God" and "Amazing Grace." It is time to break forth in joy over this land and break the fears and bondages of not being able to use the drums for the Lord. Why should they be bound to worship like a white man?

We had a booth at the Hopi Tribal Women's Health Expo and there were over 145 people who had signed up at our booth. Everyone was so suspicious of us when we first came, but the tribal office asked us to set up a booth. They provided us with an already made banner that said "YWAM New Life Fellowship," along with some balloons. Many expressed their desire to come, as they told us that they had already heard of us and how we share one another's burdens and pray together.

The Fall Festival was a big success, because I believe we followed our Shepherd's instructions, and it was He who brought the kids to us. He spoke in our hearts that we ought to make this event fun and colorful and imaginative, so as to be not outdone by the schemes of the enemy who seems to present himself in ways more deceptively alluring.

We put up lights everywhere at YWAM, got dressed up in colorful and fun costumes and had fast-paced praise and worship songs going constantly in different rooms. We opened up the staff apartment for the adults to sit and have fellowship with one another with tea and coffee, hotdogs and chips. There were so many kids and parents, that sometimes it was hard to even move around. Every child and adult who showed up was a miracle!

Danielle and I visited my good friend, Georgie. Her husband Amos, and daughter Genelle, and sometimes other family members, join this simple church. We read out of the Gospels and Psalms, and then we pray and say goodbye. They are always glad when we come. Georgie sits in her wheelchair since one of her legs was amputated because of diabetes. We always get to sing many songs out of our old hymnals, which we take with us.

Sometimes I wish we could sing more indigenous songs, but Georgie likes these old hymns. Once I tried to take away all the White contemporary Christian songs from our Puhu Qatsi (New Life) ladies group in order to encourage more Native style. I was invited out to a restaurant by two of the ladies and was politely told that they do not want me to take away these songs, for they were healing songs. I tried to introduce other songs written by other Native American Christians. But I was told that these were more plains or other Indian style, and not Hopi.

Gillie wants to come to the YWAM building and sing some songs on the "Father Drum" with some of his buddies. He said he has written some more songs for the Lord. They have been gathering at his home for worship with these songs in Hopi and English. One lady just told me that she and two other ladies got together for church to pray for a principal who is being bamboozled at one of the schools. "Simple churches"—the gathering of two or more believers—is something these new Christians can do very easily. We pray that they will do this, so that they do not have to always depend on outsiders, but read the Word together, pray for one another, take communion together and baptize one another! We are trying to model these things.

What a celebration we had back in Hopiland at our DTS graduation. When you have Islanders in your school, not just an immediate family, but entire extended families come. Ajay, our Samoan student, sang a Samoan song, which the Lord had given him. His grandmother, who looked like an island queen, with a beautiful island dress and white hat, went up and joined Ajay. She elegantly danced to his new-found Island song. It was truly beautiful. When the Word of God says that "every tribe and nation and tongue" will worship in heaven, one could get a glimpse of this at our DTS graduation.

It is a beautiful world, when we have even just one friend! "Ging-yah-ah" (meaning "come on in") is what the Hopi men say, as they shake their rattles in the kivas. Yes, we need to say, "Ging-yah-ah" to the Holy Spirit, for this Great Spirit will be our close and best friend, if we invite Him to come in.

The Hopi Economic Development office called, asking if eleven dancers could stay at our Flagstaff retreat center for the Hopi event at the Heritage Square in Flagstaff.

"This is Jesus' house, huh?" asked one of the Hopi girls, as she was leaving our center. "That means He is going to be with me all day?" "Yes," I said, "But He will be with you all day and every day, if you ask Him into your heart." A couple of the girls kept saying, "I don't want to go home, I want to stay here." It is such a good thing that they like it here. As they were leaving, they presented us with a silver in-laid helping hand pendant necklace, saying, "This is because you help others."

There are only nine small Protestant churches in Hopiland. There are now four churches in Hopi without pastors, soon to be five. And, yet, the Hopi people seem to be doing more leading themselves in a "simple church" style, where they come together to sing praises, read the Word and pray for one another. This could very well be an answer to our prayers that His indigenous church be raised up. The Hopi believers really can do it themselves, if they will only look to Jesus and try.

There has been yet another funeral of a Hopi man who had responded to the Lord in Jail some years back. His younger brother called Will asking him to perform the funeral service at the grave site. He also asked our YWAM team to sing some praise songs, as his brother had prayed to receive Jesus into his heart again two weeks before his death. So we drove out to Hopiland with our DTS and had a good service, where the Spirit of God surely was present, speaking to many traditional people and eating with them afterwards. We have no doubt that when this song was requested—"The Battle belongs to the Lord"—and his sisters joined us in singing, something lifted in the heavenlies. We pray constantly that He who inhabits eternity, whose name is Holy, would revive the spirit of the humble and those who are bruised with sorrow in Hopiland.

Nita joined us for the five month DTS with her six year-old son, Franklin, and her fourteen year old daughter, Kayla. Kayla wanted to get away from Hopi High School for a while, as there was much drug and alcohol use. She was often offered drugs by so called "friends", and she would answer by saying that it was stupid. Once she had her water bottle spiked with alcohol. When Kayla was living here in Flagstaff, she attended Sinagua High School while Nita was doing DTS. Kayla came home really hurt one day, because a White girl had called her a "stupid Indian." We all prayed with her and let her know how much we loved her. She is one of the wisest and bravest young ladies we know!

Our elderly neighbor, Lucille Namoki, a potter who lived across the street from our house in Kykotsmovi, has gone to be with the Lord. As she was passing away, she spoke out loud saying, "Oh that must be you, Jesus." In the Hopi way, when a person is dying and sees a vision, it is considered to be true. So now all her family members know that Lucille has seen Jesus. We are praying that Lucille's house would be used as a House of Prayer for many Hopis to come and receive the same vision as she did.

There is a burst of hope at times and at other times so much heartaches and tears.

A young man called at 11:30 last night and said that Will and I have been like a second dad and mom to him, and that I was the mom that he never knew. He asked me to forgive him for all the things he had done to hurt us in Hopiland. As I listened to him crying on the phone, I was able to say to him, "I forgive you." It was as though the years of pain between us were wiped away and we were both restored.

I heard about Bethany Hamilton, whose arm was bitten off by a fourteen foot shark when she was surfing in Hawaii. She did not quit. Most people would have been freaked out about going back in the water but she was more afraid of not being able to surf with one arm. She became a champion surfer amongst her peers and, eventually, a pro surfer. There are sharks on land too. I want to be like Bethany, who would not quit but became a champion.

It is so strange that in over thirty years of our full time ministry, we never ran into anyone in the film industry. But this year we have run into so many. The other week, our Digital Documentary School (DDS) team drove out to the Wupatki Ruins and Grand Canyon to film some shots. We ran into a couple who had filmed for the Discovery Channel and are presently filming for PBS. They came to our base with their RV, and taught our DDS students. This small DDS is helping us firmly establish all the curriculum, instructors and equipment needed for future schools. God is so very good!

We are seeing that we need outreach protocol in places where we have YWAM bases working with Natives. People need to be educated about going anywhere in Native American country. We are looking at producing a teaching video, interviewing Natives on that topic.

The Governor of Kykotsmovi came to chat with us at YWAM Hopi. After watching the documentary which was produced in our DDS, he asked whether we could help him. He said that the elders in the village are dying and that their stories will be forever lost, if they are not documented. The village had purchased a camera last year, but no one really knew how to use it. He asked whether we could help each other, and he would give us the permission letter to be able to film in the village. Recently another organization came to film in the village, and they were denied. We told him that we would love to teach the youth so that they could film their elders themselves, rather than having us do it. He asked when our DDS will start and how many students we can accommodate.

The Governor is also very interested in having our ropes course in the village to be used for various team-building activities. We are excited about this and the DDS, because it really seems to be the Lord's *kairos* timing for Hopiland.

We also had time with the governor of Bacavi village and the director of the elderly program in First Mesa. After seeing a couple of short DDS projects the director of the elderly program asked whether he could show a video to the Hopi elders at their next gathering. He felt that the times have changed and that the elders may be ready to be filmed, as he also felt that the stories are being lost in the other villages as well. The governor told us that her village celebrated the 100th anniversary of the founding of Bacavi. She said she had spoken with many of the young people at the Centennial Celebration and, especially those in their early twenties said they want to know more of their elder's stories. Having said all this, it has still been difficult for our students to get the interviews needed in Hopiland. The people are intimidated by what others may say critically about their statements.

Our DDS just finished the classroom phase. It was amazing to watch the documentaries which they all produced about the school. These first projects were six to twelve minutes long, and I was so impressed at what one can do with all the modern technology of cameras and computers these days. They are now working on their final documentary projects of fifteen to thirty minutes during the remaining six weeks of their outreach. They have to pour themselves into doing all the research, scriptwriting, producing, directing and editing. We believe that we are in another phase of our ministry, where the Native American students can come to learn how to film on their own reservations and the Pacific Islanders on their own islands. As Natives, they are best able to get the true stories from their own elders and chiefs, who have a rich supply of wisdom by which our Lord is glorified. We must reach all spheres of our societies in our modern days not only in science, business and government—but also in media and music.

The weekly classes for the DDS consist of these subjects: scriptwriting and editing, camera, lights and sound. Also, Documentary 101 Overview, equipment, etc. We are seeing that this is a very good beginning. We just need to be faithful with small beginnings in whatever the Lord calls us to do!

It is indeed an honor when the Hopi Guidance Center and the CPS called us, asking whether we can help with some emergency foster care. To be trusted with their children means that they trust our ministry. There is a deep joy in my heart that we're doing what we're supposed to be doing on this earth, and that the Lord has been ever so faithful to provide all that we need to do His will. Yes, it is indeed true to say, "It is a wonderful life!"

We have learned that children who don't learn to read by the time they are in the fourth grade are most likely to end up in prison when they get older. So our staff feels that they need to help in the reading program in the schools, as well as helping Hopi people get their GED certificates. Another possible need is an emergency foster child program so that they can be more connected to helping children and families.

One of our Hopi friends gifted our daughter, Naphtali, with a set of silver Hopi bracelets and earrings, saying that—in the Hopi way—she is like his niece. This is a great honor, because uncles play a huge role in Hopiland. He used to be a Hopi Tribal councilman.

On another occasion we were invited to a baby hair-washing ceremony at Mishongovi village. It was so wonderful to hold Trinette's baby boy in my arms, with his hair so black, for such a long time. Hopiland is our home.

One of my best friends is Ida Walking Bear Murdock from the village of Kykotsmovi. She is over ninety years old now. When I walk into her old house, she says, "Where have you been all this time?" A few minutes later, she asks me "What is your name?" She cannot remember hardly anything. She only plays with just one finger on the piano and sometimes she does not remember some of the hymns we used to love to sing together. I wrote about her in my first book, *The Great Eagle Calling*. She was the first Native American female student to graduate from the Northern Arizona University in Flagstaff. She became a teacher just like her aunt, Polingaysi Qoyawayma, also called Elizabeth White, who is the author of *No Turning Back,* and is also well known for her beautiful pottery.

Polingasi wrote that the Hopi life was a constant prayer—not just one day a week but every day. When she was little, she used to watch the men meditating on the rooftops, wrapped in their blankets. Her mother told her that they were praying for health and wisdom. They prayed for the well-being of their village and long life, purity, abundant crops and rain.

Her mother, Savenka told her that she would live to see a time when the "dotsi," their soft buckskin moccasins, will no longer be worn. Savenka said that her grandmother once said that there would some day be a path made in the heavens, and along it people would travel as do the eagles. She also said that people would move swiftly, their feet not touching the ground.

When these things happen, the grandmother said that it will be the time of "Suh-ah-kits-pe-oo-tani," the time when changes will come swiftly, and that will be the forerunner of the end of an age.

"I was in Jail and You Visited Me."

Jesus said, "I was naked and you clothed me. I was sick and you visited Me; I was in jail and you came to Me (Matthew 25: 36). It would be an understatement to say that I have often felt so inadequate to do the jail ministries. That was the last thing I wanted to do one Sunday night. I sat at the Coconino Jail parking lot just before going in, saying, "Lord, you must help me, for I need your help tonight." Over thirty ladies walked in, as I was waiting for them with my guitar. If you want your voice to be heard, go to any jail facility, for they are so eager to hear your message! They worshipped the Lord singing, "I have a Father, He calls me His own . . . He knows my name, He knows my every thought, He sees each tear that falls, He hears me when I call." Some ladies were crying. It was a sweet evening of reading the Gospel together (Mark 15 & 16), and He showed me, once again, that He is able to work when we feel unqualified.

It was the day after DTS another time and I did not want to go to do the jail ministry one night. In fact, I had been feeling faint that day and felt weak. I heard Jesus ask me in my heart "Would you go into town to meet Me in town?" I said, "Yes, of course," He then said, "Why don't you meet Me in jail?" I thought to myself that if I wanted to meet a special friend in town that I would quickly get perked up and go. So, I went and had a wonderful time sharing with the lady inmates and I didn't even feel faint that evening.

There is hardly a time when the Lord does not touch someone's heart, and one or more inmates are in tears. More than once the ladies have gone and hugged one another when one was crying, because they knew now that they were valuable and loved by the Creator Himself and that He deeply cares.

In the "F" pod at the Jail facility, many of the ladies are reading their Bibles, praying and singing praise songs in their cell together. Last week some of these bootleggers and drug dealers talked of their need of God to help them stop selling, for they now realize how much they have hurt so many families by what they had done. I feel like this is the greatest group counseling session or therapy when we can speak of the One who can redeem and give new and beautiful life to all who ask.

One Hopi lady who was sitting next to me said that she had to throw up. We had just finished reading Mark 1, where the demoniacs were brought to Jesus, and He cast the demons out of the man. The Lord was so good to reach out to this Hopi elderly lady for He was cleaning her up. As this Hopi lady began to pray out loud, repenting of her sins and asking God to forgive her, the other ladies (who were mostly Native), saw that God was real. They began to quietly cry also.

It is so wonderful when we do not have to tell others how to live, but they read from the Sacred Word themselves and obey. One Hopi inmate asked one night whether he should continue to set aside a morsel of food at each meal for the spirits, as many Hopis do. Before anyone could answer, another Hopi raised His voice and said, "The Bible says that our God is a jealous God. I don't think we should do that anymore." During one service, one young Hopi man burst out and cried when we told him that the Lord was telling us that he would be a good father and a husband someday. Sometimes, any words of hope can be the life line when one feels so hopeless. These Hopi men were getting together twice a day at that time, to have Bible studies and prayer in the jail.

One Navajo woman who was a school Administrator, cried out to God, asking the Lord to forgive her. She had run away from the Lord and been so foolish. She told God in her prayer that she knew that it was never too late to come back to Him. We are so thankful for Bryan Hawk, who has constantly provided us with the Bibles to take into the jails for many years now. Who knows how many lives these thousands of Bibles have saved and encouraged?

I learned a trick long ago with "magic paper" which demonstrates the forgiveness of God. The ladies at the Coconino Jail sat and wrote down their sins on the magic paper. They folded the paper tightly and I asked them to imagine that there is a wooden cross in the middle of the room. I collected all their paper and laid them before the cross, and lit a match. It made quite a scene, causing a big flame instantly. In less than a second, everything was gone, leaving not even a bit of ash. All the ladies gasped and sat back in amazement. And then the very next moment, something unexpected happened.

One by one, they start weeping. They got it! It was truly a beautiful thing to see these ladies find forgiveness deep in their hearts. Jesus forgave their sins and will not recall even one single sin which was on that piece of paper. They all left the room with tear stained but radiant faces, going back to their cell, saying "Thank you, thank you!" We have been doing jail ministry for twelve years. If just one single lady or man could be transformed to walk with Jesus all the days of his or her life, I would be very happy.

"I still really don't understand what you mean when you say that the Son of God came down," a female inmate said to me around Christmas time. I told her that we are like bunches of ants going toward the furnace of fire. We could scream all we want to these ants to warn them that they are all going to be burned. But unless I could become as an ant, in order to speak their language, they would not understand the predicament of their impending doom. I told these female inmates that Jesus came to us as a man, speaking our human language, leaving all His glory behind in heaven. These ladies at the jail understood and yet some still did not accept His gift into their own hearts.

One lady among the Native women was an aggressive Lebanese Muslim, who would not hold a Bible in her hand. She later told me that her mother was a Native American, but she had gone back to her father's country in the Middle East. She listened to all that was read out loud by the other inmates from the Psalms, Luke and Proverbs. Her eyes were soft by the end of the evening, and I knew that the Lord had touched her! The following week she came back and not only read out loud from the Bible, but prayed out loud! As she was going back with the other ladies to their cell, she reached out and thanked us for coming.

Jail ministry is so very good. Every time we go in, we feel we receive much more from them than we give. They are so hungry and thankful to be able come to church at the jail. One gal, who will be going to a prison for two and a half years, said that she was so grateful to be alive. When an inmate expressed how she was discouraged and was beginning to lose her faith, everyone else shared how their strength came from knowing Jesus. When I expressed how sad I was after hearing about what happened to Will as a little boy, and how sadness had gripped me about some other issues in my life, they all prayed one-by-one around the circle for me.

Thank you God, for my friends in jail! I know you would have visited them also.

Chapter 21

Life's Lessons

When I start cleaning one area of our house, I find other areas which need cleaning. When I cleaned out our refrigerator, I saw I needed to clean under the kitchen sink. Then the bathroom counter-tops had to be washed. Just when I think one area is clean, I see another pile somewhere else. Life seems to always present one thing or another which we need to work on—either on our character issues or in relationships.

We are meant to live with all five senses, as the Lord has made us. We want to taste, to touch, to feel, to hear and to smell. As children, my brother and I used to say, "Smell my feet." I wonder what that was about. I think this is why most of us like clean houses.

We have two little girls in a foster care situation at our YWAM base in Hopiland. The littlest one goes around smelling everything, like inside of people's shoes, dirty laundry and even people's arm pits. It is as though it makes her feel alive to have her sense of smell.

I believe that people want to feel alive in this world, so much that they are willing to take the negative things to feel something—anything other than their pain—because that is better than feeling nothing. I believe this is why there are the abuses of drugs and alcohol or any other pleasure on this earth.

Many young people cut themselves, just to feel something. More than that, they want to be in control and do penance for the shame they feel. If only they knew the thrill they could have in the One who bore that shame and bled for them on the tree!

Shakespeare, once said, "The whole world is our audience and we are the actors on the stage" (my paraphrase). Symphonies and other cultural events are one of those places where everyone seems to dress up to impress others, whom they will never see again. Once I was held back from entering a symphony at Santa Domingo, Dominican Republic, because I wore a jean skirt. It was a long and classy skirt. We had to wait until everyone else went in and sat down. I think they wanted to make an example out of me how not to dress. Give me a break. Who do we need to impress? Who is our most important audience? Have we considered how we may be able to please the Maker of the stage of our universe and love Him more each day?

Someday our bodies will rot six feet in the ground. Our flesh will be cremated and the ashes scattered into the air and on the ground. Any beauty one may have possessed on this earth will be consumed by the Grave, and Death will feed on our bodies.

Farrah Faucet and Michael Jackson passed away in 2009. Everyone who has ever seen the 70's show, *Charlie's Angels,* on TV would remember this blonde beauty. However, all her beauty is forever gone after only fifty some years. Michael Jackson, who, with all his incredible talent as a rock star and performer, made the "moon walk" dance famous, is forever gone also.

What is the use of trying to look cool? What is the meaning of fame and beauty? As Solomon says in Ecclesiastes, it is "all blowing in the wind." If we dress up at all, it should be only to present ourselves honorably as a royal child of God—simply because that is who we are!

There has been much self-hatred in my life. I am convinced that the greatest psychological, spiritual and medical need that all people have is the need for hope. Hope is indeed the best medicine, when all seems to be lost. In fact, this conclusion has been proven by scientific research. How precious is the loving-kindness of our God! I have been able to find hope in His tender love and to tremble in His presence and put my trust under the shadow of His wings.

My mother once bought a scented home-made hand lotion from a booth at a market place. The lady came out from behind the booth and gave my mother a sample, along with a free bottle of water. My mother not only purchased one, but three lotions—one for herself, one for me and one for Naphtali. She did not purchase them so much because we had such a need for this scented lotion. She purchased them because of this lady's smile, which was so contagious with joy. The lady gave us each a bottle of water. This may have been a bribe, but was kind, nevertheless, as there was no guarantee that we would purchase anything. As believers, we also need to have the scented message which is contagious. It would not hurt for us to extend a cup of water to a stranger once in awhile, as well.

We have found it necessary to build a fence around our home, mainly for my sanity. We are being pro-active, as we anticipate our base growing in numbers in the future. It has been hard, even with our small school this year, as we could not even have confidential private phone conversations. We sometimes found our students right outside our home—sometimes in front and back. As far as they were concerned, our property was all part of YWAM. I found it hard even to have a birthday party for our daughter, Naphtali, this year without feeling guilty, because we had those who so much wanted to belong to our family. We could not even have a private barbeque without some students feeling hurt and wounded, because they were invited only to have dessert and not dinner. We are situated just 45 steps away from the conference center (I counted them). As much as I am glad and grateful to be in this ministry, I must admit that sometimes I feel a bit dismayed.

We have only one life to live and every day my heart's cry is, "Oh Lord, please let me love you more."

True Confessions of a Missionary

I had just gone out to Hopiland with a friend from Flagstaff and stayed overnight, as we had many people to visit. We had a wonderful time with so many who showed up at YWAM.

The next day, back in Flagstaff, our Hopi friend dropped off her ten-year-old son to spend all day with us. When I had just cooked dinner and before I could finish eating with our dinner guests, David, a staff member, showed up at our front door with a couple of female teachers from Hopi Mission School. Before I could sit back down to finish dinner, another Hopi man from Old Oraibi showed up at our back door after dark, saying that he needed to talk. He was almost ready to cry.

Early the next morning, Saturday, this same man came knocking at our door. He wanted to have breakfast and go cut wood with Will. I had yet not finished my cup of coffee, when Merwyn, who was attending our Digital Documentary School (DDS), came in with David. Merwyn wanted eggs, not cold cereal. I got up to cook him eggs and toast. He gave the plate to David, who had changed his mind and wanted eggs also. Having run out of patience, I had Merwyn cook his own eggs. I confess, I should have cooked eggs one more time!

Someone once said, "Some people complain because roses have thorns. I am thankful that thorns have roses." I don't always see the roses, especially when the Hopi man came back the next night after midnight, and we were jolted out of bed by a phone call from one of our staff gals next door at the Retreat center.

Changing the subject, I personally feel that it is good to visit places just to be able to say, "I've been there and done that." It is no good when you see places and never feel like you could afford to stay there. It was good to make a reservation for one night at the El Tovar Hotel at the South Rim of the Grand Canyon. It always looked so grand to me, with an enormous rock fire place in the lodge. The room we stayed in was so tiny, that we could hardly walk around, but it was quaint with nice unique furnishings. I no longer have this aching feeling inside me, which told me that I was not good enough to stay there.

I discovered that I could almost always find one thing, at least one, about which I could compliment a person or thing without being too indulgent or flattering. I find that this, too, is love. It is LOVE to build up another child of God with acceptance and dignity. Some people, like John Dawson, are extravagant with this gift of complimenting others. I am not talking about some lofty words, but even simply to comment on one small thing that was good. I have not always been good at this, but I am getting better all the time, for I want to imitate my Father in heaven.

Easter Home going

Our good friend, Rod "White Eagle" Wilson, who was one of our regular speakers for our DTS, went home to be with our Lord on Easter morning. Even though I was so happy for my brother who had so gloriously finished his task on earth, I cried for his wife, Alexis, and his children and grandchildren, and for myself who would so miss him. I only wish that I had given him a harder time with some of our debates, as he seemed to thrive on wrestling with ideas that were not so tame. We had many evenings when Will and I stayed up talking with Rod.

The first time we met Rod, he was wearing a large white deer skin jacket with fringed sleeves. His large build and his cool jacket made him look like a movie star. He would not give Will the time of the day, for Rod was in a very stoic mood.

Rod and his wife, Alexis, founded a YWAM base in Africa so many years ago. He spoke fondly of his mother who used to drive down Redondo Beach Blvd in her convertible, shouting joyously at the top of her lungs, with little Rod sitting beside her smiling away. He was a Cherokee Southern Californian surfer who touched many lives for Jesus. His death on this earth causes me to want to live my life all the more fully, and find time to love on my family.

This is the story to brag on our God who gives back ten fold when we release things. My Pendleton coat is the most beautiful of all the coats I ever owned. It has striking Native American designs and colors. I was able to purchase it at the big tent at the "Gathering of the Nations" in Albuquerque. Unbelievably enough, a Pendleton store from Santa Fe came to sell their jackets for half price. It is the biggest powwow in the world, with more than 35,000 people attending every year. One may never see such an array of colors and feathers and pageantry in a whole life time, as on this one weekend.

There was an honoring of Rod's memory at our YWAM North America staff conference in Colorado. During our gathering among the Native American ministries, I sensed that I was to give Rod's wife, Alexis, a different Native American jacket. It was one of those cool leather jackets with turquoise colored beads and fringe under the arms. I had purchased it near the Crow reservation in Montana, but I hardly ever wore it because I did not want to be seen as a wanna-be Indian.

When everyone else presented their gifts to Alexis and his daughter, Psalm, I stood up to give this jacket to Alexis. But then, the Lord did it again! He always likes to challenge us and mess things up when we are feeling so smug.

He said, "No, give that leather jacket to Psalm. And instead, give your prized Pendleton coat to Alexis." A sudden panic rose up inside me momentarily. I knew I needed to give it away. Even this coat did not really belong to me. It was His anyway, and He was asking me to release it, now.

When we give things away, we cannot concern ourselves with what may happen to them. Once I gave away my favorite palm tree to a friend who really loved it. This tree had really thrived in my apartment. I found out later that it had died in the home of my friend.

Sometimes God asks us to give away things that are valuable and dear to us. If they were not so valuable, it would be easy. Also, we should not expect to receive any thanks when we give. It does not matter how important those items may have been to us. I remember when I felt a tug in my heart to give away a wide silver bracelet which we had purchased from a Hopi man. I have yet to see another bracelet as beautiful, to this day. Why does God ask us sometimes to give away the best of our things? Why doesn't He ask for something of a lesser value? Giving away our junk is not really giving. That is just getting rid of things.

I never even got a word of thanks. Whether it was the Holy Spirit or my own voice which tugged at my heart, I don't know. I would rather err to the side of giving and be sorry later than to not to give. I want to give—not because I have to, but for bringing joy to the Father.

It was delightfully freeing to give away both coats. I cannot covet anything on this earth anymore. Nothing is completely mine. I may need to release it at any moment.

But the funny thing about releasing is that so often, God gives back tenfold. Several days later, I got a phone call from Alexis. She said that she could not keep my Pendleton coat, as she was going back to work with the YWAM base in Hawaii to live. The wool coat would not be suitable there.

As we talked, Alexis realized that Will and I would love to have a small item of Rod's which we could remember him by. She said she would send something. When we received our package, not only was my Pendleton coat in the box, but two pairs of Rod's cowboy boots and a pair of moccasins with bead work which Rod did himself. She also sent a perfect ear of Hopi corn, which Rod, as an artist, had decorated with beads and feathers. If I had not listened to the Lord in releasing my coat, we would have never received these other gifts. How wonderful our God is!

True Confessions of a Missionary

Father, help me not to waste so much time doing meaningless things on this earth. Help me to know that I am a sojourner, passing through this earth, for such a brief time. Help me not to hoard things, but to let things flow out of my life.

Wahale Onaga (White Eagle) original watercolor by Alexis Wilson Russell (See her Art gallery on-line)

Chapter 22

Dream Keeper

I used to have a recurring sad dream in the first years of our marriage: I had run away. I was sitting by a stream and washing my clothes in the dream. I was alone. One day I told Will about my dream. It was remarkable how Will responded. He hardly waited for me to finish telling him the dream.

He said, "Millie, do you think I am going to let you get away that easily? I would come and look for you!"

Every time I tell this story to anyone, I choke up and almost cry, because I think it was such a sweet thing for Will to say! It was such a great relief. I think this is like our God. He will always come looking for us, just like the sheep which was lost in the parable of Jesus. He left the ninety-nine to look for the one lost sheep. I never had that dream after that time again.

Some dreams can terrorize us. For example, the Pharaoh's two dreams which Joseph interpreted. The Lord is the dream keeper who can help us with the interpretations and bring healing and deliverance and hope to us.

I had a dream that some evil person had entered my home while I was in the bathroom. I could hear him coming toward my bedroom. Soon he unlocked the door and began pushing on the bathroom door. His arm came reaching into the bathroom and the other arm came in through the window. I screamed through the open window as I was pushing against the door as hard as I could.

I could see someone coming out through a window from the house across the street. He must have been a thief. Why would he come through the window and not through the door? He looked at me but was not interested in helping. A thief would not want to help because he would not want to be caught and go to jail afterwards. I wonder who this thief represented.

I saw three young people walking by on the sidewalk but they were not interested in helping either. Just as this evil person's arm was reaching to grab me, Will awakened me and I screamed. He asked if I was okay. Will heard my distress.

Will said he had a dream as well. In his dream I was in a semi truck which was hit by another semi. I was thrown out of the truck, but he said in his dream that I was perfectly fine. Some say that the vehicles in our dreams usually represent ministries. It is so amazing while I was having a nightmare that Will had another dream simultaneously which would tell me that I was going to be alright. God is so good and faithful to show us that even though the enemy wants to harm and terrorize us, He will deliver us.

I love when we know without a doubt that the Lord has delivered us from harm. Josephine Oketta is from Uganda. She had started YWAM work in Sudan. We took walks together regularly when we were in schools at YWAM Tyler in Texas. We saw a large snake coiled, standing up with its mouth wide open like a cobra. Josephine who was closer to the snake leapt like a big frog towards my side, screaming. She said all the snakes were poisonous in Uganda. I went a little closer to get a better look saying that I did not think this was a poisonous snake. I confess I was a fool. Because what is a truth is a truth and it does not matter what one thinks at all. I found out that this snake was indeed very poisonous. There are people who are like this snake and we need not to go near or hang around them but be wise as they are liable to lunge at us and we are liable to be harmed. We are all creatures of hurts and lunge at someone one time or another. However, we cannot avoid being with people all together as God is able to grace us to forgive.

A flyer was passed out in our class that same week with all the dangerous things we should watch out for in that region. I found the picture of that same snake in that same position and I was so astounded. Water Moccasin snakes are the cobras of America. It could have easily bit us with one lunge which was no more than four feet away. It was as though the Lord froze its body. I knew that He had protected us so many times. Both Josephine and I were the founders and the leaders of YWAM bases. We both had suffered many things. One does not escape hard things in life just because one becomes a Christian or a leader. In fact, you are more of a target for the enemy when you are in the front line. God is able to protect us from those who want to harm us. He is able to save us from our own foolishness also. The Lord is indeed our deliverer!

One day we had a young Hopi man show up for our class. His head was shaved because he said that the Lord had told him to do it. He did not want to cut his hair because, like so many Hopi men, he had long, shiny black hair down to his waist. After a few different dreams from the Lord, he decided to obey and had his brother shave his head. The Lord then spoke in his heart that if anyone asked why he cut it that he should say, "The time has been long, but now it is short." This young man found that no one wanted to listen to him before. However, now he had ample opportunities to share about Jesus, as everyone was asking why he had shaved his long hair. We thank the Father, who is speaking to His children in Hopiland!

Another young lady was having repeated nightmares, so much so that she did not want to go to sleep at night. She came and shared her dreams with the rest of us. We had taught on dreams from the Bible that evening and how God can use dreams to direct people or to show them what is to come. As she shared, all the others in that room began affirming her, that God is more powerful and that the devil was trying to get her back. We all prayed for her.

Our staff person, David, had a dream. He had a dream that he was to feed his students. When he came into the house, there were foods prepared on the dining table. But the kids were eating off the floor, so he told them to stop and eat the real food. They were mad at him for saying that.

David said that when there has been much injustice, people take in certain spirits to protect themselves. These protecting spirits will come against anyone who tries to encourage and free those who are deeply wounded, so that the people will not succeed. When there is a whole community of wounded people, these "protecting" spirits will try to influence and have the people defeat this purpose from every angle. Recently, a Native American girl said, "I really want to receive Jesus, but I just can't." She knew that, with all the pressures from everyone on the reservation, she just wouldn't be able to walk the walk with Jesus.

Will and I have had some bad times also. Will dreamt that he had five arrows pierce his body and that he knew the next arrow was going to kill him, just before he woke up.

Sometimes, I feel that we are like little Frodo, who was given an almost impossible assignment in J.R.R. Tolkien's book, *The Lord of the Rings*. It is a spiritual battle which we are all in, whether we think so or not. Did we get recruited into this army, or did we voluntarily sign up? Sometimes I forget.

God has a way of changing our minds and hearts. He has a way of turning things that we think are bad into something amazing. I thought we were so poor when Will and I first married. We were not poor at all, as we had such a wonderful ministry center, full of so many people who became a part of our family.

We lived in the downtown area of Santa Barbara, California, and our ministry center was located in one of the poorest sections of town. We had a few drug dealers who lived on the same block, as well as a woman who entertained men next door.

Many Mexican families also took up residence in our block; some might call them illegal immigrants or "wet backs". They had many children, uncles, aunts and grandparents living in very small quarters. But I was always amazed how happy they all seemed and how they got along. One could hardly blame them for wanting to come to this country to improve their lives and the lives of their loved ones. I know I would if I were in their shoes. They are not lazy people. One would see almost any other color and race pan handling out on the streets, but you would never see a person from Mexico ever begging for anything. Instead they would be seeking work.

The only thing that got on my nerves was that these Mexican children kept messing up the front of our place with chalk drawings on our sidewalks, and leaving trash on our yard quite regularly. We had the biggest yard on that block which was not big at all, only big enough to lay a couple of large blankets for a picnic or something. But for these Mexican children, it was their only place to play safely.

I prayed about this and sensed that, rather than trying to chase them away, I should invite them over into our apartment to have a children's ministry. The first time they all came over we made cookies. None of these Mexican kids had ever made chocolate chip cookies or banana bread from scratch, so they really enjoyed doing it. They came weekly to learn songs about the Lord and to hear the children's Bible stories. Eventually, we got to know all their extended families and had block parties where they all came to a barbeque in our back yard. These children never messed up our front yard again. They became the protectors of our place. They not only kept the place clean, but they often babysat Clover. What I thought was such a bother became a blessing to our family.

Once I went away with a couple of my girl friends to work on this book. Lynda and Jan have been my dear friends for over a decade. When we arrived at the ranch, we found our room not well prepared and some items in the room were missing. We also found our coffee pot full of fuzzy mold. We were in a studio with two double beds and would have had to share a bed, if Jan had not brought her blow-up mattress. We were happy to just get another coffee pot. But the manager felt so bad that he up-graded us to a two bedroom cabin with our own deck right over a stream. If I could ever have another house, I would have a house by a stream. We had our own Jacuzzi on the deck, too. We stayed up until one in the morning, as we stared at all the stars in the night sky and talked away.

It was astounding how the Lord blessed us by having allowed the mold to be there, so we were able to be up-graded. What was even greater was that it was free! When I went to check out and pay for these two nights, we were not even charged a single penny. God is so good to us!

When the Lord took us out to the Hopi Indian reservation, we thought our three children would suffer. But they were greatly blessed beyond what we could have ever imagined for them, had we stayed back in Santa Barbara. All three of our kids, along with some other Hopi honor students were taken on a free trip out to visit all the Ivy League colleges—Harvard, Yale, Dartmouth, etc., on the east coast. All their expenses, including their airfares, were paid by the Hopi tribe. Two of our kids were selected to go twice! It is truly amazing how God orchestrates these sorts of things.

We can work all of our lives to have fancy houses, fancy cars and to save for the college funds for our kids, etc. In the end, it is the Lord who can bless all our endeavors. No one knows how our children will turn out. You could save all your life to send them to some famous college or university, but they may not go at all. If they do, they may go astray and do things which may be harmful to them and squander all that you saved. It is only God who can fill us and our children with the knowledge of His will, in all wisdom and spiritual understanding. It is He who qualifies us to be partakers of His inheritance.

The Lord can heal us in every way—emotionally, spiritually, and physically. He cares about our hang nails, as well as what is happening in the nations. We should not rule Him out on anything. I used to have a congenital medical condition which would make me black out. It was really embarrassing sometimes, as I did not know what had happened when I awoke. Once I woke up in the middle of a very crowded mall with the lights of an ambulance flashing and the medics keeping many on-lookers at bay. I had apparently lost consciousness and had lost control of my bowels. I was dazed, but not in enough of a daze to not be embarrassed by the smell. The reason I am sharing this is because I was at the end of my rope. I was like the woman in the Bible who had bled for twelve years. She desperately wanted to touch Jesus because she knew she would be healed. I also knew my hope of healing was in Jesus.

A portable EKG (electrocardiogram) was assigned to me for twenty-four hours, to test how fast my heart was beating. The test showed that my heart rate was shooting up like crazy over a thousand times a day. I asked my doctor what a normal person's erratic heart rate was, and he said zero. He told me that my heart was not getting enough blood. Therefore my heart was working extra hard to compensate. He said I had a condition called grand Tachycardia. I was told that some people have it so bad, that they cannot even leave the house or drive a car. It actually comforted me to have a name for my condition, because at least I knew why I was blacking out. I was put on a daily medication to regulate my heart. Here I was a very healthy, strong woman, taking medication that was usually taken only by the elderly for their hearts.

I sensed that there was a reason for my condition. I was not normally very sympathetic with anyone who was ill. I did not have much empathy for those who were sick. It is not that I did not want to be compassionate, but I could not muster it up to feel sorry for them. I can't stand self-pity.

I can't stand those who spiritualize everything either. I think it is good to talk about the colors of toe-nails and not just about "heavenly" things all the time. One can get really bored with that. It would be like someone always saying, "Buddha said this and Buddha said that." It is just nice to hear one's thoughts and how the world makes them click.

I can't stand a lot of things. I can't stand myself sometimes. Sometimes I feel bad that I can't stand a lot of things. I wish I could say it is not my spiritual gifting and not feel bad about it. But, I do feel bad. I think I could say like Anne of Green Gables said, "Only if you knew how much I don't say the things I want to say." I know the Lord is making my heart to be more like Him. One can hardly be in a full time ministry for a long time if one's heart gets hardened.

And now, I had a condition which I could not control, no matter what I did. I understood that it was not as simple as trying to eat right or exercise. It had nothing to do with confessing my sins or getting counseling.

As I prayed, I sensed that the Lord wanted to heal me. So whenever there was an opportunity for me to get prayer, I would always go to the altar. But I did not get healed. Yet I still had a quiet but deep peace in my heart that someday I would be healed. So I never gave up hope. I never stopped praying and never stopped getting prayer.

One day I felt an annoying sense of pain on my right arm like someone had a firm grip on me. I thought I was having a heart attack, as I heard that is one of the symptoms. I prayed, and I heard the Lord gently say in my heart, "You are healed. But you are continuing your medication, which is actually doing you harm." I went back to my doctor for another EKG. This time there was not one single eruption! My heart beat was totally normal and had returned to a steady and perfect beat. It was proven without a doubt and in black and white on the chart. It was amazing! On the other hand, this is not that amazing, as our God can do anything. I will not rule out God's physical healing in this present day.

We all have a dream to have health, joy and happiness on this planet earth. But this is all temporary. It all seems like a dream. And it is. There is a world which is much more real than what we see.

My physical needs and appetites are great, but often carnal.

Great Eagle Rising

Dietrich Bonhoeffer said in his book, *Life Together—The Classic Exploration of Faith in Community*, "God hates visionary dreaming [carnal]. It makes the dreamer proud and pretentious . . . It is true, in so far as these are devout people that they do this with the intention of serving the highest and the best, but in actuality the result is to dethrone the Holy Spirit, to relegate Him to remote unreality." As we enter another new year, we truly desire to only do what is in the heart of the Father and not our human (carnal) dreams!

Going down San Juan River
I used to dream of towering cathedral rocks
Now I am in my dream world

Chapter 23

Blessed is the One who is Full of Quiver

There was a time that I was sorry I named our first daughter, Clover. Names are important. Abram to Abraham, Sarai to Sarah, and Saul's name was changed to Paul in the Bible.

After finding out what I named her, a friend said, "What? Are you kidding? Clover? That sounds like a cow's name!" Boy, she's got some nerve. My friends' name, which I will not bother to mention, sounded like a hillbilly name which should be in a *Hee Haw* show (for those of you who are old enough to know what this show was in the seventies). She had some fancy degree in counseling or in psychology, as far as I could remember.

How this so called "friend" responded, does not help my psyche, and I would never sit in her counseling seat, because she does not like Clover's name. But then, again, she is entitled to her own opinion.

I must admit it would be nice to have beautiful last names like "Nightingales" or "Fields" or "Sing" rather than "Eehns" (pronounced as in "*in* and out.)" Toms is not much better and is boring as could be. Names like "Diamond" (like Neil Diamond), "Sterling" or "Lovejoy", "Loveland" or simply "Love" are pretty nice too. "Cousteau" or "Fitzgerald" is distinguished perhaps because there are legends behind the names. Those names would not be admired if there was a mass murderer behind it. If one cannot have beautiful names, they could have audacious names like "Hogg" (pronounced "Hog") or "Leaky" (What did he leak?) or "Drooly" (Was he drooling?) or "Outhouse" (a Navajo name) which will always be a conversational piece.

I never really knew why I liked the name Clover, other than that every time I saw it in the 5000 name book, I felt refreshed. Will was not particularly pleased with this name. After having had a home birth and a very hard and long twelve hours of labor, Will said I could name her anything I want. Many years later, I realized the meaning of her name when I ran into a lady from Ireland. She said that they seed Clover into the ground to replenish the earth when the ground is out of nutrients.

Our daughter, Clover, is in social services, working with foster parents and children. She helps facilitate a special display, called "Heart Gallery," in different cities featuring older foster kids who are beyond the ideal age for adoption. This exhibit was featured on the TV program 20/20. Photos of the children, taken by professional photographers, are beautifully displayed with a short story of each child. This is in hope that someone who sees the photos would adopt these older kids who desperately need a family. Many get adopted, but so many more families are needed.

I thought I was going to be just like some Native American ladies whom I read about. I read that they go behind a bush and have the baby, and then come out and go to the field the next day to go to work. (I don't know a single Native woman who has done that.) It was not like that at all, and I have a great respect for woman kind throughout all history. How were all those tiny ladies able to give birth? I just don't know. I suppose not every woman lived through it. I was almost sure that I was going to die.

The curse of child bearing is really not fair, but I would not want to be a man who has the responsibility of being the head of the family. When Will is gone for a long period of time, I feel the heavy burden, even when my circumstances have not changed around me. I don't like the thought of making some hard decisions for both our ministry and our own affairs. Will once had some kidney stones which were so painful to pass, that he said he could only compare it to a woman giving birth. I don't think so!

However, I feel sorry for the men. It must be hard to be a guy because they have to wear such boring clothes. Ladies can wear frilly, pretty and lacy things. Guys can't wear pink hats or party dresses, all color shoes and jewelry. If a man were creative, it would be extra hard to wear the same old type of pants and shirts and jackets all the time. At least in the old days, men wore powdered wigs and fancy jackets with lace sleeves and collars. The men now a days could only wear tuxedos for proms or a few special occasions. But there is not much variety in tuxedos either; they are all pretty much the same, except the ones with a long tail. Poor guys! If they were peacocks, they would get to have the fancy feathers. If they were lions, they would get to have the beautiful mane. But they are just men.

I worried that our children may not marry, as if a marriage was everything in the world. Is it not better to be single and have self-respect, than to be married and be unloved or abused, only to end up hating oneself and life with no escape? Is it not better to be poor and have a life of dignity, purpose and happiness than to be married to a prince who does not love you (like Princess Diana)?

There are so many miserable people who are in marriage who have no respect for one another. Their children resent the parents and they are no good to society. They do not honor the One who created and loved them. So, I wondered why I wanted our children to marry as though it was the only way to be truly happy.

It is nice to have someone to sit with and enjoy each other without saying hardly a word. It is better than having a dog. Dogs can't be the bread winner or help with a ministry. It is true that a dog would let you have any opinion you want to have but it cannot discuss Shakespeare or music. Will and I sat together and watched a leaf in a pool of water at Oak Creek near Sedona once. Will wanted to take a video of a leaf floating gently into an eddy and then out again. We must have sat for at least twenty minutes. It was not a thrill or anything to watch a leaf floating in circles but it was a quiet joy of having someone who had stayed with you for over thirty years and still loving you.

I admit that there is something very nice about having a permanent date to go out to restaurants or to go for a hike in the woods and not have to wonder whether the date of the month was good or bad. And there is something very nice about playing toesies in bed; you can't just do that with anyone. And it is nice to have children calling to talk to you when you are old. I have prayed for the spouses for all our children ever since they were born. I prayed for God's guidance for their lives and for protection and blessings wherever they may be walking or sleeping on this planet earth. I hope they show up sooner rather than later. I know that they are maturing in the Lord and getting ready.

It was a beautiful thing to watch our daughter Clover wait in such quiet confidence for the Lord to bring the bridegroom of His choice. When she was only twenty, a youth pastor from Norway came soon after her DTS in Australia, with a serious intent to pursue her. She quietly refused.

Then Tim came to ask for our blessing to court her. We sensed his great passion for our Lord. We soon realized that this was the very young man whom we had prayed for throughout the 27 years since Clover was born. He came to us in the month of September, six months later, and asked for our blessings to have Clover's hand in marriage.

If there is ever a need to try on a dress, it should be your wedding gown! Our Heavenly Father provided our daughter with the most beautiful wedding dress. We first went to a local bridal store, and Clover tried on many gowns. They seemed a bit worn from having been tried on by so many others, and the store was not particularly clean. Then our daughter found a beautiful wedding gown online and ordered from China instead. What was she thinking? When it arrived, the gown came wrinkled and carelessly stuffed in a paper bag, and did not have the right measurements. She wanted to prepare and present herself to her bridegroom, but she knew that she did not feel like the perfect bride in this gown.

In order to save money, she found someone on the East coast who could share the cost of an $800 dress. I did not even know that there was such a thing as a "share a wedding gown" computer site. We are definitely in a new era, with all the computer technology! It is a great idea for those who don't care to keep their wedding gowns. It is such a sentimental idea to hope that your daughter would someday get married in that same dress, but who is to know what the fashion would be by a few decades later, and what size the daughter would be. Anyway, Clover would not be able to keep this dress after the wedding, as the other girl wanted it, although Clover would pay just a bit less. I knew that the Lord had something better and prayed.

We had a mother-daughter trip to Scottsdale, Arizona. As we browsed, we found a gorgeous designer gown, so elegantly sown with costly tiny beads that it made all the other gowns look plain or frumpy. This was even more stunning than the gown she was going to purchase with the other girl. But, what was this? It had been marked down so low that it would make your jaw drop open. When we went to purchase it, we were informed that the store was taking 10% off every gown in the store that day! Since a wedding gown is the most extravagant garment a girl would ever wear in her life, it almost seemed sinful to have it be on some special sale, but we did not care. We remember that nothing is too big for our God who gives so superbly out of the treasures of His amazingly kind heart! After all, we are HIS bride!

The Wedding was almost all about worship unto our King! It started out with three songs, "How Great is Our God," "We Cry Out," and the "Revelation Song." This last song says, "Worthy is the Lamb who was slain; Holy, holy, holy is He! Sing a new song to Him who sits on heaven's mercy seat . . ." We were sitting on the very front row as the parents of our daughter, Clover, the bride, so we could not see. But we heard that almost all the hundreds of people were standing to praise Him who is so worthy indeed. It sounded and felt like a bit of heaven.

How beautiful it was to see the sun on the day of the wedding when we had a blizzard which shut down Interstate 40 the night before! We are truly thankful for all our friends who came from so far away. More chairs had to be brought out at the wedding. The reception at the Museum of Northern Arizona was maxed out, so we had to plan a second reception at our YWAM Retreat Center.

I cried when I had to tell our island and Native American friends that they could not come to the main reception. Ours, Will's and mine, was a very simple hippie wedding under a big weeping willow tree in someone's backyard. We were so poor that we had everyone bring a picnic blanket to sit on the lawn and it was a pot-luck meal to share. No one was left out. The guests threw a flower on the isle which was marked with white ribbons so the bridesmaids and I walked the flower lane. Someday in heaven, we will have enough room for everyone, and we will laugh and reminisce together about how we were stressed about nothing.

During the vow exchange, Clover thanked Tim for initiating so many of their prayer times, and for being the man to give her the very first kiss! She was truly the Proverbs 31 lady, "Who does him good all the days of her life" (Verse 12). "All" the days meaning even before they were brought together in marriage, she thought of him and kept herself pure. What a beautiful picture of a bride!

It was a few months later that Will and I were invited to hear our son-in-law, Tim, share the message at a Saturday evening service. Our son, John, led the worship that evening, and my heart was overwhelmed to see both our son and son-in-law in charge of the service. Tim spoke of how the Lord had touched him profoundly through the Word of God and shared many scriptures. He was able to share from his heart, and with certain love for our God.

Afterwards, I was able to give him a hug and a kiss on his cheek. I knew when he asked for our daughter's hand in marriage, that he loved her. I thought that was good enough. However, that night for the first time, I saw that God had answered all the years of my prayers—that our daughter would marry a man of God, who would be able to influence many others with the word of God!

I do not know what Abraham felt when the Lord required the sacrifice of his only son, Isaac, to be put on the altar. But I believe I have a glimpse of it now. I panicked when our son, John, said recently that he wanted to go do a DTS (Discipleship Training School) somewhere. It was in our hearts to see our Wilderness program revived, and John is very good in wilderness skills and working with youth.

I cried out to God, "Do you know how humbling it is to be on support, never quite knowing month-to-month how much will come in? Did you not also call our daughter, Naphtali, to Hopi Mission School, with her meager salary? Now you want our son as well?"

The Lord had me go into a deep time of repentance. I wept because I saw all of my insecurities, hanging onto this world's standards. If they want to go into missions full time, because that is their passion to serve Him with all their hearts, I should trust the Lord to provide.

Our lives are so short, and yet I wanted our children to have the comfort of this world, when eternity is just right around the corner.

When John was born, Will told me that it was the best anniversary gift I could have given him—a son after two daughters. It is not as if I had anything to do with when a child could be born—you know what I mean. Will was actually quite happy with our two girls.

Will never wanted to give Johnny a toy gun to play with. He said that the boys in this country are set up to be in wars. He realized this when he was a Navy Seal. At one point, Will realized that the war was not just a fun game, but that he had been ordered to kill the "gooks," (a name given to de-humanize the enemy), as though they were not even human beings. Fortunately he got to Vietnam right at the end of the war. It seems to me that men need something to fight about. There is glorifying of wars as though if men need something to do.

He did not want to glorify war for our son, Johnny. But we saw that Johnny did not need to have a toy gun to play soldiers. He was making a gun with his hands and shooting things with it. Finally, we realized that this might be a warrior and a protector instinct which the Lord has put into our son and all men. We said to each other that we need to not stifle this gift, but to redirect it in the right way. I think we did finally get Johnny a toy gun, but told him he couldn't use it to ever shoot people.

Our son, John, is possibly the most handsome young man God has ever produced. He is one of those sons that every mother dreams of having. Mr. Mentzer, at Hopi High School, once said that Johnny was the most renaissance young man he ever had in thirty years of teaching. I did not know what he meant. I think it is more than being a Shakespeare although he wrote some clever stuff. How can anyone who wrote things like, "Romeo, Romeo, wherefore art thou, Romeo?" have been good in sports and other things? A renaissance man is someone who sought to develop skills in all areas of knowledge, in physical development, in social accomplishments and in arts.

I am not going to pretend that I am not proud of our son. He could have become anything he wanted to be with some hard work. It became apparent that John found the most joy whenever he was in a ministry setting—whether in worship with his songs on his guitar, or ministering and praying for others.

He is presently serving the Lord in South Asia where over 95% of the population is Muslims. He can understand and speak their language. We miss him terribly, but this is how we raised our son. We cannot complain, since he has the greatest privilege of telling the people of this earth about the love of Jesus.

It was in October when the Aspen leaves in my garden were beginning to turn bright yellow when our son John brought Kayti Grace home to us. They first met while John was doing his DTS in Australia. They both had a long term calling to Southeast Asia as full time workers of our Father when they fell in love. So many young people are waiting for their mate in this world, not willing to do the work of God until their longing is fulfilled. They are afraid that they may miss their chance. They think that they have to make this happen themselves. But while our son was about the Father's business, the Lord provided a bride for him. How faithful our God is who brought our son John from Arizona and Kayti from California to Australia and gave them both the calling to Southeast Asia to fall in love. It is God who orchestrated this union and brought them together in His perfect timing.

It was Naphtali, out of our three children, who had the hardest time at first, being in Hopiland. And yet, she chose to go back to teach at Hopi Mission School after she received her teaching credential. It did not seem important to her to have a good teaching position in a city with all the benefits and retirement plan. This note from Naphtali will give you a beautiful picture of what the Lord is doing with the children in Hopiland.

Dear Brothers and Sisters in the Lord—God is so good! He has brought me out to the desert place once more to serve Him, and I feel so very blessed! I could go on forever about the faithfulness of our Lord and Savior! About the goodness and PERFECT judgments, and disciplines of our heavenly Father—for that is the testimony that He has stamped on my life to speak of, but I know I must let you go. Thank you for letting me share this bit of my life with you, and I would so appreciate any prayers you could offer up on my behalf, as well as the kids and the rest of the staff here at the school. The Lord is moving.

I am including a few journal entries from students in my class from our daily journal writing time. Most of the entries are talking about what they heard from God during our "3 minutes of listening to God's voice," which we do every morning. I have their permission.

Dear Jesus, please Lord, be with my family right now. We already went through a lot. My grandpa passed away, now my auntie. Why is this happening to my family, my cousin and my uncle, too. They don't need this. Please help us. Please be with us. We need you right now. This is a very hard time for us, especially my uncle and my cousin. Help us, Lord, please.

Sincerely, S . . .

Dear Jesus, this is what I heard from God while our 3 minutes of silence. "My love is everlasting. I have so much love to give. Tell everyone about my love. My love will conquer the Devil. My wish is to have all my children come to heaven with me. Show my love to the world, and everyone in it." Blessed be your name.

Sincerely, L . . . .

Just now, we listened to God's voice, but I didn't hear anything. Instead, I got a picture. It was like an angel lifting Jesus up from the grave! I was amazed that God sent me a picture

Sincerely, A . . .

This is a picture of God that He showed me. He said, "The Devil is a fool!" Then, He showed me an angel in heaven. The angel said, "God's love is stronger." God told me that the Devil doesn't believe in love. He said, "The Devil thinks he's stronger even though I'm stronger." That's what he told me.

Sincerely, D . . .

A sister in Christ, Naphtali Toms

The Lord has delivered us in more than one way! Our son and daughter, Johnny and Naphtali, were in a car accident when someone in a pickup truck hit their car from the rear. They were seen by a doctor and they are both fine, other than some back and neck-aches for the first couple of weeks.

Three weeks later, Naphtali's car was hit by a tow truck, right behind her on the driver's side. Now, her car is totaled in a junk yard. However, she is doing fine. We believe the Lord really protected her from the enemy, for she could have easily died.

Prior to these accidents, Naphtali called us at home at 1:30 AM asking for prayer. She felt such a dark presence in the century old stone house, where she lived alone, while working at Hopi Mission School. Curiously, several others felt that same presence that same week. They are not just ordinary believers, but those who know how to do spiritual warfare. They all said they felt a heavy evil presence.

We believe that the enemy is trying to make some last efforts to act as though he is powerful. But not one of them are budging from under the shadow of His wings and trusting in His faithfulness and His shelter.

Adoption is in God's Heart

I never knew how incredible a loss of a child on this earth was until I found out that one, perhaps even two of my sisters, were aborted many years ago. I always had a deep longing to have a sister, deeper than I could ever begin to explain. I would often feel a bit jealous when I would see other sisters together.

One day I was talking to my mother, as I caught a glimpse of a beautiful blonde girl in a newspaper article. When she was a baby, she was found alive in a bucket, among all the other aborted babies at a hospital. A nurse found her still moving in this bucket and rescued and adopted this child. Now she was speaking at many high schools about how she was saved and God's grace over her life.

My mother looked at me and said that she had aborted two times while she was in Korea many years ago—the one after me and another after my brother, Daniel, who is two years younger. She said that someone came from America and set up clinics and many of the Korean ladies had abortions for it had become normal.

This news hit me like a deep wave of sorrow, deeper than I could have ever imagined. The truth had finally revealed itself. Now I knew why I had so longed to see my sister, like when twins are separated at birth. I knew then that at least I had one, or even two sisters, who were supposed have been here on earth with me. We could have done so much together; play house, run, play "hide and seek," cry and take joy in one another. We might even fight once in awhile and pray for one another. We would be in each other's weddings, and watch each other's children play together.

I found tears stinging my eyes for many days after finding out about these losses. It was not that I wanted to feel sorry for myself, because I can't stand people with self-pity. I genuinely felt that it had broken God's heart also. I wondered what their names might have been. Could it have been Lisa or Anne or Melody? I knew now, that even though we would have no memories of this earth together, they would be there to welcome me into heaven. They would come running with open arms, and, without introducing themselves, I would know who they were and that they were my sisters all along.

One beautiful thing about the Hopi people is that they do not seem to believe in abortions. They have a great respect for a birth of a child.

There is a great sadness. In this nation alone, millions of babies have been killed before they are ever born. I have heard that these babies, who are aborted, go to be with God in heaven. I could understand this from the story of King David's baby in II Samuel 12:23. The fact that all babies go to heaven does not justify their destruction in the womb. There is a calling for each human being to fulfill something on this planet, which no one else can—if only to bring joy to the Creator who knits each one with such unique beauty.

I want to see our children produce many children to populate the earth. I pray that they would bring hope and the glory of our awesome Lord to this earth. I want them to populate this earth with those who would bring joy to God. People say this earth is a hard place to bring children. I believe all the promises of blessings the Lord has put in His sacred Word for His children. I believe our children and grandchildren will not be only blessed but bless others. They would not only be provided for but provide for others who are in need.

Chapter 24

Can we ask the Wildest Questions?

Is there a place in the body of Christ where we can ask the wildest questions without fearing the consequences of being ousted by the church? Should we have questions but not be allowed to ask? I think sometimes the Christians and the Muslims and the religious people are the only ones who cannot ask the questions they have in their minds. If you are not a religious person, you can think or ask anything. It is like what Communism is about. They must always be on their guard, because they do not know who would turn them in. One could be sent to the work camps, if they are found asking any questions or say anything contrary to the regime.

Will said that God let him know that he was in a trance once. I think sometimes we get scared of certain words and concepts and end up throwing out the baby with the dirty bath water. Didn't the Bible say that Peter was in a trance, when the sheet came down from heaven? We are afraid to hear anything out of the ordinary, as though we may be taken captive by every idea that comes our way. We are so afraid that it might sound New Age or Eastern—and, of course, everything about their music and ways are evil, right? Of course not! That would be like saying all Rock and Roll and Country or Celtic and Soul/ Jazz songs are evil.

In this line of thinking, we should also throw out the music of Mozart and Beethoven, because they were heathens and only listen to Bach who wrote his music for the church. We should not appreciate the paintings of Van Gogh, because he was crazy. I believe all good things come from God. This means all creative and wonderful things—music, art and dramas, etc. We end up doing a huge disservice, when we throw out all excellent sources of beauty in life, simply because they don't fit into our own boxes of thinking. We live in constant fear-based theology, that if we ask any questions at all out of our own fundamental Christian thinking, we may be labeled a heretic in some way.

The first thing I saw when I opened my eyes in bed, as I turned towards Will, was a bald man. I knew that I had gone to sleep with a man with lots of hair. I saw that it was just Will and went back to sleep. I knew that the Lord must have spoken to him about shaving his hair in the middle of the night. In the morning, he explained that he woke up about 2 AM, with the Lord speaking in his heart to cut his hair. So he stood in front of the mirror and cut most of his hair, and then asked the Lord "Is this enough?" He felt that more needed to be cut. He asked again and realized that what the Lord wanted was for him to cut it all off. He said that when he returned to bed, he was wondering what this had all been about. He then heard in the Spirit, "Long-Haired Kachina," with no further explanation.

What in the world was this about? Could these kachinas possibly be a good symbolic thing of something good and humble? Can we ask these questions and still be a Christian? This was the night after Will had come back from a river rafting trip with Clover. On their way home, they saw clouds with dark rain streaks coming down. Will mentioned to our daughter that it was for the Hopis a "Long Haired Kachina." We were both very perplexed about this. Will, especially, was seeking God for more understanding, which we later received. Was this like the time when Peter was presented a sheet full of unclean food and was told to eat of it?

When we asked our Hopi friend, she told us that the long hair kachina is the first one they met when they came into this world, which they call the "fourth world." They believe that a remnant was saved from three prior worlds and that they came from the Grand Canyon through a hole called the "Sipapu." Another Hopi friend told us that the long hair kachina is the most humble of all kachinas.

To be very honest, the looks of some of these kachinas scare me. Sometimes I don't understand their looks at all. I wonder, however, whether the Native Americans were very frightened, when they saw tall, blond, white-skinned Europeans—especially when they wore full armor and rode on big horses (which they had never seen before). It is really easy for outsiders to peg everything as evil if we are not familiar with certain things in another culture. However, we need to be slow to judge, praying always for discernment and testing the spirit.

Can we release the women to minister in the church? Women in America could not even vote until 1920. Women missionaries still cannot serve communion, and they cannot speak in many churches in front of the men. This same issue of not being able to release the women in the body of Christ is similar to not being able to release Native American believers into their own ministries.

There is much misogyny (hatred of women) on earth. I do not think that Jesus hates women. He brought dignity—not only to the Jewish but to the Samaritan women. He brought honor to every sphere of women's lives, both to the rich and poor. This would be impossible in almost all other religions, where women in the twenty-first century are considered less than animals. Many are unjustly killed by men.

How about "name it and claim it" theology? It is good to claim all that God wants for us on this earth, but when does this hurt others? Once we had a staff gal who babysat a Down syndrome child. She went to her church and was badly criticized for mentioning that the child had this syndrome. A woman in the nursery got mad and told her she should not ever say that. She said the baby was healed and that she should believe. Our staff gal came back confused and hurt. What is faith? Hebrews 11:1-2 says it is the substance of things unseen. But there are times we simply have to face reality. It is horrible when someone is told they do not have enough faith or they are in sin, when they have tried their best to believe. Can we be transparent and say that we have a headache without being condemned? This "name it and claim it theology" stems from desiring to have greater faith to believe what God has for us on this earth.

The fact is that we are made of body, soul and spirit. When you get a bad headache, you may need to take a couple of aspirins and pray. When the headache is gone, you can give God the glory either way. Or if the ache stems from emotional issues, you may need to get some counseling. Why do we think that we can fix ourselves all the time? It is biblical to get counsel. It may not necessarily mean you have to go to a professional counselor. Just go to those who are wise and godly. If someone does not know how to clean house, they need to learn how to do that. If someone does not know how to organize, they need to learn how to do that. If someone does not know how to deal with their emotions, they may need to get some counseling.

When someone eats a family size pizza and a whole gallon of ice cream in one sitting, one would most likely feel pretty awful unless one is a real glutton. I had seen some pizza drenched in Coke after it sat out for awhile and some ice cream that had been left out. They looked disgusting—like blubber monsters. You could almost hear the sound that they made, saying, "blurp, blurp, blurp." I don't know how our stomachs can take all that stuff. God has made our stomachs to endure a lot.

When we have a bad stomachache or a headache from eating too much, it is not a spiritual matter where a demon needs to be cast out. Someone can tell us that we don't have a head or stomachache, but the fact is we do. Someone may want to cast out some blubber monster spirit from us. But it was our fault, because we ate too much. Sometimes we just need to own up, rather than blame demons for everything. I think we just need to change our eating habits, and those bad spirits will keep away.

How about the *prosperity* theology? We all have so much to learn from one another. I understand that we need to know all the scriptures which talk of God's riches and how He desires to bless His children. I am not certain that we are all supposed to have millions of dollars and some fancy cars. All of God's word must apply to all generations and nations. I am certain Jesus did not have fancy Roman chariots. If a person in some poverty-stricken country is happy with one bowl of soup or rice a day, we should not make him feel guilty because he does not have Rolls Royce in his garage.

How about the concept that God is not omnipotent because of our free will? Does this mean that God is not all-powerful, because of our own will affecting our destiny? Is our God not in control, since He can only do as much as man's free will allows? If God is not in control, how is the universe able to go on and not be destroyed into oblivion without planets colliding into one another? Some say that God has given us the power of free will and that God's power can go only as far as the free will of the human race. Doesn't God change His mind when the people repent? Does this mean that nothing is ordained from the beginning of time, but that history is made with the choices we make?

How about speaking in tongues? Is it of Satan, or was it just for the time in the book of Acts? I have seen an old grandma who never spoke in tongues in church, but I knew that she was a lover of our Lord. She sat quietly and worshipped God, and her life was a sweet aroma to everyone around her. I have also seen those who spoke in tongues whose joy was contagious. The one who stirred me to want more in life was a young doctor's wife, who helped out in the kitchen up at Idyllwild Pines summer camp when I worked there. She was always singing. Sometimes, I could hear her break out in her prayer language quietly. I have also seen those who speak in tongues who are full of anger and bitterness.

Is Jesus coming back before or after the Tribulation?

Can Native Americans play their own drums and rattles? Can Native American believers chant their songs in their language, rather than only translated hymnals?

Some people think worship is only when we sing. Others think it is when we close our eyes and rock ourselves in prayer.

Perhaps, it is also when we are washing dishes, taking showers, changing a baby's diapers, accounting, grocery shopping, mopping the floor and even when we are cleaning toilets.

And how about the Simple Church concept, that the church is not buildings but where two or more are gathered together? Is this a rebellion against the Orthodox Church theology? The Greek word *ekklesia* derives from two words: *ek,* meaning "out of", and *klesis,* meaning "a calling." It came to refer to an assembly because people were summoned or "called out" to assemble. *The word* church *derives from the Greek word* kuriakos which means "belonging to the Lord." When early believers heard *ekklesia,* they didn't think of a building but of a ruling body. Would it be more profitable to teach the tribal peoples to do simple church at homes like in the New Testament days? Or do we insist that they must go to a building to meet on Sundays and Wednesday evenings to be considered a Christian?

I do see the danger of someone who may get out of fellowship for the lack of a bigger community. I believe the Word of God, which admonishes us not to forsake the gathering of the saints regularly. We all need to get rid of our pride of putting down any parts of the body of Christ who may do things differently. That pride is worse than anything. That is how Lucifer fell. I think God put within the body of Christ what seem to be opposing views, so that we would be challenged to consider what the opposite camps are saying. Proverbs 26:12 says that there is more hope for a fool than a man who is wise in his own eyes. I don't want to be a fool. Worse yet, I don't want to think I am so wise.

God brings two opposite kinds into one thing and makes beautiful things. Look at the dragonflies with ugly bulging eyes with delicate wings. He makes rose petals with such tenderness and puts sharp thorns on them. I don't understand Him. He mixes everything up—something gentle and soft with something ugly and rough, something beautiful and tender with something dangerous. Yet it all perfectly makes sense somehow.

If you come to me to prove your point one way or the other, I will tell you that I am not interested. I am willing to have open dialogue, because we need to be able to discuss things. I am willing to do it, if I am not going to be damned to hell by them. I suppose one could think me damned to hell, but that is only the prerogative of God to decide where I go when my life on earth is done.

Everyone seems to have their passion in different corners of God's theology. This is a good thing, but we as YWAM Tribalwinds cannot do it all. We cannot meet every person's agendas for us as to how we should do this ministry. Some would want us to all do 24/7 prayer all the time. If everyone did that, no one would do any work, and we would all starve. No one would go out to talk to others about Christ.

It is exhausting to hear all the demands and suggestions. Some feel the book of James says we need to be helping with community transformation. Others would say that we need to do prison ministry and visit the elderly. Spiritual warfare and deliverance is tops for some others—we are told to go and tear down the strongholds over the Hopi reservation and San Francisco Peaks. However, if the people continue to invite the spirits, they have the right to be there.

I wonder whether our God is intimidated by any question. There must be a place where any young people and intelligent adults can ask these questions, without being burned at the stake. I think this is the problem with many young people turning away from Christ when they leave their parents' nest and go off to colleges and universities. They are bombarded by the secular teachings of their professors who allow any questions to be asked. They are told by their professors that no question is a stupid question. These kids are now open to a vast world of new information. They are able to delve into many different ideas and concepts. They no longer are satisfied with pat answers, which are not answers at all. They want to try any out-of-the-box thinking as their minds have been opened.

If we give permission for our young sons and daughters and the new believers and converts to ask any questions, we may not lose them to the secular universities. This world presents the body of Christ as rigid, self-righteous, judgmental and divided. I know I have been there many times myself and am still seeking the Lord to help me to think His thoughts.

So much of our Christianity is based on scriptures which tell us that we are sinners and wicked. These days, when one is asked how they are doing, everyone seems to say, "I'm good." This is just not proper English. If my English teacher, Miss De Jane at Hollywood High heard this, she would have a holy fit, as she would say every sentence needs a noun and a verb. We would have to say, "I am doing well." However, this is not why this bothered me. It also bothered me, because I used to majorly focus on the scripture that says, "The heart is deceitful above all things and beyond cure. Who can understand it?" (Jeremiah 17:9). And Jesus said, "No one is good, but one, that is God." (Luke 18:18-20) We are not good according to these verses. So, I used to say, "No we are not good. God is good." Our flesh is wicked, but Christ in me is good!

There is certainly truth in these verses. However, we would be missing a huge piece of who we are, if we do not look at some other things. We also need to read all the other hundreds of scriptures which tell us that we are made in His image and He is good—therefore, we are good. I don't understand what it is that makes us want to feel bad and beat up on ourselves. We need to claim all that we are as a child of God. We are a dwelling place of God, holy, dearly loved, forgiven, accepted, chosen, have the mind of Christ, secure in Him, blessed with every spiritual blessing, etc., etc. This is especially those who are in Christ, as He is in us, the hope of glory!

I have friends who believe they can worship the Lord in their own Native American style of music and those who believe that they cannot do anything Native. I have friends who would not be welcomed in many churches. They are my friends, simply because I believe it is our calling to love them with the love of our Lord.

I know the word "God" is not even a good translation of Adonai. It is a Germanic word for not even a supreme God, but a lower god. So, should we never call Him God from now on? Should I go look up every place in this book where I have the word "God" and replace it with the Creator?

Christmas replaced a pagan holiday and Jesus' birthday was sometime in the fall of the year, not December. So, should we call the birthday of Christ by another name and pick another fall date? Does Jesus care? Or does Jesus care more that we remember that He came to earth to die and rise for us and that we love one another?

Is it okay to use blue spruce trees to decorate during the birth of Christ, and hang lights to celebrate? My question is "Are we bringing honor to Christ? Are we declaring Christ's birth through Christmas, as the world now knows it? Are we making our home or our environment more inviting? Do these things and customs bring our families and loved ones together in shalom or do we push them away? If the lights and the pretty decorations make our home more inviting and give a warm environment, is anything wrong with this?

Shalom is not just about peace in our heart but encompasses so many other aspects of living on this earth—spiritual, physical, mental and even environmental.

What does it mean to love our neighbor as ourselves? Can we hear others, as we want to be heard? Are there mind-boggling thoughts that can be discussed without fear of being excommunicated? Should we ex-communicate any who ask questions like, "Would Jesus go down to hell at the end of age and bring back the host of captives once again, as He did after his death on the cross? Could He possibly bring everyone out and empty hell?" We are going to find out when we get to heaven whether who was wrong or right.

Some people ask, "When the Bible says that every knee shall bow, every tongue confess, does that mean only the ones who confessed Christ with their mouth or does it mean literally "every knee" or does it mean "almost all or some knees?" "Does the word *eternity* or "the end of age" mean something else than forever and ever and ever, or does it have a time limit like some thousand years as some Greek theologian profess?"

Others have asked, "Is there any possibility that the demons will someday be reconciled back to God?" I recently heard that there are really no demons and that the evil on this earth is myth and that these are attitudes, mind-sets, and pathologies which bind us and from which we need healing and deliverance. Are demons "spiritual entities" that God created, or is the term "demon" a name for an unseen spiritual or mental force? When we are casting out a demon of lust out of someone, is "lust" a demon, or a mindset—something that has become an addictive way of thinking? I think this is a reasonable question. The King James Version of the Old Testament uses the word "devil" only four times.

If there are no demons, what did Jesus kick out of the demoniac by the tomb? (Matthew 8:28-34) When the demons had come out, they went into a large herd of pigs. So, did this man's attitudes all go into these pigs which made them act so violently to jump into the sea? Boy, talk about multiple personality! How does this work? Did the man have any personality of his own left after this or was he just a big blob? I know that we blame the demons for many of the areas which we all need to take responsibility for. One does not have to say or shout saying, "I take authority" over anything because either you have authority or you don't.

The Sabbath really should be Saturday and not Sunday so if we are to do everything according to the law, we should be going to church on Saturdays. "I won't run on Sunday" said Eric Little during the Olympics in the thirties. The world said Eric was "A man of principal" because he did not want to run on the Sabbath in the Olympics. It seemed like such a noble thing to choose not to run on Sunday. This meant that his Olympic metal could not be attained. He would not run even for the sake of his own nation, Scotland. I couldn't help but to wonder whether one day was more important to God than another. Is someone godlier because he/she goes to a church on Sunday morning only to live all the other days for self? Every day is holy, not just Sundays. One, however, could hardly not respect Eric Little for sticking to his convictions. We sure need more of them.

Someone else also told us that we are doing Communion wrong. He said we needed to now include the oil and salt to every Communion. He was very serious.

Colossians 1:16 & 20 says that, *By Him, all things were created, visible and invisible . . . and by Him, reconcile all things to Himself, by Him, whether things on earth or in heaven.* What invisible things? Could there be other created beings on other planets, who had not sinned? Does it really matter if we ask and whether the answer is "yes" or "no" to these questions? Would it take away our salvation?

Our indigenous friends ask, "What about our ancestors?" Can someone go to heaven, if they didn't receive Jesus into their heart? How about the people who never had a missionary come to their town? How about Paul, who saw a stone plaque "TO AN UNKNOWN GOD"? How about, "Blessed are the poor in Spirit," who may have truly called out to the Lord but didn't have a missionary come to tell them about Jesus? Is it possible that these people have been delivered and are in heaven now?

I have seen those who believe in eternal hell, who never share the love of Jesus with anyone. They live for themselves. If one thinks that their parents or loved ones will go to hell forever and ever, why don't they preach the Good News of God's salvation? Why do they sit around comfortably and never share the love of Christ, when they can warn the loved ones from hell? If they know the truth and don't do anything to rescue their loved ones from going to hell for zillions of years, perhaps they should also go to hell themselves.

I want every single person on earth to know and experience the sweet fellowship with Christ. My question is, "Are we helping others to walk on this journey with our great and awesome God? Are we leading them to get on this sweet path?" Why do we sit around and argue when this time could be used for good?

Easter also originated as a pagan worship of the "queen of heaven—Ishtarte". So, should we now condemn everyone who calls the day of resurrection by that name? I do think it is okay to study the origin of these names but to expect the world to have to change may be unrealistic.

I have no problem with having Easter egg hunts because I personally don't look at it as some heathen ritual. I do it with kids because it is simply fun to do. If this draws our neighbors or some others to be with us and feel loved by us, I think that is more important than getting the idioms right.

Why is it okay for us to sing "a mighty fortress is our God" which Martin Luther composed from what was originally a bar tune? Is it okay to sing Amazing Grace to the tune of The House of the Rising Sun? I wonder if God is going to come down to earth and say, "How dare you sing that song to that terrible tune? You have really offended me. Therefore, I am going to have to zap you to oblivion." How about singing "Hotel Hallelujah" to the tune of "Hotel California"? Are we honoring God with these songs or not?

It is not the form which our Father is examining. He is more concerned about our heart condition. Jesus said that we should love the Lord with all our heart and love our neighbor as ourselves.

Americans have a lot of Idioms. But, unless we explain, the other nationalities would not understand what in the world we are talking about. If we say, "kick the bucket," or "hit the ceiling," it would not make any sense to some others. We also have many idioms within the body of Christ—their own interpretations and their doctrines. The church divides itself with these idioms. I am sick of all the hyper fears of Christians.

I remember how the Christians lived so much in fear just prior to Y2K. There was so much fear mongering about how the world was going to be.

The Christians were told to burn all the Rainbow Bright and Cabbage Patch dolls in the seventies because of some fears that the dolls originated from satanic groups. How ridiculous it is to think that our God is not powerful enough to cast out a thousand demons out of these dolls? The regular people in the country must have thought we were really stupid because those dolls were expensive. Many Christians were also told to burn all the rock and roll records just as all the Native Americans are still being told to throw away or burn all their jewelry and clothing as though all the records and the Native American items are full of demons.

I think I have heard it all. I get really upset talking about some of these controversial subjects with my friends sometimes. Yes, they are my friends still, even though I don't agree with everything they believe. I love them, because they love the Lord and reach out to more people with the love of Christ than do many staunch so called "Christians," who are prejudiced against other races and peoples.

Sometimes I concentrate too much on those who do not love and disapprove of us. In fact, a few times, I simply wanted to die. I am not suicidal but I wanted to be taken out of this earth because being in ministry and being on this earth has been so arduous sometimes.

He loves me, he loves me not. She loves me, she loves me not, is the question. I wonder whether the other missionaries love us or not because they disagree with us sometimes. I go round and round in my mind. One could waste a lot of time and energy that way. The better question is "Who loves me?" I need to concentrate on those who genuinely care for us, speaking the truth in love.

Chapter 25

"Every Bush Is a Flame with the Fire of God"

People think they are so smart. I know I do. If people are so smart, I used to wonder why they could not come up with disposable toilet seat covers that do not have to be torn in three places before you put it down. Why couldn't they invent a machine which would cut it completely all around, so we don't have to stand there over the toilet seat trying to get those un-cut places torn in order to sit down? And then if I was so smart, I would know that I could put the seat cover down without tearing anything at all. I bet it had something to do with folding and packaging. And then someone finally did come up with the ones which could be put down with no trouble but I bet they are more expensive for the store owners.

I did not understand my Geometry teacher. I don't understand my kids. I don't understand my husband. I certainly do not understand my God, who made them all. God is a Great Mystery.

As you do not know what is the way of the wind, or how the bones grow in the womb of her who is with child, so you do not know the works of God who makes everything.
(Ecclesiastes 11:5)

I think there are a lot of tensions in the Word. I don't need to know how to figure everything out to put God in a box, so I can feel secure.

Margaret Browning once said, "Every bush is a flame with the fire of God, but only those who see take off their shoes. The rest just pick the berries."

We live in a strange and incredible age. We can sit in our own living room with a full symphony to serenade us. If that is not enough, we can travel to almost anywhere, sitting comfortably on our chair or a couch with accompaniments of reporters and singers and bands, with heat in winter and air-conditioning in summer inside closed windows. We can stand under the water falls to clean ourselves or a small pool of lake to sit right inside of our own homes. We take it for granted but it is quite amazing how with a turn of a knob, a flame of fire can be turned on like magic. It happens in an instant. Poof! And there it is. And as though that is not enough, we can adjust these flames so we can cook several different dishes at their own speed. It is hard to see the burning bush sometimes, with so many things to comfort and occupy us.

We cannot put God in a box. We may find it wrong when we say, "God will never do that." I don't understand God's ways at all sometimes. He had Ezekiel lie on his left side for three hundred ninety days and on his right side for forty days for the sins of Israel and Judah. God also told Ezekiel that He was giving him cow dung instead of human waste and to prepare bread over it. (Ezekiel 4)

How about when Jesus spat on the ground and made clay with the saliva and anointed the eyes of the blind man? (John 9) That would not have been considered kosher in Jewish culture or any other culture for that matter.

How about when Jesus put his finger in the ears of the one who was deaf and mute and spat and touched his tongue? (Mark 7:31) If I was God, I would not have chosen this method either. But, I am not God.

I don't understand God, who brought His Son through the line of David and Bathsheba. I don't understand how Bathsheba could live with a man who murdered her own husband. I am glad that she at least mourned for Uriah, when she found out that he was dead (II Samuel 11: 26). Who knows what her marriage to Uriah was like? I would want a husband who was not so staunch in his duty that he would sleep outside the king's gate. I would want a husband who would want to come and sleep with me, his wife, instead. It does show that he was an amazing servant of the king. I have always prayed for someone as loyal as Uriah to be sent to our ministry. Sam Wise in *the Lord of the Rings* by J.R.R. Tolkien is also like Uriah.

The first child born of David and Bathsheba died, but the second was Solomon. I understand that the Lord forgives the greatest of our sins. But did God have to bring His only Son through this sinful union? Could God not have chosen the line of Jesus through another wife of David instead of Bathsheba? Of course He could have but He didn't.

I don't understand why the Bible presents Solomon as the man of such wisdom. He was such a fool in the end to worship the idols of his foreign wives. It showed me that, even with all our wisdom, we have the freedom to be loyal to our Father or satisfy our own desires on this earth. I don't understand a lot of things.

The serpent tempted Adam and Eve in the Garden of Eden. The bronze serpent was lifted up by Moses to save the Israelites in the desert. It is not for us to question God why He did not use a bronze lamb or an eagle rather than the snake. Or can we question God? I believe we can, as long as we want to know the answer because we love Him, and not because we want to rebel.

Many of us act like we have the corner on all the systematic theology and subjects concerning God and the body of Christ. We react to others, as though we are the only ones who love God, and the others don't love Jesus at all. We believe our opinions are the only ones that are one-hundred percent correct. I don't know whether all my opinions on the Bible are always right. But I'd like to believe they are. We lash out at one another, almost in violence, as though we would be betraying our God if we did not. We act as though we are the only protectors of the perfect knowledge of our God

It would be such a pity to get to heaven and see all the moments I missed out and messed up others by arguing. It would be such a pity that we wasted so much time with those things which would have been what they are, no matter how we all thought. I know I have been wrong more than once concerning matters on which I was certain that I was right one-hundred—or at least ninety-nine—percent. That really aggravates me.

So much of our Christianity is canned, like the typical wedding vows. The bride and the groom are expected to simply say, "I do," to all the extravagant promises which they can never keep. If one does not respond, "I do," one is liable to not be announced as husband and wife—even though one or more of those vows could be broken in the first week, or perhaps, in the first day or the first hour.

I think it would be refreshing to hear someone say, "Are you kidding? You must be crazy. I can't promise all that! But, I will certainly earnestly try to love my spouse, even though I tend to be selfish. But with God's help, I surely will try my best."

I like having a full spectrum of the body of Christ. It is like having all varieties of food, because one type of food gets really boring after awhile. But no matter how delicious the food is, one can have only so much of the same thing. Likewise, we will be unhealthy, if we neglect all the other parts of the body of Christ. It is like bearing unhealthy babies, when someone is too in-bred within the same family.

Just think if you have to have steak or lobster or spinach every single night for a whole month, you would get sick of it. One of the best ways to get cured of any one food is to make a glutton out of yourself and eat that, until you are absolutely sick. I think we also need all the varieties of the body of Christ.

It is good to have desserts, as well as steak. We need the encouragement as well as admonishment and discipline. When I used to nurse our babies, I found out how sweet my milk was. Once,

I had to go away for a few days and pumped my milk to freeze it in bottles. I wanted to taste my milk. I couldn't believe it was so sweet, that it tasted almost like evaporated milk. So, there is no way I am going to believe that God does not want us to have sweet things.

God meant for us to have sweets. I believe in having all food, even banana cream pies, chocolate cream pies, pecan pies, rhubarb apple pies, rocky-road and mint chocolate chip ice cream, Snickers candy bars, lemon drops, etc.—in moderation. God would not have given us honey to eat, if He didn't want us to have sweets.

I have a friend who ate six pounds of chocolate all in one day. She had promised her kids she would bring some treats home. She bought three pound of chocolate. Now, that is a big bag but she ate the whole thing by the time she walked home. I like chocolate, too, but this is ridiculous! So she had to go back to the store to get another three pound bag of chocolate since she promised her kids. I couldn't believe it when she told me that she ate the whole thing again! If I had doubted her integrity and character, I would have said that she was lying. She got sick to the point that she had to make a radical change in her diet. Just because God gave us sweet milk and honey does not mean that we have to go ahead and eat six pound of chocolate all in a few hours. That is just not wise.

Americans are obsessed with food. I never saw buffets until I came to this country. I never saw any obese people until I came to America; I was shocked as a child. I think the Americans are the only ones who "super-size" their meals at the fast food restaurants. We are the only ones with mega size cups for soft drinks and coffee and get refills on top of that. It is amazing how greedy we can be. The Americans are not satisfied. The problem is the more you drink coffee and tea, the more you have to go to the bathroom. It is distracting to have those who always have to get up to go to the bathroom during our Discipleship Training School (DTS) classes.

When you go to England, they give you a tiny cup of coffee for three or four dollars which is gone only after a few gulps and they don't even give you a refill. Either they have much self control or they are really cheapskates. Americans are gluttons compared to the rest of the world. We have to get a grip on ourselves or we could all get hypertension and diabetes and there will be no one left in this country.

Once we did twenty one days of a "Daniel fast" with our DTS. We decided that we would have no meat, desserts, spices, salt, pepper, coffee and tea. We all agreed that we would only have grain, fruits, vegetables and juice. It is amazing how we can get so ingenious when it comes to food. The students made "Smoothies" in the blender with fruits and juices, having hot water with juice so that it tasted like tea, made pop corn and ate more mixed nuts than we could hardly keep in stock. One student made some potato salad by boiling rice to make a substitute mayonnaise. Whole grain *Ezekiel* bread and tortillas were brought in and sandwiches were made with almond butter, bananas and halves of cherry tomatoes. It was quite a work of art! It seemed there was hardly anything we were not having. I began to wonder whether any consecration or sacrifice was being made until I realized I lost fifteen pounds during this fast. Some people eat like this all the time. Good for them! I don't want to. I will only eat like this if the Lord convicts me to do so.

Grits and oatmeal without any butter or sugar should be outlawed. Oatmeal is the most boring and bland food there is. I don't know why something which is so healthy for human beings has to look so dismal. It only looks semi-good if one puts raisins and nuts on top of it. Otherwise, it is not fit for human consumption. It is too bad oatmeal does not look like a banana split sundae or a cream puff with custard inside.

I really care too much about what other people think. One night, I was at the *Wild Flower* restaurant after I had just finished doing the church service at the jail in Flagstaff. I like that restaurant with its reasonable prices and simple menus. I just wanted a cup of tea and nothing else as I was fasting that night. I wanted to be there to work as I needed a change of atmosphere. After a little while, I needed some coffee. I hoped that they would let me refill my cup with coffee, but the gal at the register didn't get the hint. I hate that when people don't get the hints. You either have to be blunt or you have to forget about what you wanted in the first place. So I had to order a cup of coffee and pay.

The restaurant was closing so I asked if I could have a "to go" cup to refill with coffee. He was not pleased about giving me a to-go cup, but he did anyway. I am such a pain. I think the manager thought I was still on my tea bit, because he didn't know I paid for the coffee. I thought he acted like I was stealing. I even put a good tip in the jar. This really annoyed me. I had to think about why this irked me so much. It was because I did not want to be a bad witness. I hope that gal told him I paid. Either way, God knows I paid.

Sometimes, I never feel like I do enough, even when there is hardly time enough to be alone. The only way to truly get rest here is to simply get away from our own home, which sits right next to our YWAM center. But the Lord is saying to me that if I did not do one other thing this week, but visit with the few inmate ladies who came to the Thursday evening worship service, that was enough for Him.

No, doing is not everything! We are not human doings but human beings. It is good to sit and fast. *Psalm 131:2 says, "Surely I have calmed and quieted my soul, like a weaned child with his mother."* I don't know whether you ever saw a weaned child but they are not crying for mother's milk. The child can be held quietly close to the bosom of the mother. The weaned child just wants to be where the parent is and stay close.

True worship is intimacy with this incredible Creator who loves us beyond our own pathetic imaginations.

Here below are the words of Tatanga Mani, who was born on *March 20, 1871, in Alberta, Canada*. These words are worth pondering, as it may help us get under their skin a bit more.

"Do you know that trees talk? Well, they do. They talk to each other, and they'll talk to you, if you will listen. Trouble is, white people don't listen. They never listened to the Indians, and so I don't

suppose they'll listen to the other voices in nature. But I have learned a lot from trees, sometimes about the weather, sometimes about animals, sometimes about the Great Spirit. It's not right raising kids so far from nature. I suppose your boys and girls have never seen pussy willows, robins building nests, or grass-covered hills. This pavement is fine for cars, but it is hard medicine for children."

I do understand that we don't have to agree with everything, when Tatanga said the Whites never listen to the Indians. Obviously some white people do listen. So, we can decide not to learn anything from Tatanga and just shred apart all the other things he said, or we could glean some truth from him. Rather than focusing on one sentence about which we may disagree, we can choose to see all the other matters on which we do agree. The Native Americans are a lot more holistic. Their lives touch every aspect of life. If the words of Tatanga Mani bother us, because we feel it is too New Age, we may also be bothered that the Bible says the trees clap their hands and, if we do not praise the Lord, the rocks will!

Tatanga Mani said, *"Nobody tries to make the coyotes act like beavers, or the eagles behave like robins."*

In the seventies, Simon and Garfunkle came out with a song called, "El Condor Pasa." Some of the words in this song go like this:

> *I'd rather be a sparrow than a snail*
> *Hammer than a nail*
> *I'd rather be a forest than a street . . .*
> *Yes I would, if I could, I surely would.*

It is all about something that is stronger and more beautiful than the things which are ugly or weak. But the chorus says:

> *Away, I'd rather sail away*
> *Like a swan that's here and gone*
> *A man gets tied to the ground.*
> *He gives the world its saddest sound, its saddest sound.*

This song became a theme song in my life. It broke my heart when I first truly recognized what these words meant in my teen years. I walked down the aisle at our wedding, to live flute music of this song. This is also true worship—knowing our Father's heart and doing His will to help those who are on the ground and giving their saddest sounds.

I heard an incredible story of an experiment of the three bowls of rice. One bowl of rice was given positive attention and affirmation of speech by the people. Another bowl was given bad attention and spoken to harshly by the people. The third bowl was completely ignored. After some time, the bowl of rice which was given positive comments stayed fresh. The second bowl of rice, which received bad attention, had turned stale and black. The third bowl of rice, which did not receive any attention, looked awful and worse than the rice which got negative attention.

I realized from this experiment how important it is to acknowledge people. So, when I come into a meeting, I try to greet people by name as much as possible. I always try to wave at hitch-hikers, even if I cannot pick them up, so that they may know they are not invisible.

When I am old, I want to be gracious and not a cranky old woman. I want the shrew of a woman inside of me to be tamed like Katherine in The Shakespeare's *Taming of the Shrew*. I want to leave a legacy of beauty and integrity and everlasting hope and prayer. I want to have all those around me to be like the bowl of fresh rice.

Before we ever came to Arizona, our pastor invited the leadership team of our church in Santa Barbara to come to a meeting. He said that a prophet was coming to speak to us. I was not feeling particularly spiritual that evening, as I had a bad day. I was skeptical about prophets. Who are the prophets anyway? Will was not available to go to the meeting, so I went alone. When I went and sat down and heard the prophet, I was not very impressed. When he had hardly finished his teaching, he immediately put his hand over someone sitting in the front row and began to prophesy.

The fear of the Lord is a strange thing. One cannot explain what it is, but one knows it when it fills a room. It came over everyone in that room within a matter of moments. As this man of God continued to prophesy over each one in that room, and began to get closer to me, I was shaking in my boots. I desperately cried out to God for mercy with all my might. I asked that I would not be put to shame. Finally, the prophet came and put his hand on my head, which was bowed.

He said, *"The Lord saith unto thee* (I don't know why he spoke to me in King James style, when I don't even speak modern English that well), *I shall make you a witness even in peculiar places, even in the market place.* (Everyone laughed because they knew I was doing ministry at "Winter House" in downtown. They thought that this word had already come true. But, I knew God had something else in mind. I did not know that He would bring us out to the Hopi reservation in Arizona.) *And where thou doest labor, thou shalt be a light and thou shalt have a word that speaks of the savory and saltiness of His grace. Rejoice, rejoice, thou shalt count the numbers later, not now."*

I wept like a baby, after only the first sentence of his prophecy. Oh, I was spared. I was not doomed. Not only was I spared from shame, but I knew that my God was so good and merciful, even though I did not deserve His kindness. He was calling me extravagantly into His service, just as He had called Gideon and the prophets of old. I came into that room very casual, as if life did not matter and how God thought of me. I left that room with all my desire to love this incredible God, who saw me—not as I saw myself but worthy to serve Him. I think our God is like that with everyone. He has huge prophecies for all those who love Him.

It is amazing what God calls us, when we don't think we deserve it. He is always trying to reconcile us to Himself and calls forth the best in us as individuals and nations.

Will says that he just wants to stand before God like a little toddler with a diaper on! Jesus said that we cannot come into the kingdom of God, unless we are like a child. A toddler is not embarrassed by the fact that he may not have anything else on but a diaper. I think King David was like that, and I think that is why God called him a man after His own heart. He was stripped down and danced without shame, when the Ark of the Covenant came into Israel. I had to be stripped of much of my own systematic theology in living among our Native American friends.

Sometimes I see Him riding in His chariots in the clouds! No, I am not crazy, or at least I don't think I am. Imagination is the key. We will miss a whole lot of things in life without imagination, which is the mind's eye. We have the mind of Christ. Psalm 104: 2 says that He covers Himself with lights as with a garment, He stretches out the heavens like a curtain. He makes the clouds, His chariots. It is so cool to think of Him! He walks on the wings of the wind. Yes, sometimes, I could see God reaching into his bag and scooping a big handful of diamonds and throwing them out onto the curtains He laid down in the heavens. He is indeed fantastic!

I have a Father who paints the skies for me. He is extravagant! I am hugely impressed by Him. He not only paints the skies with different strokes each time, but He thinks up hundreds of geraniums and hundreds of rose species as well as hundreds of colors of translucent dragonflies and butterflies.

He created human beings to be able to create dances—ballet, river clog dance, waltz, country, Native American and a thousand others. He created us to create music in all sorts of ways, design clothes with such interesting colors and fashion, etc., because we are made in His image to create. This Creator, my Father, loves me. He loves me. All is well, because He loves me.

Living this life is like trying to walk on a circus tightrope. In our spiritual journey, we can either agree with God, or live in rebellion moment-to-moment, day-to-day, week-to-week. Our time is not our own. Our money is not our own. Our love is not our own. When our hearts are being nudged by His voice, we can either keep or give away our finances, time, love, etc. I desire to know when it is His pleasure for me to have things, or when I should forego purchasing a one-dollar item. These dollar items can add up to support another person or a couple, doing His work on this earth.

A friend was in the hospital in our town of Flagstaff. She was very ill. As I was driving to see her, I looked around the world all around me. The hills and the mountains, the Ponderosa pines, the blue sky and the clouds all seemed more beautiful than ever. I want to live and not die. I wonder how this world would look to me, if I knew I only had a short time to live on this earth. The truth is that our lives in this world are indeed brief. What is one more day, one more year or thirty years? I want to be fascinated with every pine cone and every dragonfly and every kind of roses, as though I was a child all over again. I want to be useful to fulfill the dreams of my Father's heart.

I am calling out to the Lord to equip me with a greater heart for Him, self-discipline, dying to self, loving others more, speaking kinder words, not judging others and asking for His grace to think the most beautiful things of others. It all sounds very grand, but I know I cannot do these things without His help. I desperately need Him.

I do not understand how I could find such a simple joy in washing and folding the towels and sheets from the guests in our home. I do not understand how our thoughts and actions affect our heavenly Father's heart so much here and in the next world to come, and yet I know they do!

Recently I was taken to a Himalayan restaurant in Flagstaff. But I think no food is as delicious as Thai food. I love Thai food. It is the only kind of food that is so euphorically heavenly, that I just want to close my eyes and float far away on a balloon ride. But nothing on earth compares to our God, who is beyond beautiful in my opinion. I am not saying it is always glorious or euphoric. Sometimes, walking on this path can be daunting and outright hard. I have sat in His presence and walked the garden with Him. I would not trade all the Thai food in the world for a moment of sweet fellowship with my good Shepherd—no way!

About the author

They were surprised when Will had a sudden "Right of passage" Native American experience in the wilderness which was followed by two years of dreams and visions. They then received a clear calling to go to the Hopi nation in Arizona after being in a full time ministry for seventeen years in Santa Barbara. You can read about it in Millie's first book, The Great Eagle Calling.

Millie was born in Seoul, South Korea. She came to US in the late sixties and grew up in Los Angeles and attended Baldwin Hills Baptist Church. She went to Le Conte Jr. High and graduated from Hollywood High School as an Art Major. She went off to Orange County to attend Fullerton Jr. College and then to Cal State Fullerton and majored in Teaching. She fell in love with a Navy Seal, Will Toms who was in a full time ministry in Santa Barbara, California with youth at risk in "Sea & Summit Expeditions." They were married on May seventeenth of 1980 under a big tree in Whittier, CA. Will and Millie Toms eventually brought the ministry of their outdoor adventure program, Sea & Summit Expeditions and the discipleship house under Youth With a Mission. Will and Millie have three grown children, one who became a social worker, another, a teacher, and another became a full time missionary in south Asia.

True Confessions of a Missionary

To order Millie Toms' first book:
The Great Eagle Calling
Please contact: YWAM Tribalwinds
www.tribalwinds.org or call 928-527-0104
E-mail us your order at: tribalwinds@hughes.net or contact

Kingdom Enterprises International Publishing
& Destiny Center at www.DestinyCenter.com

Or you can also order through: YWAM Publishing
www.ywampublishing.com or call 1-800-922-2143

Great Eagle Rising- True Confessions of a Missionary
in e-books and Kindle is also available
through booksellers or by contacting:
iUniverse- www.iuniverse.com 1-800-Authors (1-800-288-4677)

The audio books of The Great Eagle Calling &
Great Eagle Rising- True Confessions of a Missionary
(Both read by the author) are available through YWAM Tribalwinds.

Please inquire about Tribalwinds ministries and schools:
DTS (Discipleship Training School)
DDS (Digital Documentary School)
ESL (English As Second Language)
Sea & Summit Expeditions

Printed in Great Britain
by Amazon.co.uk, Ltd.,
Marston Gate.